Fifty-Eight Events That Will Change Our World

Noel Tyl predicted the exact dates of the Gulf War, the fall of the Soviet Union, the Israel–P.L.O. Oslo Accord, and many other events of historic change. Now he gives you an entire book filled with strategic insights into vitally important world events that will continue to change our world.

Noel Tyl, the "Master of Astrological Prediction," makes fifty-eight dramatic predictions for the years 1996–2012, each one founded on historical trends and exact astrological indicators.

How will these events affect the global economy ... the centers of world power ... how will they affect *you?* The new millennium is a pivotal time in our history. We who care about the fate of our world need the crucial information in this book.

About the Author

Noel Tyl is one of the foremost astrologers of the world. His eighteen textbooks have led the teaching of astrologers for two generations; he is counsel to individuals and corporations and is a popular lecturer throughout the United States and Europe. He is a graduate of Harvard University in Social Relations (Psychology, Sociology, and Anthropology). He also founded and edited *Astrology Now* magazine.

Noel wrote *Prediction in Astrology* (Llewellyn Publications, 1991), a master volume of technique and practice, and edited Books 9 through 16 of the Llewellyn New World Astrology Series, *How to Use Vocational Astrology, How to Personalize the Outer Planets, How to Manage the Astrology of Crisis, Exploring Consciousness in the Horoscope, Astrology's Special Measurements, Sexuality in the Horoscope, Communicating the Horoscope,* and *Astrology Looks at History*. In 1994, his master opus, *Synthesis and Counseling in Astrology—The Professional Manual* (almost 1,000 pages of analytical technique in practice), was published, and *Astrology of the Famed* appeared in 1996. Noel lives in the Phoenix, Arizona, area.

To Write to the Author

If you wish to contact the author or would like more information about this book, please write to the author in care of Llewellyn Worldwide, and we will forward your request. Both the author and publisher appreciate hearing from you and learning of your enjoyment of this book and how it has helped you. Llewellyn Worldwide cannot guarantee that every letter written to the author can be answered, but all will be forwarded. Please write to:

Llewellyn Worldwide, Ltd.
P.O. Box 64383, Dept. K737-4, St. Paul, MN 55164-0383, U.S.A.
Please enclose a self-addressed, stamped envelope for reply, or $1.00 to cover costs. If outside U.S.A., enclose international postal reply coupon.

Free Catalog from Llewellyn

For more than ninety years Llewellyn has brought its readers knowledge in the fields of metaphysics and human potential. Learn about the newest books in spiritual guidance, natural healing, astrology, occult philosophy, and more. Enjoy book reviews, New Age articles, a calendar of events, plus current advertised products and services. To get your free copy of *Llewellyn's New Worlds*, send your name and address to:

Llewellyn's New Worlds of Mind and Spirit
P.O. Box 64383, Dept. K737-4, St. Paul, MN 55164-0383, U.S.A.

PREDICTIONS
FOR A
NEW
MILLENNIUM

Noel Tyl

1996
Llewellyn Publications
St. Paul, Minnesota, 55164-0383, U.S.A.

FIRST EDITION
First Printing, 1996

Cover Design by Lynne Menturweck and Tom Grewe
Editing and Interior Design by Connie Hill

Library of Congress Cataloging-in-Publication Data

Tyl, Noel, 1936–
    Predictions for a new millennium /Noel Tyl. — 1st ed.
        p.   cm.
    Includes bibliographical references and index.
    ISBN 1-56718-737-4 (pbk.)
    1. Predictive astrology.   2. Twenty-first century—Forecasts.
I. Title.
BF1720.5.T855   1996
133.5'890983—dc20   96-24922
                                                            CIP

Llewellyn Publications
A Division of Llewellyn Worldwide, Ltd.
St. Paul, Minnesota 55164-0383, U.S.A.

Note for Readers

My plan for this book is for it to bring you information in a way that is interesting, useful, and memorable.

This time now is especially important: the Millennium is a key Earth-birthday—a time in which to take stock, to understand the meaning of time's passage and how that affects our life.

When we see themes of history clearly, the strategies that propel affairs in the world, we can understand change. We can form opinions and we can plan ahead. Most importantly, we can appreciate more who we are in the scheme of things.

I am an astrologer, and astrology supports this entire book, the analysis of nations and their futures; the details are confined to 40% of the footnotes. (Those footnotes are identified by an asterisk.) For astrologers, then, this volume becomes two books in one. For the general reader, however, the astrology will not intrude.

Indeed, there is a portion of imagination at work here as well, just as it is in any body of analyses and projections. This imagination is born in past history and refreshed for future time. I have worked hard not to be fanciful, but to be realistic in the transition from times-that-were to times-to-come.

Noel Tyl
Fountain Hills, Arizona
January 1996

Other Books by the Author

The Horoscope as Identity

The Principles and Practice of Astrology
- *I. Horoscope Construction*
- *II. The Houses: Their Signs and Planets*
- *III. The Planets: Their Signs and Aspects*
- *IV. Aspects and Houses in Analysis*
- *V. Astrology and Personality*
- *VI. The Expanded Present*
- *VII. Integrated Transits*
- *VIII. Analysis and Prediction*
- *IX. Special Horoscope Dimensions: Success, Sex and Illness*
- *X. Astrological Counsel*
- *XI. Astrology: Mundane, Astral and Occult*
- *XII. Times to Come*

Teaching Guide to the Principles and Practice of Astrology

The Missing Moon

Holistic Astrology—the Analysis of Inner and Outer Environments

Prediction in Astrology

Synthesis & Counseling in Astrology: The Professional Manual

Astrology of the Famed

Edited by the Author

How to Use Vocational Astrology for Success in the Workplace

How to Personalize the Outer Planets:
  The Astrology of Uranus, Neptune and Pluto

How to Manage the Astrology of Crisis:
  Resolution through Astrology

Exploring Consciousness in the Horoscope

Astrology's Special Measurements

Sexuality in the Horoscope

Communicating the Horoscope

Astrology Looks at History

Contents

The Pacific Basin

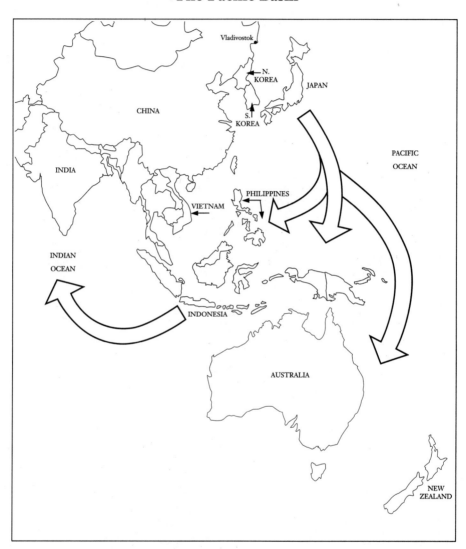

See Chapter 3, The Pacific, page 39

The Middle East

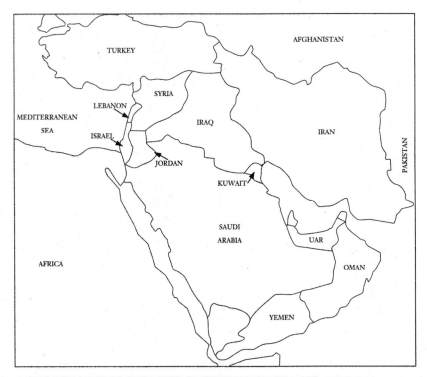

See Chapter 4, The Middle East, page 103

Europe

See Chapter 6, The Union of Europe, page 149

The United States

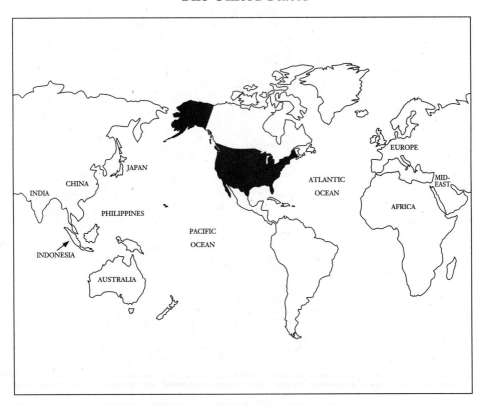

See Chapter 7, The Lone Super Power, page 225

1

ORIENTATION TO THE MILLENNIUM

The Rigorous Growth Toward Globalism

During the decades from the First World War through the Second, the twentieth century saw unprecedented world economic crisis. This crisis threatened capitalism with delusion and potentialized Communism with rationale. There was warfare on a world scale for the first time in history.[1]

Overkill boggled the statistical mind and shamed the sensitive spirit. The revolution of Communism came into being and grew to dominate over one-sixth of the world's land surface and, as well, after World War II, over one-third of the world's population. The convulsions of economics, the carnage of war, and the revolution of politics provided the stage on which democracy was traumatically challenged and eventually exonerated.

Throughout history, accompanying the thrust of change, is the perspective held by each successive generation that the immediate past is horrible. The world at any given time works

---

1 The First World War involved *all* the major powers of the world and, indeed, most of the states of Europe; excepted were the Netherlands, Spain, Switzerland, and the three Scandinavian countries. Troops were sent from countries holding alliances with besieged countries to fight on distant war fronts. The Second World War was similarly global among the major powers. Only South America remained nominally above the fray.

  Along with the two World Wars, the Japanese war with China (1937–1939) and the Korean War (1950–1953) all totaled the highest number killed of the seventy-four international wars that occurred between 1816 and 1965. [See Hobsbawm, 24, 7.]

exceedingly hard to forget that past.[2] Defensive amnesia in the present generation has been encouraged and vindicated by some twenty-five years of extraordinary economic growth and social transformation, highlighted by the commercial trade partnerships, the "unifications," among the former world enemies, Japan and North America and Germany.

But, with an inexorable sense of cycle, at the close of the century, old restlessness and new facts are indeed reviving painful memories: Japan is conducting and winning trade wars, engendering the United States' resentment; there is the United States' need for Japan's apology for World War II; West Germany's unification with East Germany has drastically depleted West Germany's financial strength and threatens to fracture the spirit of the German people; Iraq has revived virulent animosities against Israel which date back to the reign of the Babylonian monarch Nebuchadnezzar II, who destroyed Jerusalem and Judea in 586 B.C.E. (Before the Common Era, formerly B.C.).

How far into renewed conflict will these and many other conflicts of old take the countries of the world? Will history inexorably show repetitions?

New Considerations

There are new considerations that are important for us in answering those questions. Our world is no longer *Euro*-centered. With atomic weaponry and germ warfare on the market, small countries—countries less developed and more distant from venerable Europe—*are now equal in threat to large countries.* While the sizes of arsenals are different, the weapons are similar, the devastation power is identical, and distances are negligible. It takes only a singular explosion to make one's point and assure one's place in history. Guerilla and terrorist tactics, born of the stand-off in Vietnam, increase exponentially the presence, leverage, and potential of many nations. The voices of more countries than ever before are being heard, commanding attention, and necessitating response and intercession by other countries whose interests are threatened.

---

2 Poll results indicate that many adults do not know against whom the United States fought in World War II. A majority do not know to what "D-Day" refers. In a nationwide history test of high school juniors in 1986, it was found that one-third of these young adults could not find France on a map of Europe. In the year 2000, these "juniors" will be thirty years old. *New York Times* report, December 3, 1995, Section 4, page 5.

The meetings at Versailles in June 1919, Teheran in 1943, Moscow in Autumn 1944, Yalta in early 1945, Potsdam in occupied Germany in the late Summer of 1945, and the establishment of the United Nations brought the victors of World War II together to divide up the winnings and to plan their cooperative futures. Arbitrary and contentious new boundaries were established for the countries that had been involved—like Palestine, East and West Germany, Poland, Yugoslavia's Republics and Provinces—and new scenarios were put into action for colder wars among the major powers.

The totality of war—involving whole societies to produce what is required to deliver the war and to recover from attack—spurred to an extreme the growth of technology and innovative management of national resources. In fact, the advance of technology, especially in terms of miniaturization, calculation, information processing, and physical transportation of goods and people, has become so valuable to the world's prosperity, productivity, trade, and future development that the devastation of the twentieth-century crises can appear as almost *necessary*. It is as if some inexorable purging was required to reveal, to call forth new strengths and potentials; the muscles of nations flexed before they relax; the Winter before the Summer.

The Past was the Same

Fatalistically, we have always understood our history that way; some 5,000 years ago in ancient Mesopotamia or in present-day England, for example: the good *must* surely follow the bad, i.e., we must suffer these rainy weeks for the sunshine yet to come. Indeed, the corollary grows clearer as well: the bad *must* follow good.

The ancients and their millennia of progeny were all "moderns" unto themselves and their epoch. Each ancient culture, for the most part, at one time did indeed rule the known world. The position as the finest culture of the known world, practically by definition, carried with it a powerful conviction, a sureness of any current point of view. There was an arrogance of knowing how things are supposed to be.

In fact, when people have obtained what they believe to be absolute truth, they have, in their own terms, *a moral obligation* to impose their standards of behavior and principles on other people.[3]

---

3 This is a well-developed thesis of scientific philosopher Karl Popper, as studied by Campion, 11.

Any leader and his people, any nation, that opposed/opposes the prevailing truth became/becomes the enemy, threatens the sunshine of the present Summer with the cloud and storm of Fall, and then, Winter rushes in.

As well, there are always those who then are targeted traditionally as scapegoats for the suffering of bad times, perhaps as propitiating sacrifice to dispel the clouds. Appreciation of this fact illuminates much about the present-day resurrection of mystic Jewish evils cast yet upon the modern state of Israel, born from British Mandate on May 14, 1948.[4]

Group conviction and leadership (tribe, people, kingdom, nation) have always been inspired, fortified, and justified by religion. There is no change in history that is not somehow led or condoned by religious rationale. In ancient times, religion was government. Government was religion. Kings were themselves divine; they were intermediaries of the gods.

In modern times, when people have no voice in government, they collect for power within the voice of their religion. Extremism defines these people, justifies their difficult life, and gives them power. Holy War, pronounced as concept in the Koran, is as much a reality at the close of this Millennium as it was at the close of the last Millennium when Islam ruled the western world (see "Considerations of Islam, Judaism, and the Christian Crusades" beginning on page 136).

Cycles of Tension

The following graph presents the twentieth century in terms of cycles of tension. It is astrologically based: these cycles are determined by consecutive notations of the averages of the ten arc-distances among the planets Jupiter, Saturn, Uranus, Neptune, and Pluto. In astrology, without any possible doubt, these slower moving planets correspond to emphatic and highly significant events on

---

4 The time was 4:00 P.M., local standard time. The meeting to proclaim independence from British rule began precisely at 4:00 P.M.. The reading of the proclamation ended at 4:37 P.M., but Ben Gurion regarded 4:00 P.M. as the critical time and recorded it as so in his diary: "At four the Proclamation of Independence." This time in Tel Aviv has been tested by astrologers for over thirty years; by me for seventeen years. There is little doubt about the efficacy of this time in astrological work. It is one of the most reliable Mundane charts in the literature.

See MacCoby, 27, for the careful illumination of Hellenistic antisemitism, the prevailing idea that "the Jews are doomed to be expelled from their land as punishment for their sins in killing their own prophets and, as a culminating crime, Jesus himself."

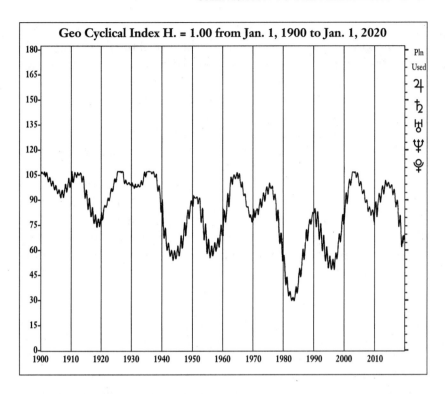

Geo Cyclical Index H. = 1.00 from Jan. 1, 1900 to Jan. 1, 2020

earth; the closer they are to one another, i.e., the lower number, *the more powerfully focused is disruptive activity.* Their index synthesizes an enormous amount of the synchronicity between planets and time.[5*]

Note that the values for 1910–1913 are uniformly high, above 105. Then in 1914, there is a precipitous drop from 109 to 83, with the plunge continuing to 75 in 1917. This period, of course, defines the time of World War I.

In the time period 1940 to 1946, World War II, the index is clearly at a low, from 90 to 55. Similarly, from 1950 to 1958, there is a drop from 90 to 56: the Korean War, war in Indochina, the Maw Maw uprising in Kenya, Castro and his guerrilla movement against the Batista regime in Cuba, warring against the French in

---

5 This Cyclic Index graph is computed by measuring the degree distances from Jupiter to Saturn, Jupiter to Uranus, to Neptune, to Pluto; Saturn to Uranus, Neptune, and Pluto, Uranus to Neptune and Pluto; and Neptune to Pluto, and then adding the averaged totals for each planet's arc distance to the others, for the first day of every year in a series. Enormous shifts from high to low measure the fall from good times to bad, from peace to war.

The Cyclic Index was developed by astrologer Andre Barbault of France and introduced into this country through the work of Ken Negus of Princeton, New Jersey.

North Vietnam, the anti-communist revolution and the Russian invasion in Hungary, Israel's forceful takeover of the Gaza Strip and the Sinai Peninsula, the Laotian Civil War, terrorism against the French colonial government in Algeria, and more.

In the late 1960s (1965–1973), the time of the Vietnam War, there is a synchronous drop of the index from 105 to 75.

There is a dramatic drop from 1978 to 1984 (the *extent* of the drop is not relevant in reading this index; it is the *relative* drop that appears to be significant): the Russian invasion of Afghanistan, rebel uprising in Colombia, civil war in Chad, revolution in Iran and the U.S. hostage crisis there, labor revolution in Poland, the Iraq-Iran War (1980–88), the attempted assassinations of Ronald Reagan, Pope John Paul II, Anwar Sadat, and Indira Gandhi, U.S. preparation of neutron warheads designed to kill people rather than destroy property, Argentina and the Falklands, Israel and Lebanon, Vietnam and Cambodia, civil war in Yemen, turmoil in Haiti, United States air-attacks on Libya in response to international terrorism.

The period of this closing decade of the century shows another clear drop in the index, from eighty-five in 1990 to fifty in 1998, which is certainly echoed by the Middle East Crisis, the fall of the Soviet Union, the further fractures throughout the communist world, uprisings in Haiti, Cuba, Somalia, and the complete disappearance of Yugoslavia (the Serbo-Croatian war). The period of 1997–1998 promises great world tensions and United States military involvement in Israel, Iraq, the Balkans, with domestic upheaval as well about the nation's imperialist/custodial outreach to other countries. There will be tremendous upheaval in Japan and in China, as the former heads for social revolution and the latter aims for a change of political positioning and market leadership, coming to a peace with its satellites, Hong Kong and Taiwan. These outlooks will be constructed and annotated carefully in the sections dealing with the specific countries in detail later in this book.

These are the tensions that take us into the next Millennium. There is recovery indicated several years after 2000, but with yet another dip in the index bottoming out in 2010. This graph record has earned respect in historical record and must be assimilated as a backdrop to our projections in this book for the times ahead.

The World Growing Smaller ... and Meaner

The political dissolution of the USSR allowed the subdivision of its land and rule into many autonomous states. The communist world literally fell apart. The fall was forced by the rebirth of *intense nationalism* and the rearrangement of borders, as in Yugoslavia, for dramatic example. There are borders under perpetual contention in the Middle East; there is the loosening of borders throughout Europe in formation of the European Union[6]; there is the loosening of trade barriers now beginning between China and the West— all of this change is working to give people nationalistic security and bring people of the world closer together.

Earlier, kingdoms had borders that were constructively flexible to the inroads of marriage, religious movement, trade routes, bribery, and pacts of peace or cooperative aggression. All this has given way in the twentieth century to static, self-possessed nations. The First World War ended Europe's internal empires (the Ottoman, Austro-Hungarian, and Prussian). The Second World War ended the extension and emulation of European ways, i.e., expansionism, colonization, the European overseas empires.

And behind all these pages of history is the memory of the "universal empire" of the Arabs, which, at mid-Millennium, ruled the world from the western borders of China to the western borders of Spain.

The grand process of this global change has been dual: there has been an explosion of *ethnic political autonomy* and, second, an *implosion of interdependency.* Look at the nationalistic break-up of the Soviet Union, the divisionism and consequent eradication of Yugoslavia, the press for nationhood by Canadian Quebec, the cries for recognition by the Basques in Spain, and so many more pockets of ethnically focused people seeking to fulfill their autonomy. Nationalism appears to be a modern right. Is it a signal of the times that forming a nation is the only way to have a voice in government? Does the smaller and smaller and smaller unit lead to anarchy, to the *absence* of government?

---

6 Originally, a "club" of European nations convened through agreements to form the Common Market, then the European Economic Community, which gave way to the concept of the European Community following the Single European Act of 1986. This development of a free-trade area became the European Union (EU) in 1994.

The original members were France, West Germany, Italy, Belgium, the Netherlands, and Luxembourg. The United Kingdom, Ireland, and Denmark joined in 1973, Greece in 1981, Spain and Portugal in 1986. Austria, Finland, and Sweden in 1995.

Yet, national populations and their resources then inexorably *interact* with each other through war, acculturation, religious conversion, intermarriage, and through resource exchange, price wars, embargos, trade-quota manipulation, etc. Enormous changes gradually emerge and gain permanence ... until the next revolutionary stage.[7]

As the world gets interactively smaller and busier, the nation-components collide more often, like massive molecules slowing down and getting closer to one another, like water becoming ice. Israeli statesman Abba Eban, writing in *Foreign Affairs* magazine, echoes this view: he sees the world "integrating and fragmenting" at the same time. Internationally syndicated columnist William Pfaff, author of *The Wrath of Nations*, sees the technological and economic integration of modern international society coexisting with the national struggle of the most primitive kind, e.g., among Serbs, Croats, Bosnians (and he provides a long list of evidence), all otherwise members of the advanced industrial world.[8]

Communications, trade, and tourism now expose us all to one another in ways and to extents beyond the imagination just two generations ago. Within vastly increased interaction, the modern western nation founds itself upon the practical bases of defense, social order in society, justice, structured economy, and social services. All are provided to the citizens. The empowerment of religiousness given to nationhood justifies its existence. To the citizens, this nationhood is worth dying for.

In this smaller world, now so repeatedly wounded with global conflict, all national acts are literally witnessed and evaluated immediately through modern information and communication technologies. The nationalism strength of the major powers, after the global wars, has switched from war to commerce. Now, *how* we interact, *how* we exchange which resources, *how much one nation needs another*—just as much as which political or religious doctrine we feel is the real truth—these are the considerations that determine national peace or unrest, Summer or Winter. The goal appears to be a

---

7 Britain's monarchy, for example, is German—before that it was Dutch, and before that it was Scottish. There has been no "English" king since the eleventh century. (See "England," 210.)

8 Pfaff, 30.

world community of independent states; the Millennium consciousness of planet earth.[9*]

Financial editor, broadcast commentator, and world market expert Hamish McRae, in *The World in 2020*, sees an overwhelming inexorability in "the economic logic pressing towards an integrated European economic space. It will take place. The only issue is the time scale over which this happens. Just how quickly Europe will unify, and the extent to which it can unify, will turn on its more general ability to adapt to change."[10]

And what will happen when China culminates in *its* new season? Later in our predictions, we will study the takeover of Hong Kong scheduled for July 1, 1997, about China's inevitable governmental reorganization and leadership of the Pacific Market.

Russia and now China will have moved far away from a centrally planned marketing system (and government). There are similar signs in the Koreas as well. When will all of this mature? Will the agonizing growing pains continue; will there be new collisions between old countries and new ones? Is the millennial time schedule going to witness an entire world playing by the same economic rules? McRae seems to think so; and he adds logically that the rewards will go to those who best understand the rules. It *seems* peaceful.

At the same time, what will happen between Syria and Israel? Will the peace treaties already concluded in the Middle East—and the new ones—hold up? Are we anticipating a grand market in the Middle East, a consolidation of resources involving Syria, Lebanon, Israel, Jordan, and Egypt? Will this be inspired by the grand market now building in the Pacific Basin, overseen by China, involving Hong Kong, Taiwan, North Korea, Japan, Indonesia, Australia, and New Zealand, and potentially India? Will these balance the European Union?

Does the religious spirit of being the chosen people in the Promised Land yet prevail in Israel or is that just the projection of minority fanatics? In the Balkans, will the warring factions be admitted into an *extended* European Union to safeguard the return

---

9 For the astrologer, signal to this thrust is the entrance of Pluto into Sagittarius, involving the significances of world trade, tourism, as well as the Internet, the Information Highway, and, again, the interplay to an extreme between government and religion. We can expect the concentrated formulation of international ethics and justice to dominate the international scene, all working toward world government—bureaucracy—when Pluto enters Capricorn in 2009.

10 McRae, 65.

of civilization to that area? Will the concept of a grand Europe reach eastward to the Ural Mountains in (western) Russia?

And Africa. Africa's borders have been determined more by family, community, tribe, ethnic group, and religion than by nationhood, by politics. Indeed, there were "liberation" movements at the close-out of colonialism in the 1960s and 1970s, but historians see these movements as westernized elitist activities, of Europe(ans) bringing the sense and infrastructure of nationalism to Africa. But "nationhood" is confusing to the African sense of tribe and history. It is independence that the people want, *as an extension of historically nomadic ways.*

It is no secret that South Africa, while setting a stirring example of tenacity and patience within the European system, will have much ground to cover once again when Nelson Mandela is no longer in power, and *North* Africa presents an imposing list of changing governments and borders, a dangerously unstable picture for the future.

Pfaff suggests what is perhaps a majority view among social historians: that the sense of international community should be aroused in Africa through reimposition of a form of "paternalist neocolonialism," i.e., the Africans are not yet ready for nationhood.[11]

Will South America continue to look to the north for political and economic rescue, and North America to the East *and* West for trade supremacy and enforced political hegemony? Do two vast oceans protect the United States in particular from the implosion of the world? The United States still remains an extension of Europe, no longer through ancestral origins and immigration, but through protection alliances born in the First World War, matured in the Second, and gone gray in Vietnam and Iraq.

History Has Signals

Perhaps the most clear-cut historical example of a change of eras is the time long ago when archeo-historians say the Bronze Age ended and the Iron Age began. History looks back specifically to 1205 B.C.E. and defines this end and new beginning in unequivocal terms of catastrophe. Mycenaean Greece disappeared; Anatolia (ancient Turkey) came to an end; the Hittite (ancient Jordan) empire disappeared.

---

11 Pfaff, 158.

Everywhere in the ancient world, urban life was set back drastically. In Egypt, the Twentieth Dynasty marked the end of the New Kingdom and almost the end of pharaonic achievement. The average temperature of the desert area rose 3 degrees Centigrade and rainfall diminished overall by 20%. Historian Robert Drews and many others point to this time as the "worst disaster in ancient history, even more calamitous than the collapse of the western Roman Empire" which followed much later, of course.

The legendary Sea Peoples, marauders probably from Sicily, Sardinia, and the western coast of Italy, joined with Lybian mercenaries and, with new warfare tactics and technology, invaded many lands in the Mediterranean region. They finally settled in what is now the Gaza Strip on the southwest coast of Israel, probably the precursors of the ancient peoples (Philistines) later called "Palestinians" by the Romans.[12]

History already looks back similarly upon the twentieth century, to the years between 1914, with the beginning of World War I, and 1991 with the collapse of the Soviet Union, and sees calamity and enormous world reorganization. Country after country—the USSR, Romania, Ethiopia, Yugoslavia, Somalia, Haiti, Cuba, Afghanistan, areas of India, Sri Lanka, San Salvador, Peru, and more—all erupted in revolutionary bids for justice, change of government, improved ways of life. Boundaries and leaders were changed. A new World Order was born.

There were signs for both these epochs—as there are, indeed, for all epochs—*astrological* signs. In 1205 B.C.E., two mighty planets in rare conjunction (Uranus and Pluto arriving to the same longitudinal degree in the heavens; occurring every 112, 143, 112, 143, etc. years) signalled the turnover of all centers of power.[13*] Early in

---

12 See Drews.
   As well at this time of 1205 B.C.E.—not covered by Drews—in the reign of Ramesses II, the Exodus of the Jews out of Egypt has been placed; inaccurately and without proof, as we shall see in our discussion of Israel's future (See "Israel," page 103.)

13 See December 2, 1205 B.C.E. (computer entry, -1204). The conjunction occurred at 21 Scorpio 59. Modern occurrences of this conjunction occurred in 1850 (June 26 at 2:40 A.M., UT) signaling the Taiping Rebellion (twenty million killed), the Crimean War (France, Turkey, Russia, Great Britain, Sardinia, Austria), the twelve-year Maori War in New Zealand, the American Civil War (breakup of the Union, Emancipation Act, over 600,000 killed); and in 1966 (April 4 at 8:05 P.M., GMT), signaling the height of American bombardment of Vietnam (some 500,000 U.S. military personnel involved), France's withdrawal from NATO, the beginning of the Cultural Revolution in China; Quebec separatists working for independence from Canada; Soviet forces invading Czechoslovakia.

1993, the planets Uranus and Neptune conjoined for the first time in 170 years, and similarly signalled a tremendous upheaval through worldwide revolution, a direct response to the people's sense of entrenched injustice.[14*]

Astrologers *knew* there would be a new World Order organized in the mid-1990s, completing this century, and introducing the next. Astrologers were able to relate this phenomenological occurrence in the heavens to the birth charts of specific nations (the horoscope, the imprint of the heavens, the planetary positions at the moment of national "birth," the ruler taking power, the signing of a constitution, etc.) to pinpoint which nations would be swept up in the eruptive furor. For example, the Uranus-Neptune conjunction occurred at an extremely important place in the horoscope of the nation of Iraq.[15*]

This rare and powerfully symbolic conjunction of Uranus and Neptune connected strongly with other national horoscopes as well. Throughout the globe, revolution began and continues still.

Century Signatures

There is also the planetary Astro-profile of the twentieth century itself, that moment when the calendar turned at 00:00 hours on January 1, 1900.[16*] This horoscope promises enormous international struggle, the international clash of national ambitions, the restructuring of nations; the dissolution of administrations throughout the world; conspicuous emphasis on war and a tremendous concern with right and wrong.

The most focused synthesis of this aggression of internationalisms is what astrologers see in the technical formula of

---

14 First conjunction occurred on February 2, 1993, at 12:51 P.M., GMT, in 19 Capricorn 34.

15 Iraq was formerly recognized as a kingdom with the assumption of the throne by Faisal on August 23, 1921, precisely at 6:00 A.M. in Baghdad. A great gathering was witness to the event. Sir Percy Cox read the proclamation of the kingdom and brought personal best wishes from England's King George. The Iraqi Moon is at 19 Aries, *squared by the Uranus-Neptune conjunction.* Please see Tyl, *Prediction in Astrology*, for a time-specific scenario of the Gulf War, "Desert Storm," written *before* the War took place.

16 Astrologers are alerted to a calendar bias in New Year horoscopes since the 00:00 hours time always places the Sun at the fourth cusp. Additionally, the Sun is *always* in Capricorn and Mercury and/or Venus are usually in Sagittarius, Capricorn, or Aquarius. The New Year/Century chart will always be midnight for whatever area on the globe it is cast. It is the tension structures among the planets that can be telling in projection of the century ahead, as well as the tie-in of those structures with subsequent phenomenological charts like Mars-Saturn and Jupiter-Saturn conjunctions.

"Saturn equaling Sun/Pluto" (Saturn aspecting the midpoint position of Sun and Pluto), "the illumination of power needs; the needs to control; new perspectives to be confirmed through struggle and ruthlessness."[17]*

This picture is in great contrast with the horoscopic portrait of the first moment of the *nineteenth* century which focuses conspicuously upon a planetary picture Mercury=Jupiter/Uranus, "the excited presentation of ideas, curiosity and invention; sudden inspiration and discovery; learning, communications, international travel."[18]* There is a war signature as well, but not on the world scale of the horoscope indications for the twentieth century.

There are other sensitive and detailed astrological measurements that guide astrologers to understanding trends in the world and specific developmental occurrences in and among nations.[19]*

The Century Ahead

"Umbrella" Predictions: The horoscope—the Astro-profile—for the century ahead, drawn for 00:00 hours on January 1, 2000, promises eruptive explosion out of frustration, *along with international peace treaties being broken.* Not surprisingly, the countries that are decidedly highlighted by the planetary picture are the United States, Israel, Iraq, and China. There are other countries specifical-

---

17 This twentieth century horoscope has 7 conjunctions, 5 oppositions at a New Moon conjoined by Mars. Jupiter is unaspected and dominant in Sagittarius. Saturn = Sun/Pluto within 1' orb; Aries Point = Moon/Saturn (within 4'): ambition, strategy, overkill on public display.

Additionally, the Century Mars opposes the United States Sun (July 4, 1776 at 2:13 A.M., LMT in Philadelphia, and is exactly conjunct the Ascendant of the French Third Republic (September 04, 1870 at 4:00 P.M. in Paris; relevant 1870-1946; Campion, *World Horoscopes*, 132); the Century Saturn is square Japan's Meiji Constitution Mars (February 11, 1889 at 12 noon LMT in Tokyo; relevant until its Sovereignty was confirmed April 28, 1952, 1:30 P.M. GMT; Campion, Ibid, 172); the Century Pluto squared the England Saturn (December 25, 1066 at noon LMT in London; Campion, *Ibid*, 287); and squared the Sun-Moon midpoint of the Nazi Germany horoscope (January 30, 1933 at 11:15 A.M. in Berlin; *Ibid*, 140). Midpoint picture synthesis: Tyl, *Prediction* and *Synthesis*, Appendix.

18 The chart focuses on the T-Square Mercury/Jupiter in mutual reception, the axis squared by Uranus in Virgo, disposited by Mercury. Additionally Mars squares Pluto, an aspect of belligerence. Midpoint picture synthesis: Tyl, Ibid, Appendix.

19 A chief one is the Great Conjunction of Jupiter-Saturn occurring every 20 years or so. Next occurrence: May 28, 2000 at 3:59 P.M. GMT. A chart cast for the time of this signal conjunction from the perspective of a capital city suggests its future development. See, Tyl, "Jupiter-Saturn Synthesis—20-Year Cycles of History in the Making," *The Mountain Astrologer* magazine, July 1995, 39–49.

ly keyed, and they will come forward in the predictions later in this study.[20*]

The overall picture clearly involves the *eruption of radicalism;* authoritarian doctrine imposed in the name of religion, protected somehow with the ethics of religion or national philosophy. The portrait is inescapably one of *the painful use of force in the name of radical doctrine;* wars of the spirit as well as the breakdown of spiritual order. As we will study in further detail later, it is suggested by this century horoscope that the United States will prevail as a "lesson-teacher" throughout the next 100 years, an enforcer, a mediator.[21*]

■ Prediction ...

Internationalism and Regionalism—The outbreaks of treaty upsets and wars will disrupt an overall, extraordinarily well-defined emphasis upon the political power of international trade and tourism, i.e., the press for internationalism (liberalism) over nationalism (conservatism), affecting the Vatican and world Catholicism (its tenets and lifestyle and expansion), Japan, China, the Koreas, and the Middle East especially. Dramatic regional alignments—nations grouped together by common needs and even a common currency: the expanded Pacific Basin, the expanded European Market, an allied Middle East, the Americas—will be defined en route to clear consideration and formulation of world community, world government around 2008–09.[22*]

---

20 The dominating planetary picture in the twenty-first century horoscope is Uranus= Moon/Saturn (eruption out of frustration) and Mars square Venus in Sagittarius (breaking the peace). Neptune squares the Moon, adding deception, duplicity, bewilderment. The Scorpionic Moon suggests the control factors of religion, and the whole complex introduces *radicalism*, certainly a dimension of Pluto in Sagittarius as well.

  Note that the key Uranus is conjunct the United States Midheaven and opposes the Israel Saturn; Neptune opposes the Israel Moon; the Sun opposes the Iraq Pluto, illuminating a power struggle; and the Century Sun-Moon midpoint at 8 Sagittarius 34 equals the U.S. Uranus and Ascendant (in Gemini) and the Iraq Uranus as well. The China Mars opposes the Century Uranus exactly.

21 The Century Jupiter in Aries, a powerful echo of the ethical egocentrism of nations, is square the U.S. Mercury-Pluto axis, i.e., teaching lessons, gaining a good reputation, persuasion and publicity. And in the background, of course, the presence of Pluto in Sagittarius, i.e., dogma.

22 The passage of Pluto through Sagittarius into Capricorn.

■ Prediction ...

The Environment—Additionally, as much as sporadic battle skirmishes will allow, there will be global, cooperative emphasis on proper management of the environment. Population explosion and a geometric increase in energy consumption have caused much damage over thousands of years, most markedly, though, since the Industrial Revolution. World population tripled during the twentieth century and world production jumped from $0.6 trillion in 1900 to $15 trillion in 1990, a twenty-five-fold increase. Consumption of fossil fuels also surged eleven-fold in the same period. This is an awesome drain and attack upon the planet that sustains us. World intelligence will be called into action as never before to deal with the problem of greater human activity causing increased environmental destruction.[23]

■ Prediction ...

Aging—Nations will now confront the problem of aging population segments dominating their society, i.e., with the older levels of populations growing excessively, thanks to greater protection against disease and fewer and shorter wars. For example, Japan, in just two generations, has gone from being the youngest nation to the oldest; there are similar rises in Canada, France, Germany, Italy, the United Kingdom, and the United States. This problem will be severe and will surely dominate world fitness consciousness (much as the AIDS epidemic did in the '80s and '90s) in the period late 2001 and all of 2002.[24]

---

23 Additionally, note that in 1650, world population was approximately 500 million with an annual growth rate of 0.3%, reaching 800 million in the eighteenth century. The number doubled in the next 100 years, and projections to the middle of the twenty-first century are to 10 billion. *Foreign Affairs* magazine, Vol 74, No. 5, September/October 1995, Eisuke Sakakibara, "The End of Progressivism," page 12.

24 See McRae, Chapter 5, page 100, graphing several OECD report findings. In 1950, just after World War II, 5% of Japan's population was aged sixty-five and over; in 1995, 17%, projection to 2020, 24%. For the United States in the same period: 8, 12, 17%, respectively. Note transiting Saturn conjunct Pluto late 2001, 2002.

■ Prediction ...

Education—Concomitant with the aging issue will be the education issue, the crucial fortification and inspiration of the young for realization of progress in the future. Studies and statistics abound to show that it is not the *structure* of education that is deficient, i.e., foreign students do better in the United States educational system than do American students. Rather, studies suggest that *the cultural attitude toward the need to learn* and the rewards of learning; and a nation's deficient attention to the *earlier levels* of education (research and university-level education are far and away the more emphasized) are the problem areas. The quality of research (higher-level education), for example, in most fields in the United States is the best in the world, while the average level of attainment by pupils leaving school is the worst in the industrial world.[25]

■ Prediction ...

Religion and the Spirit—In its relation to attitude and future orientation, religion will be part of the education power-moves in industrial societies, especially in the United States and Japan, each facing social renewal programs of grand scope. Formal religious movements will come into politics more and more and more. This is the way of human history; it is a dominant statement in global life transiting the Millennium, and it will punctuate practically every point of information and prediction established in the pages that follow.

In conclusion of this orientation to the Millennium, we can appreciate that the tie between astrology and world events can be discovered and developed strongly, that there are astrological signals ahead that should be studied carefully. We can know that there will continue to be wars and that they will be propelled fervently by religion (ethics, righting wrongs, affirming history) cloaked in nationalism. We can know that there are cycles that seem to alternate good times and bad, the past and future, with ancient enmities living still in our modern times. We can know that global activity is

---

25 McRae, 42.

birthing a younger world, with regions of diverse personality traits warring and working to meld in unified character.

There will be no technical astrology presented in the text of this study of our world buildup and entrance to the future; the astrology, in abbreviated, technical detail, is annotated in many of the footnotes to the text. What is presented within the text has as its foundation my work with astrology. And that work is seasoned by courage born of thirty years practice and my full awareness of how much we astrologers yet do not know.

I work with a deep conviction that astrology can help us understand the world in which we live. While astrology certainly articulates history startlingly well, the future is the greater challenge.

The objectivity throughout these pages is not presented as a proof of any kind—astrology is beyond that—but to be informative and stimulating, to present the exercise of one astrologer's learning, intuiting, measuring, and sharing. So remember with me, please, that, even with the substantive insight and temporal guidelines of astrology, I am still participating within the fallible human condition to understand the purpose of time.

Let's see what we can learn.

2

LARGE ORGANIZATIONAL CHANGE

The Breakdown of the United Nations

After the cataclysm of the protracted world war period between 1914 and 1945, it was crucially evident that there was a need for global co-ordination of international governmental agendas. The key powers at the time, the United States and USSR, could not be allowed or, indeed, relied upon to decide the ways of the world, what with the socio-political tensions continuing and growing between them.

The United Nations was organized late in 1945 with the same noble purpose as its predecessor, the League of Nations, which had been formed after World War I and subsequently swallowed up into impotence during the following war. The consensus of historians and journalists worldwide is clear that the United Nations has fallen into similar ineffectiveness.

The former United Nations representative from Israel (1948–59), then serving concurrently as Ambassador to the United States (1950–59), Abba Eban, has stated this consensus simply and poignantly: (in reference to the United Nations' founding conference in San Francisco in April 1945) "Many who attended the sessions may have felt that expectations were being set exaggeratedly high, but few would have predicted that after five decades the peace organization would resemble the chorus in a Greek drama, expressing consternation at events it has no power to control."[26]

---

26 *Foreign Affairs* magazine, Vol 74, No. 5, September/October 1995, "The U.N. Idea Revisited," by Abba Eban, page 39.

The United Nations began with fifty-one country-members and has grown to 185 in 1995—and as a testament to the viral surge of nationalism rampant throughout the world, it is significant to note that only some twenty of these members, nearly all European or American, *possessed national consciousness before 1914.*

The United Nations' initial budget in 1945 was $147 million. That budget has grown to over $1.3 billion in 1995. The formation of international organizations working to coordinate peace-keeping and health-maintenance activities throughout the world has grown in grand scale as well: some 265 inter-governmental organizations and no fewer than 4,615 non-governmental ones were formed by the mid-1980s.[27]

However, as Abba Eban puts it, the role of watchdog (nurse-maid) to the world fell initially and most pointedly into the illusion that the American-Soviet-British alliance that had won the victory *would command the future through the United Nations.* Then the highest expectancy for catalytic action was directed toward the United States, the United Nation's most powerful member.[28*]

Three Birth Defects

To astrologers, the horoscope of the United Nations reveals three major birth defects, if you will—shortcomings that were visible instantly at the end of 1945 from the horoscope and all too soon from the record of activity thereafter.

First, the organization is unable to administer force; it is dependent on the force given to it by its member nations. Bureaucracy and caution stifle any organizational autonomy and drive.[29*]

Abba Eban sees the United Nations' formation of the austere Security Council (the United States, Russia, China, Britain, and France) as the first time in history that collective security would be

---

27 Hobsbawm, 430.

28 While the signatures of fifty participating nations were collected at the San Francisco Conference on June 26, 1945, the United Nations came into existence with the final signing by the U.S. Secretary of State of a protocol deposit of ratification at 4:45 P.M. on October 24, 1945. See Campion, *World Horoscopes*, #359.

  It is most telling to note that the United Nations Midheaven is almost exactly opposed the United States Sun and the United States Mars energizes the United Nations Moon through exact conjunction. The United States was/is the U.N.

29 Mars (force) is the ruler of the U.N. Ascendant and is conjoined with Saturn in Cancer in the 4th, with no other aspects. This is a stagnating "island," dedicated to the enforcement of security but unable to do anything about it.

institutionalized.[30] Now, fifty years later, Eban sees this as a "hollow doctrine," it being very unlikely that *collective* security will ever again regain preeminence as an aim of international politics. The loyalties built around the nation-state are not transferable to any notion of world community, according to Eban: *what is aggression for one is self-defense for another and national liberation for a third.* Eban feels that world community is not the spirit of our present age. "There are no collective solutions to individual crises."[31]

Another assessment of this flaw of impotence in the United Nations infrastructure is the organization's "well-demonstrated capacity to be seen to fail." This view is presented by Conor Cruise O'Brien, Irish statesman, a delegate member to the United Nations and former editor in chief of the London Observer. The United Nations becomes a scapegoat for international crisis: for example, the United States supported the revolt in Hungary late in 1956 but could not come to the Hungarians' aid because of the threat of triggering a world war with the Russians; the case was handed over to the United Nations in whose General Assembly debate and condemnation of the Russians were aired with no action mustered among the members. The United Nations then "took all the blame for the ignominious passivity through which the Eisenhower Administration had avoided a war."[32]

Another example of the powerlessness of the U.N. came crucially to light in the 1980s when the government of Iraq killed thousands of its citizens by poison gas, breaking one of the clearest-cut international bans contained in the Geneva Protocol of 1925 against the use of chemical warfare (not ratified by the United States, by the way, until fifty years later in 1975): no action was taken against the offender. The protracted and, some would say, clumsy surveillance of Iraq with regard to atomic power would be another example, let alone the administrative muddling with Bosnia, which, according to Eban, represented not a failure of power but a paralysis of will among the European nations and the United States.[33]

---

30 The People's Republic of China was admitted to the United Nations on October 15, 1971, against the idea pressed by the United States that there should be a "Two-China" membership. President Nixon's courageous and historic trip to China took place February 18–21, 1972. Formal diplomatic relations with the United States followed seven years later on January 1, 1979.

31 *Foreign Affairs* magazine, Vol 74, No. 5, September/October 1995, "The U.N. Idea Revisited," by Abba Eban, page 43, 46, 47, 51.

32 O'Brien, 86–87.

33 Ibid, page 52.

Second, there is every indication that the United Nations is incapable of being fiscally healthy and clear in its financial records.[34*] It has been a long-continuing media event to try to unravel the U.N.'s finances and track their management: "The United Nations is going broke," according to Secretary General Boutros Boutros-Ghali, stated at the U.N.'s fiftieth anniversary celebration. The Secretary then predicted that the peacekeeping debt could rise from the $800 million in June 1995 to $1.1 billion by December 1995. The deepening financial crisis could force the U.N. to stop reimbursement to countries for their troop and equipment contributions to keep the peace. This trend projects a difficult future indeed.[35]

The member nations are constantly behind in their payments to the U.N. Russia owes nearly $599 million, as of 1995; France, more than $81 million; and South Africa nearly $113 million, as examples. One of the chief delinquents is the United States, owing *$1.18 billion* as of May 31, 1995, approximately one-year's operating costs for the organization (which sum the United States is disputing, claiming arrears of only $955.5 million).

Hamish McRae notes signs of a United States cut-back in financial support for multinational agencies, specifically for the United Nations. He sees this as (the beginning of) the United States' retreat from global leadership.[36]

While it is undeniable that a nation's growth in its economy increases its political influence, the indication here is that the United States can have more effect on the world *on its own*, overseeing the world, than it does working through the United Nations. Witness the transferral of "responsibility" over the Bosnian crisis from the United Nations, to NATO, to the United States.[37*]

---

34 Venus rules the 2nd and the 7th, and is in tight conjunction with Neptune and Jupiter in Libra.

35 *New York Times*; Christopher Wren, June 25, 1995, page 4.
   Egyptian Boutros Boutros-Ghali is the sixth Secretary General of the United Nations: preceding him were Trygve Lie, 1945–53 (Norway); Dag Hammarskjold, 1953–61 (Sweden); U Thant, 1961–71 (Burma); Kurt Waldheim, 1972–81 (Austria); Javier Perez de Cuellar, 1982–92 (Peru).

36 McRae, 221.

37 This role of international nursemaid, watchdog, humanitarian caretaker portrays vividly, classically, the United States' Sun in Cancer and the Moon in Aquarius. (See "The Lone SuperPower," page 225.)

And third, the United Nations is unable to establish an informative and compelling public image.[38*] The public relations problem faced by the world organization is formidable. Its popularity rises only at times of highly visible open conflict, such as after the Persian Gulf War (with 67% of those polled by Gallup and Roper saying the U.N. was doing "a good job" and the previous high of 42% logged after the Korean War). In June 1995, in the depths of involvements in Bosnia and Western Africa (Rwanda, Burundi, Tanzania) and other places on our restless globe, the poll shows 42% of Americans favorably impressed, with 46% saying the United Nations is doing a bad job.[39]

Most of the world population does not know that the United Nations is deeply active in disease control and disease elimination, feeding the hungry and maintaining some seventeen missions around the world, all costing many millions of dollars. The United Nations does not *appear* successful; it can not claim success in world situations that are clear enough and dramatic enough to impress upon the world the value of the organization.

After the fall of the USSR in October-December 1991, there was a surge of optimism about the future of the United Nations, but that fresh impetus seemed to dissipate quickly.[40*] Astrologically, the beginning of the end of the United Nations as we have known it coincided with the eruption of the Rwanda-Burundi incident on April 6, 1994.[41*]

The United Nations has been strongly criticized for not being able to head off the uprisings in Rwanda and Somalia, Haiti, and Cuba. The apparent confusion and ineffectiveness of the U.N. in

---

38 The United Nations Sun is in Scorpio (inscrutable) and is peregrine (not making a Ptolemaic aspect), placed in the 7th House of the Public. Venus rules the 7th and is muted by conjunction with Neptune. Mercury, ruler of the communications 3rd, is in the 7th and is squared by Pluto (public anxiety). The Sun and Pluto are in mutual reception, reiterating a frustration in identity fulfillment.

39 *New York Times*, June 25, 1995, page 4.

40 SA Sun opposed U.N. Uranus; SP Moon trine Uranus; *tr Uranus exactly conjunct the MC*; tr Saturn square the Sun. Important Note: Solar Arcs (SA) define the progressed Sun's distance from birth to any given future time, determined by subtraction of the natal Sun from the Secondary Progressed Sun position; the SA is then applied uniformly to all birth planetary positions and points, advancing the horoscope into time, preserving its relative birth interrelationships. In effect, 1 degree equals close to one year. Orbs are kept within 2 degrees; for Transits (tr), orbs are conventional. "SP" is Secondary Progression. For Solar Arc theory and Practice, see Tyl, *Prediction in Astrology.*

41 SA Moon exactly square the U.N. Pluto; SA Ascendant conjunct Moon; SA Pluto conjunct Aries Point=Uranus/Midheaven; with tr Uranus-Neptune square the U.N. Ascendant and tr Mars square the Moon.

the Bosnian War have pushed public opinion into a trough of disregard for the institution. The end seems imminent.

■ Prediction ...

New Secretary General—Boutros Boutros-Ghali will not continue in a second term as Secretary General. He will face reelection at the end of 1996, at the same time as the United States will have picked its president. To be reelected, Boutrous-Ghali needs the backing of a majority of the 185 countries in the General Assembly and the tacit or open support of the five permanent members of the Security Council: the United States, Russia, China, Britain, and France. Four of these Security Council members have been involved with the Bosnia crisis. In spite of the fact that every preceding Secretary General has been reelected to a second term, the horoscope of the United Nations indicates much confusion and an impulsive bid for change focused in November–December 1996, which should correspond to the ouster of Mr. Boutrous-Ghali (or his studied withdrawal) after his first term. A death may figure prominently in the course of these events.[42*]

■ Prediction ...

Financial Exposé—The next Secretary General of the United Nations will have a very difficult time with the same problems that have plagued the U.N. since its inception. There could very well be a major inspection and exposé of the U.N.'s finances in August 1997, which will be very drawn out and inconclusive. The build-up of continuing dissatisfaction will be extreme throughout 1998, when the U.N. will be called

---

42 In the United Nations horoscope: *SA Sun opposed Moon, SA Pluto semisquare Sun; SA Saturn=Pluto/Ascendant; tr Neptune opposed Saturn*, ruler of the 10th throughout 1995 and 1996; tr Uranus square the Sun in February and September-November 1996; tr Saturn applying to conjunction with the Ascendant, exact in July 1997.

Boutros Boutros-Ghali was born November 14, 1922 in Cairo, Egypt. In March-July 1996, he experiences transiting Uranus opposed Jupiter positioned within a powerful Water Grand Trine that does not include the Sun or Moon: this suggests a new direction for Boutros-Ghali, one that will bring relief from tension and emotional pain. Things will happen quickly in this time period for him and lead to a new direction in his life, perhaps conspicuously spiritual: SA Neptune conjunct Jupiter exact in July 1997.

upon to mediate crises in the world and will fail through administrative and financial disorganization and impotence because of the dissatisfaction of its constituency. Between June 1999 and September 2000, the United Nations as we know it will be no more.

The new, more practicable goals for the United Nations—following positive indications in its Astro-profile—would be best focused in public information and teaching, leading the battle against malnutrition that affects half the world population, leading the battle for literacy (with some 800 million adults illiterate throughout the world), leading the promotion of science, technology, and industrial progress in nations 3,000 times less developed than the most affluent nations. Information and practical deployment of energy will keep our planet alive, will vitalize the concept of world community, and fulfill the concept among nations to be united in good health and prosperity. This could well be the new direction for the United Nations at the beginning of the next Millennium; a new way of global caretaking conceived out of a big-money collapse and the impracticality of enforced collective security, put into trial operation early in 2001.[43*]

Historic Change in the Papacy: "At the End of the World"

The Vatican is the smallest sovereign state in the world: just under six square miles, with some 1,500 people and a budget of about $182 million (1993). The Vatican has commanded the attention of the world for well over a thousand years. It grew into being from the Papal State of the Middle Ages that was created gradually through battles between the Bishops of Rome (part of the title given to the Popes) and their rivals, chiefly in the East, and the slow accumulation of massive wealth by the Roman Church.

The Papacy seated in the Vatican has inspired much history, much of it complicated, tyrannical, and sordid, from the Crusades

---

43 SA Saturn square Uranus (8/97) with tr Neptune square the Sun and tr Uranus opposed Pluto; tr Saturn opposed the Sun, SA Pluto=Saturn/Uranus (6/99); SA Uranus conjunct Pluto (1/00), SA Pluto conjunct Neptune (9/00), and SA Mercury conjunct MC (2/01). All to fulfill the Gemini Moon in the 3rd House, conjoined by Uranus, trined by Jupiter.

of the late eleventh, twelfth, and thirteenth centuries to recover Muslim-annexed holy places in Palestine (See "Crusades," page 138) to the autocratic denial, excommunication, and execution of scientists and competitive politicians in the fifteenth, sixteenth, and early seventeenth centuries.

The Vatican is the focus of the Roman Catholic Church and some one billion Catholics. The pope is the Church-proclaimed infallible spokesperson of God and perhaps the most prominent person in the world.

Refocusing the Vatican Position

The twentieth century saw a crucial refocus of the Vatican and its global political position. In 1919 in Italy, Benito Mussolini organized his *Fasci di Combattimento*, the black-shirted ex-soldiers set to overthrow the government through aggressive nationalism, through street rioting and general unrest among the people. This insurgence led to the formulation of the Fascist Party in 1921, lasting for twenty-three years, to the end of World War II. Fascism put the party and the state above the individual, demanding absolute obedience from citizens and the glorification of a singular leader (Mussolini). It was a movement against the so-called "Enlightenment" of democratic liberalism, the foundation of the epoch of the French Revolution in the mid-and-late eighteenth century that influenced the mind-set of European nations for well over a century (see "Enlightenment," page 176).

The Roman Catholic Church was caught in a political middle ground: large countries of the world adopted Fascism—notably Portugal, Austria, and Spain—and, while these countries were Roman Catholic, the Vatican was remaining neutral. This middle-ground position is the basis for the ambiguity about the Church's position (and that of Pope Pius XII, 1939–1958, most pointedly) during World War II, specifically in the light of Hitler's and Mussolini's policies of mutual cooperation.

Additionally, the Church was also struggling against the waves of Enlightenment that had illuminated intellect and independent thinking throughout Europe: Church tradition was being questioned; liberalism was tugging on conservatist anchors to the past.

The modern papacy came into being on June 7, 1929, at 11:00 A.M. in Vatican City when Vatican Secretary of State Cardinal

Pietro Gasparri and the Italian Prime Minister, Benito Mussolini, exchanged the instruments of ratification. This was the formalization—politically motivated by Mussolini to attract favor from the Church—of Italy/Vatican policy established in 1871, on May 13, when the Italian Parliament passed the "Law of Papal Guarantees," separating Roman Church and Italian State and *guaranteeing the pope great freedoms and independence.*[44]

Up to this time in the early twentieth century, to build, assert, and protect its position, the papacy had continuously built defensive barricades of doctrine against "the superior onslaught of modernism."[45] The modern papacy, with its accurately timed horoscope, projects a continuation of intense intellectual focus protected in a closed circuit of motivational self-sufficiency; in other words, the Vatican will "do its thing" as sole arbiter of truth, but as the Vatican has learned the ways of modern information management to preach a powerful doctrine to its people—international travel, publications, media management—it has also come glaringly face to face with dramatically changing values in the outside world.[46*]

Modernization Pressures

The Astro-profile of the Vatican—which is the Astro-profile of the Roman Church as well—shows that modernization is always the challenge; there seems to be a fragility, a loneliness of point of view, that lives more in shadow than in light. The cerebrated idealism endures, wrapped in chains of tradition, and must be protected *at all costs.*[47*]

The pressure is *not* new: for example, in the 1960s, '70s, and '80s the voice of a revived feminism assailed the Church, out of Italy and Poland, and then from the United States, to loosen divorce laws and anti-abortion doctrine. The Italian bank scandals of the

---

44 See Di Scala, 126-127, 230-231. Even in the light of the freedoms accorded the Vatican, Pope Pius IX complained bitterly that this internal Italian measure could be unilaterally revoked at any moment. He called himself the "prisoner Pope" within his 11,000-room Vatican. Popes after him kept the fears alive in the background of state dealings until the modern Papacy was clearly confirmed in its separation and freedoms fifty-two years later.

45 Hobsbawm, 110.

46 New Moon and Mercury, the triple conjunction in Gemini; Mercury ruling the Virgo Ascendant; the Fire Grand Trine. Tr Pluto opposed the MC 1995.

47 Note that Pluto is peregrine; the Sun-Moon blend is intensified in symbolism by its New Moon occurrence and angularity, supported by Mars in Leo (carte blanche for the application of dramatic energies). There are the square of Neptune to the Midheaven and the Aries Point=Moon/Pluto (self-absorbed intensity and zeal projected to the public). The Grand Trine in Fire does not involve the Sun or Moon; Mercury dominates as ruler of the Ascendant and final dispositor of the horoscope.

1980s, tied to the Vatican and to underworld assassinations, cast epic shadows upon the Church. The international decline in the influence and number of adherents to Catholicism suggests that the pressure is very great indeed for the Church to change, for it to accommodate the future.

There is more, much more, very deep within the Vatican's spirit: the horoscope of Pope John Paul II (the first non-Italian pope since Adrian VI of Utrecht elected in 1522) shows so very, very clearly the internationalism of his personal projection but, as well, it shows his stymied position between the conservatism and tradition of the past and the liberalism and innovation of the future. There is the indication that he will evade dealing—or not be able to deal—directly with the left-right factions (forces), that he will appear ineffective, off the mark in the human terms of expected programs and achievement. It is clear consensus that the pope has *substituted global politics* for the healing of the splintered factions of the Church.[48]*

The issues of modernization involve "two Churches," if you will, the old and the new, which concept of schism is phrased in extremism by some to see liberals as satanists, those prelates having infiltrated the leadership of the Church and insidiously spending their energy to go against ancient conventions.[49]

The Catholic World Report states that "liberal theology no longer recognizes any transcendent religious authority; it treats the historic teachings and practices of the Church as matters entirely subject to changing human needs. Simply put, in the debates that divide Catholics today, 'conservatives' believe in revelation in the classical sense, while 'liberals' do not."[50]

---

48 Pope John Paul II was born on May 18, 1920 at 1:00 P.M. EET at Wadowice, Poland (18E30; 49N53). New Moon birth and decided 9th House concentration *square the axis of Saturn (conservatism) and Uranus (liberalism)* upon the Virgo-Pisces Ascendant. Mars is *peregrine* in Libra and *retrograde.*

49 "There subsisted only a faithful remnant of practicing Catholics. His (the pope's) own Vatican chancery and the various diocesan chanceries throughout the Church were in the hands of the anti-Church partisans. Heresy and grave error resided in the seminaries. An intricate and self-protective network of actively homosexual priests, nuns, bishops, and some cardinals now throttled all attempts to reform morals." Martin, 632; conjecturally stated in extreme, issuing from the substantive reality of current problems.

50 *The Catholic World Report,* December 1995, page 40: "Catholicism and Modernity: A Time for Decision," by James Hitchcock, professor of history, St. Louis University, a founder of the Fellowship of Catholic Scholars.

Much of the factionalism revolves about reforms installed through the epic Vatican II Council:[51] the relaxation of the issue of the Roman Catholic Church's having exclusive possession of the means of eternal salvation; recognition of the local "community of faith" to provide guidance and authority, instead of a hierarchic body of bishops answering to the pope; clusters of "communities of faith" to cooperate with mankind to build and assure the success of world peace and world reform; and fourth, the resolve to bring into alignment with the practices of the world at large the Church issues of conception, marriage, death, and sexuality.[52]

To study the observations of Malachi Martin—theologian, Catholic Church expert, former Jesuit and professor at the Vatican's Pontifical Biblical Institute, a close associate of Pope John XXIII—the schism in the Church is broad, deep, and perilous. He describes the imminent potential of a pope elected by the liberal contingent of cardinals, "cutting the entire visible body of the Church loose from the traditional unity ... that the Church has hitherto always believed and taught was divinely established: the shudder that will shake the Roman Catholic body in that day will be the shudder of its death agony. For its pains will be from within itself, orchestrated

51 The First Vatican Council was held 1869–70; summoned by Pius IX. *It reinstated traditional dogma* against materialism, rationalism, and liberalism. It declared the pope to be infallible. The vote on infallibility was boycotted by 20% of the over 600 bishops present. The unanimity of the remaining was declared at the same time that a violent electrical storm burst over St. Peter's, with thunder and lightning. *How the Pope Became Infallible*, August Bernhard Hasler; Doubleday, New York 1981.

The astrology of the announcement—July 18, 1870—is telling: Sun-Uranus conjunction squared (rationalized) by Neptune; Moon in Aries (singularity of authority) and conspicuously peregrine; with Saturn dramatically opposing Mars-Venus (renunciation and contention), signalling the enormous resistance to the doctrine voiced in the Council and the split between the conservatives (The "Old Catholics") and the resistant liberals.

The Second Vatican Council was held 1962–65; summoned by John XXIII, to renew the Church, the updating of its organization and attitude to the modern world, and the ultimate reunion of all Christian churches.

The astrology for the Second Council, focused on its conclusion in early December, 1965, revealed extraordinary measurements of confirmation and empowerment, as well as new perspectives in the Vatican horoscope: SA Sun-Moon conjunct Pluto; SA Uranus square Mars; tr Pluto-Uranus square the Vatican Mercury; tr Saturn square the Vatican Sun-Moon conjunction in the 10th House and tr Jupiter conjunct that New Moon just before the close of the Council.

52 Martin, 682. A related issue of tremendous importance is the Pope's adamant refusal to alter the Vatican's male-dominated hierarchy and empower women with greater rights, including ordination to the priesthood. One instance of the outcry: in October, 1994, American nuns marched in St. Peter's Square, defying local laws, straight to the windows of Pope John Paul's apartment to protest. (*The Washington Post*, October 27, 1994, A33).

by its leaders and its members. There will be no one on earth to hold the fractionating members of the visible Roman Catholic body together as a living compact organization."[53]

Global Politics and the Vision at Fatima

On another level of tension, the collapse of the Soviet Union and Yugoslavia—the chaos of the Balkan region—is seen as breakdown of the global politics engineered by John Paul II (with Gorbachev), beginning with the pope's countryman Lech Walesa rising on the shoulders of the Solidarity movement to reach the presidency of Poland ... and losing reelection to that position late in 1995.

Very importantly, this crumbling of the global politics program of John Paul's papacy is *framed within the celebrated prophecies of the Virgin Mary* delivered to three Portuguese peasant children in Fatima on the thirteenth of each month from May to October 1917. The final visitation occurred before the world press and a crowd of 75,000. There were miracles of proof that day: a dancing sun of varied colors, instant climatic change from mired mud and heavy rain to brilliant sunshine, the instant drying of all attendees' clothing, winds blowing with no foliage response, and more.

The Virgin Mary had given the children *three predictive messages:* the first one warned that society was following a path of sin; the second predicted the outbreak of World War II and asked that the Church formally consecrate the Soviet Union to her, under threat of error, evil, and death spreading throughout the world.

The third and key message is still officially secret and was kept sealed until 1960, for the Pope's eyes only. Pope John XXIII was the first pope to read it; he decided to take no action on the prediction and on the directives of the message; and so did his successors Paul VI, John Paul I (in office only thirty-three days), and John Paul II. The major detail that has leaked out from the third message is that enormous geopolitical change is imminent, with Russia as its womb, its focal point. Russia was/is to be the main agent (signal) of change, the source of a universal blindness and error.[54]

All of this has been deeply personalized for Pope John Paul II through two paranormal occurrences. First, on May 13, 1981, in St. Peter's Square, in the presence of some tens of thousands of people

---

53 Ibid, 684.
54 Ibid, 634.

and eleven million television viewers, Pope John Paul escaped an assassin's bullet (later traced to Russian/Bulgarian, Middle East interests); at the moment of the shot, he had leaned forward and escaped death; he had leaned forward to greet a child *wearing a picture of the Lady of Fatima*, and that day was *the anniversary date* of the Virgin's first visitation to the children in Portugal.

Second: in August 1981, the Pope had a supernatural vision, repeating in detail the sun's changes and dance in the sky, the miracle that had occurred in the grand display at Fatima on October 13, 1917.

The Sexuality Issue

All of this supports Papal/Vatican conviction that the world is in turmoil, that the Pope's Global Politics Program has failed, and that worse is yet to come. Conservative and Liberal factions in the Church structure are dealing with these matters seriously and strategically, and the rift in the Church's foundations is widening.

The laity of the Church reflects the unrest too, especially on the issues of celibacy, birth control and abortion, and papal infallibility: 70% of United States Catholics polled recently *favor* allowing Catholic priests to be married; 60% *favor* allowing women to be priests, 69% *favor* allowing divorced Catholics to marry in the Church; 75% think it is not always wrong for unmarried people to have sexual relations; 79% feel it *is* possible to make up their own mind about Church teachings on moral issues such as birth control and abortion; 80% say they *can* disagree with the Pope's official positions on morality and still be good Catholics![55]

These statistics reflect the modernization of the Church that was pursued by Vatican II, and they define the horror seen in the Church by the traditionalists. The alarm is deeply complicated philosophically, ethically, and with regard to Church doctrine; the Pope is caught in a middle position; this has been his fate. The world is changing and the Church is in shock.

Thomas C. Fox, Editor of the *National Catholic Reporter*, writes: "On the eve of its third millennium, Catholicism seems unsure of its identity. An uncertainty affects many of the nearly one billion

---

55 TIME/CNN poll, September 27-28, 1995 by Yankelovich Partners, Inc., reported in *TIME* magazine, October 9, 1995, page 64: "The Catholic Paradox: In America the Pope will discover a mystery of faith: a block both rebellious and intensely loyal."

people who call themselves Catholic and who look to the Church for guidance. Discontent festers; Catholics are divided. Meanwhile, in the past quarter century a rift has grown between official Church pronouncements and the practices of tens of millions of Catholics. Many have simply stopped listening to their bishops."[56] Fox—and many others—point to the Catholic Church's teachings on sexuality as the heart of the divisive issues.

Since the Second Vatican Council which aligned the Church more than ever before to current cultural ways, the issue of priestly celibacy has been blamed for the 40% drop-off of ordination rates, with projected rates of 32% per decade overall within the second half of the century by the close of the Millennium. Additionally, compounding these statistics is the datum that by the year 2000, one of every three aging priests in some dioceses will be retired. This condition is global. It is a phenomenon the likes of which the Catholic Church has never experienced.[57]

Ironically, celibacy is *not* a theological Church requirement. Pope John XXIII reportedly once said he could end sacerdotal celibacy with "a stroke of the pen." All of Jesus' apostles, including Peter, the first pope, were married. The earliest Christians operated in the main in family settings. It was in the fourth century that laws of sexual abstinence emerged, which were tied to liturgical services with sex supposedly causing impurity—women contaminating men; a day of abstinence was required before the priest was "clean" enough to celebrate the Eucharist.

At the Second Lateran Council in 1139,[58] the law of *mandatory* celibacy was officially ratified. No marriage was thereafter valid. Those priests and nuns already married were told to separate from their spouses.

In the Second Vatican Council, many bishops wanted mandatory celibacy to be on the agenda, *to have it repealed.* Pope Paul VI forbade the Council to discuss the subject. And so the issue remains.[59]

In summation, Fox states that "the Catholic renewal [adjusting to new values in society] of the Second Vatican Council, fol-

---

56 Fox, 3.

57 Ibid, 173–174, citing the sociological survey conducted by Richard A. Schoenherr of the University of Wisconsin and Lawrence A. Young of Brigham Young University.

58 "Lateran" is the name of a district of Southeast Rome. The district was given to the Church by Emperor Constantine I in 311. The Lateran palace was the papal residence until 1309.

59 Fox, 178–181.

lowed by strong reactions to that renewal, most notably during the pontificate of Pope John Paul II, have ripped Catholicism from centuries of safe moorings. The Church, meanwhile, is being propelled into a modern age radically unlike anything it has ever experienced."[60]

The Call for Unity

On another issue, in his continuing effort to fulfill the call for Christian ecumenical unity made by the Second Vatican Council, John Paul II issued on May 30 1995, an encyclical entitled *Ut Unum Sint*, "That They May Be One."[61]*

In this encyclical, John Paul stated that the Christian denominations in the world (some 2,500 of them) can not remain divided. He noted the burden of mutual misunderstandings of the past and the need to accomplish the "necessary purification of past memories."

John Paul recognized present day Patriarch Bartholomew of Constantinople, citing the schism of the Church between West and East, which reaches back some 900 years in history [the mending of which has been part of the pope's global politics], and John Paul noted as "significant and encouraging *that the question of the primacy of the Bishop of Rome [the Pope] has now become a subject of study which is already under way or will be in the near future.*" This is a clear reference to the infallibility issue. John Paul referred to himself above all else as a servant of unity.[62]

The force of time is for the world to grow closer together; the world of markets, the world of spirit. And conservative and liberal factions will collide in the increased proximity.

---

60 Ibid., 385.

61 This Encyclical coincided with the transit of Pluto exactly in opposition to the Vatican Midheaven and tr Jupiter opposed the Sun-Moon conjunction in the 10th House; SA Uranus was precisely upon the Vatican Moon.

62 *The Catholic World Report*, July 1995, pages 50–55. In echo in November 1995, Patriarch Bartholomew of the Eastern Orthodox Christian (Catholic) world called the primates of the fifteen independent Eastern Orthodox churches together, representing more than 170 million faithful, meeting together for only the second time in history since the early Middle Ages. The convention was to discuss coming together "to speak with one voice."
The epic split between West and East occurred in 1054 after long years of arguing about language and doctrine (Latin/Greek), when the Roman Pope (St. Leo IX) ordered excommunication of the Patriarch of Constantinople because of theological differences. *International Herald Tribune*, November 9, 1995, Marlise Simons.

There *is* a level of John Paul II's internationalism that thrives: the growing importance of the *Third World*, because of the Church's dramatic numerical growth in parts of Asia and Africa. Speculation about the next pope being elected from the Third World can not be overlooked.

A Prophetic Voice from the Past

On the periphery of this enormous struggle between tradition and change and the lone position of John Paul II, working for global politics at the expense of extraordinary problems within the Catholic infrastructure, caught between tradition and modernization, appearing ineffective to the consensus of critics, there is another voice from the distant past still heard in the Vatican's present, for its future: the voice of St. Malachy (Mael Maedoc Ua Morgair) who lived 1095–1148 in Armagh, Ireland. While this string of events told here is discounted by parts of the Church, it must be included in the same spirit perhaps as the emphatic Fatima dimension presented above as so important to understanding John Paul's reign.

Malachy O'More was the son of a school teacher. He was ordained a priest when he was twenty-five and faced turbulent challenges in his rise to status as powerful bishop and then as papal legate to Ireland. Though credited with many miracles, including the healing of the gravely ill son of King David of Scotland, and apparently constantly caught up in politics and travel, Malachy wanted to lead a meditative life as a monk.

During a trip from England, from King Stephen there, back to Rome in 1148, Malachy stopped off to see St. Bernard in Clairvaux. He was "stricken there" and died in Bernard's arms. At his requiem Mass, Bernard then proclaimed Malachy a saint, which action was formally confirmed by Pope Innocent III in 1190. It was the first canonization of an Irish saint.[63]

Important for our analysis of the Vatican now is that Malachy was also a *clairvoyant*. He created—projected—a list of Popes which began with Celestine II (d. 1144) and extended "to the end of the

---

63 The "Patron Saint of Ireland," Saint Patrick, predated Malachy by 700 years. He converted most of Ireland to Catholicism in the middle of the fifth century and is credited with establishing the practice of education in Ireland and harmonizing civil laws with Church doctrine. He became the center of legends that flourish still. There is no formal date of his canonization. See Delaney.

world." Malachy described each successive pope in symbolic terms, with accuracy that was extraordinary through 1590, but less specifically thereafter.

For example, for the modern period, Malachy predicted—in succession—*Pastor et Nauta* for the papal time filled by Pope John XXIII (1958–1963, 810 years into the future) as "shepherd and navigator" of the Second Vatican Ecumenical Council. Then *Flos Florum*, referring to John's successor, Paul VI (1963–1978), whose coat of arms was indeed *flos florum*, the fleurs-de-lys.

Only four more Popes were noted to complete Malachy's list, and his keys for the two popes who have followed Pope Paul VI are not (yet?) immediately clear: *De Medietate Lunae*, "From the Half-Moon," surely referring to the Middle East, to persecutions of the Church and to the pope falling victim to his enemies. Could there have been some covert force behind the sudden death of John Paul I, Paul's successor, whose term lasted just thirty-three days? His successor then, John Paul II, was the target of an attempted assassination by occluded Middle-East forces, on May 13, 1981, by Turkish terrorist and murderer Mehmet Ali Agca.[64]

De Labore Solis, "From the toil of the sun," Malachy's reference to the next pope, must then relate to Pope John Paul II, but it too is not a clear reference. Malachy suggested that this pope would take the name Gregory XVII! This may refer to the *succession* of Gregorys, i.e., honoring their work: Gregory XIII (1502–1585), for example, promoted the counter-reformation through his pledge to execute the decrees of the Council of Trent which refined Church doctrine. Gregory XVI (1765–1846) strengthened the papacy by aligning it with Austria under Metternich.

Fascinatingly, in John Paul's latest Encyclical (see above), May 30, 1995—surely his last major philosophical pronouncement to guide the Church—he says, "In the beautiful expression of Pope Saint *Gregory* the Great [540–604, reorganizing vast spread-out papal states], my ministry is that of *servus sevorum Dei* (servant of

---

64 This is not journalistic conjecture. There is suggestion of a power-play within the astrology of John Paul II and the Vatican and their world, hinging on the planet Pluto, empowerment, force. See Tyl, *Synthesis & Counseling*, page 538.

John Paul II (born May 18, 1920 near 1:00 P.M., EET in Wadowice, Poland), at the time of the assassination attempt upon him, had SA Pluto almost precisely conjunct his natal Saturn in the 12th; SP Saturn exactly conjunct the Ascendant, SP Neptune exactly conjunct Jupiter; Tertiary Progressed Moon square natal Pluto and TP Sun exactly square Mercury; tr Pluto was exactly conjunct natal Mars; tr Uranus was opposed his Moon.

the servants of God). This designation is the best possible safeguard against the risk of separating power from ministry."

Pope John Paul II has been the most visibly hard-working pope of recent times, toiling in the public light, making over forty trips to more than fifty countries of the world, the first pope to publish a book, promoting the Ecumenical decrees of Vatican II. John Paul II's reign occurs at a time of waning popularity for Roman Catholicism, and Malachy's symbolic Latin label could be also be translated "from the Lonely Labour."[65]

According to Malachy, there are two more popes to come: *Gloria Olivae*, "Glory of the Olive," will take the name Leo XIV (or follow in the tradition of Leos, i.e., Leo XIII (1810–1903) *reconciled Roman Catholicism with science and liberalism and applied Christian principles to the religious and social questions of his time*, most sensitively to the working-class movement. This next pope is to unite humanity under Christianity in one last brilliant explosion, clearly a reference to world community. The olive reference could mean peace or—if not a selection from the Third World—a specific region of Italy from which the next pope will come.

Then, *Petrus Romanus*, "Peter of Rome," is to preside over the destruction of Rome and the End of the Age.[66]

After hundreds of years of accuracy, Malachy's prophecy for the present day papacy seems to break down in clarity, or we can not yet understand it. One theory is that these prophecies were forgeries of the conclave of 1590 to support the aspirations of one of the papal candidates, i.e., a list of arcane symbolisms with great retrospective accuracy created to project the immediate future as well and favor a particular candidate.

Another theory is that the list is a compilation of idle occult musings conjured up over the years in the papal archives by caretaking monks. Catholic academia considers the prophecies spurious.

---

65 Mann, 80.

66 The paraphrased explanations of Malachy's prophecies come from *The People's Almanac*, David Wallechinsky and Irving Wallace; New York: Doubleday, 1975.

■ Prediction ...

Succession and Policy—As of this writing late in 1995, John Paul and the Vatican are in the midst of a crucial time of adjustment, trying to reach a modern perspective—all of which is precisely recorded (and was predicted) by astrology. We will learn that the Pope has been near death on several occasions, quite possibly in January-April 1994, October 1994, in mid-January 1996, or in mid-April 1996. It is difficult to see the pope surviving successive health crises in January, June, and November, 1997. He will die a peaceful death.[67*]

It is reasonable to report that the astrological profile of papal succession is very clearly established within the modern papacy.[68*] That John Paul II endures approaches the supernatural, as so much around him and his activities do. The astrological measurements show enormous newness in the Vatican and its doctrine for the Catholic Church. There can be no doubt that a change of policy is being prepared now, that it is an alarm that will fracture the Church's infrastructure, that all issues must wait until the death of John Paul II and be focused upon the election of the new pope. This election will surely be the most crucial and significant in Church history in this Millennium.

The new pope—*Gloria Olivae*—will face tremendous onslaughts of public opinion with regard to the coming together of Christian denominations, the change of doctrine with regard to celibacy and related issues, and the diminution of the papal power position. The probability is very high that the new look of the papacy will be formalized around July 1997, will focus strongly on its being the active, precedential agent for ecumenism, following John Paul's vanguard reiteration of Pope Saint Gregory's statement that the pope is the "servant of the servants of God" (see above).

There will be a major event in church history, quite possibly occurring dramatically between October 15 and November 22, 1997.[69*] Should, by the grace of God, Pope John Paul live

---

67 Measurements keyed to the Pluto transit opposed the Vatican Midheaven, conjoined by John Paul's New Moon birth; the Vatican's SP Moon also opposed the Midheaven and square Neptune in February 1996; Tr Pluto square John Paul's Saturn and Ascendant.

68 See Tyl, *Synthesis & Counseling in Astrology*, 532–541.

69 Tr Pluto square Vatican Ascendant; SA Uranus conjunct Sun, many midpoint pictures; TP Sun opposed Sun, TP Moon opposed Mercury, TP Midheaven opposed Midheaven.

through his times of stress until this period in Vatican history, his end then will imbue the time even more with ecumenical significance. The point here is that *a new era is beginning, definitively:* anticipated in Vatican II led by Pope John XXIII and brought along into maturation by Popes Paul VI, and John Paul II ... and the new pope, bringing a peace offer of unity to the spiritual world *(Gloria Olivae?).*

■ Prediction ...

Serving All Denominations—A second extremely demanding period falls upon the Vatican from Spring 1999 through July 2001: during this period, in Spring 1999 or August 2000, the new pope, John Paul II's successor, may be taken out of office by premature death. The "final" pope—if we follow St. Malachy's projections—will take up the banner to preside over an *administration* of Christendom rather than an inspiration of the Church, and this may well be taking place within the emergent structuring of world-community government.

The Vatican will become a holding company of spiritual investments by all Christian denominations. This extraordinary development will occur throughout the period January 2002 to December 2003, with the proclamation focus quite possibly occurring in May 2002. It will be poised, powerful, and successful. The history of Christian religion will have changed completely, and it will be a new Christian world as a result.[70*]

■ Prediction ...

The Vatican's Possible End—In September 2003–April 2004, it is extremely likely that the pope at that time will decline the concept of his singularity, the third stage of radical change, and the papacy as it has been for two millennia, now with the world smaller and closer, will be no more.[71]

---

70 Transiting Pluto opposed the Vatican Sun 2002–2003 with tr Saturn conjunct Sun in May 2002. Tr Pluto goes on to oppose the Vatican's very powerful Mercury.

71 SA Pluto square the Vatican Saturn, tr Uranus opposed the Ascendant.

3

THE PACIFIC

Japan: Setting Sun in the East

Kublai Khan (1215–1294), the great Mongolian emperor of all of China, grandson of Genghis Khan, failed many times to take over Japan, not because of Japanese resistance, but because of the treachery and caprice of weather, the *kamikaze* "divine winds" of the Sea of Japan.[72]

Geography insulates Japan, protects it. Within this security, for all its early history, Japan indulged itself with separatism. After Portuguese exploratory visits in the mid-sixteenth century finally intruded on Japanese space, the country adopted a formal policy of isolation, closing itself off in its tortured waters to all but a few Dutch and Chinese traders. This lasted for some 300 years. Historically, Japan is a lone country.[73]

The Japanese archipelago is about 2,000 miles long and comprises some 3,500 islands (the four major ones are Hokkaido, Honshu, Shikoku, and Kyushu). While geography protects Japan, the land threatens the subsistence of its modern population: about 80% of the country is mountainous, with more than 190 active volcanoes. Lowland is scarce; *only 16% of the land is cultivatable*. The climate is monsoonal. And, most important: the island(s) of Japan has *almost no natural, mineral*

---

72 Fernandez-Armesto, 136. Japan is on average approximately 700 miles away from China across the Sea.

73 In 1853–54, U.S. Commodore Matthew Perry negotiated a trade treaty with the Shogun (military dictator) government of Japan, and similar treaties with Britain, France, the Netherlands, and Russia followed.

resources, a vital consideration in terms of industrial productivity and social progress.

Reliance on Imports

Japan's reliance on imports, which climbs constantly with industrial and social growth, is life-significant and creates a tremendous dependency upon its seapower outreach throughout the Pacific and into the Indian Ocean. Japan must import over 90% of all its coal, oil and petroleum, natural gas, iron ore, copper, nickel, bauxite (vital in the manufacture of aluminum), lead, manganese, and titanium. This extreme dependency on its imports of raw materials—more than any other great nation in the world—is the contingency from which the lifeblood of the Japanese economy and Japanese prosperity issues. The Japanese economy is extremely vulnerable to any interruption in the supply of these minerals, and also to any sharp rise in prices.[74]

Additionally, in 1991, Japan imported 53% of its food (measured by caloric intake), which is up from 21% in 1960. Economist Hamish McRae points out that memories of millions dying of famine two generations ago haunt the Japanese still. McRae calls attention to the fact that countries which can not feed themselves are liable to feel more vulnerable than others. This is the background of national fear that easily motivates aggression.[75]

Geographic isolation and indigenous vulnerability exist together: while the make-up of its geography supports Japan's cultural way of self-isolation, on the one hand, there is an ever-growing need to relate commercially to the world, on the other. The growth of this need and the dilemma—a split in national personality—have not abated since the Industrial Revolution. Today, political factions are strongly divided in terms of conservative nationalism and international liberalism.

---

74 "If oil imports were cut by 70% for 200 days, three million Japanese people would die and 70% of all property would be severely damaged or completely lost, with results more tragic and devastating than the losses in World War II." Nobutoshi Akao, *Japan's Economic Security* (New York, 1983), p. 17; see Friedman & Lebard, 8-9.

75 McRae, 85. Even in the late sixteenth century, Japan raided China for grain almost every year from 1545 to 1563! Fernandez-Armesto, 228.

Treaties Made with Japan

Immediately after World War II, under the directorship of U.S. General Douglas MacArthur, a Far Eastern Commission, representing eleven Allied nations and an Allied Council in Tokyo, oversaw occupation and rehabilitation of Japan. Due to rising tensions between the Soviet Union and Western nations, the Commission was hampered in its role, and the occupation became virtually a United States operation.

In 1946 a new Constitution was adopted and in 1947 it was put into effect. Emperor Hirohito of Japan disclaimed divinity.

In 1951, a security treaty was signed between Japan and the United States, providing for U.S. defense of Japan against external attack and allowing the United States to station troops in the country. The role of Japan's geography was a key consideration *vis a vis* the former Soviet Union (and China and Korea): with U.S. installations in Japan, Soviet naval bases in Vladivostok on the Sea of Japan were denied easy access to the Pacific. Similarly, China and Korea could be watched. Japan was/is vital to America's protection of its western front on the Pacific.

Finally, on April 28, 1952, a peace treaty was signed between Japan and the United States, giving Japan its sovereignty.[76*]

The security treaty caused a strong division of opinion in Japan and in the United States: many Japanese thought that military ties with the United States would draw Japan into further war(s). United States officials still feel that the United States depletes its resources with the promise of defense. Now, at the close of the century, the security treaties (two subsequent treaties reinforced the first), still evoke tense debate and consideration. They are often openly (and threateningly) discussed as a final straw of leverage for the United States to use to affect negotiations about imbalanced Japanese trade practices with the United States.

The Japanese Astro-profile is dominated by a planetary signature that is very telling. It suggests that there is "Great tension between the old way of thinking about things and a new way; anxiety about change of the status quo."[77*] This identifying signature introduces consideration of Japan's customary withdrawal into a

76 Accurate timing of the signing sets the Sovereignty horoscope of Japan at 10:30 P.M., JST, with 00 Capricorn 31 rising at Tokyo.

77 Uranus=Mercury/Saturn; see Tyl, *Synthesis* or *Prediction*, Appendix.

self-isolating position, a posture of self-deprecation—showing a "national masochism" or "self-flagellation" as some political and cultural analysts put it—that is inscrutable to the West in the light of Japan's *extraordinary* industrial growth to world leadership during the decades since mid-century.[78]

The Major Problems

This contradiction of ways—anchored to separatist social mores and tightly tethered to international import programs—this struggle, builds an ethos of communalism in Japanese culture that strongly subordinates individual expression to community success. As long-time Japan commentator and critic Karel van Wolferen puts it, "The Japanese individual must accept as inevitable that his intellectual and psychological growth is restrained by the will of the collectivity."[79]*

Japan constantly seems to be in some kind of self-therapeutic mode, studying everything about itself to improve national standards in every way. Its education system has been a model for the world, having fortified a grand young population which literally rebuilt the country and forged a future in manufacturing and technology, in big-money services such as insurance, and in savings in terms of foreign investment and import/export.[80]*

But these important indices of growth changed course dramatically late in the 1980s, and Japan has developed distinct problems in the 1990s. Beginning in 1991, Japan has experienced four consecutive years of near-zero growth, and banks face a bad debt burden estimated at as much as $1 trillion, nearly a quarter of the country's

---

78 Retellings of the war in Japan depict more and more the suffering of the Japanese people, with little mention of the tragedies inflicted by the Japanese. The concept of Japan being a victim is gaining ground in public memory. Hiroshima is a monument to martyrdom. (See Van Wolferen, 426–430).

  Astrologically, note as well that, in the Japanese horoscope, Saturn is retrograde and rules the Ascendant; *that Neptune retrograde is conjunct the Midheaven;* that Mars is retrograde in Scorpio and opposes the Sun, the energy internalized, censored, redirected before it is expressed.

79 Van Wolferen, 3. Astrologically: again a statement of Saturn retrograde ruling the national Ascendant with a Gemini Moon (the collectivity) dominant and conjunct the Descendant, opposite the Ascendant, sextiled by Jupiter and Venus in Aries.

80 Mercury rules the 9th (education; internationalism) and is in Aries square Uranus (technology, intensity) in the 7th, ruling the 2nd (money); Mercury also rules the 6th. Indeed Mercury is opposed by Saturn retrograde which, in the 3rd–9th axis, suggests a deeply serious purposefulness and, as well, a depression of individualistic mind-set.

Gross Domestic Product.[81*] To bring revenue back to Japan to help stabilize the economy, Japan is now selling off property investments abroad (especially in the United States) at great loss.

Education

In education, while Japan registers more patents than any other country of the world, these patents are created by its industrial machinery *rather than by its universities*. Analysis of the originally glitteringly successful educational system in Japan reveals an over-balanced emphasis on rote memorization of fact and computation. Examinations are, in the main, multiple choice rather than essay dependent. Recall is at a premium; creativity and intellect lag far behind. Van Wolferen observes, "when a Japanese resident of the United States won the Nobel prize for medicine in 1987, many press comments pointed out that he would never have won it without the stimulation of decades of study and laboratory work abroad. Scientists at Japanese universities are hampered by an extremely rigid academic hierarchy that keeps talented researchers in sub-servient positions, and by excessive regulations decreed by education bureaucrats."[82]

Social Resources

In social resources, Japan's population is aging quickly with almost three times the number of people over sixty-five in 1994 as there were in 1950, with the projection to over 25% by 2020.[83]

According to van Wolferen, Japanese society has become "hopelessly deformed: children hate school, women marry late and many married women choose not to have children. Indeed, the fertility rate of Japanese women is now the lowest among the major

---

81 *Foreign Affairs* magazine, September-October 1995, Edward W. Desmond (*TIME* magazine Bureau Chief in Tokyo), page 118.
  The astrology: SA Pluto square the Japan Ascendant (exact May 1995), with tr Uranus-Neptune square Venus, ruler of the Midheaven, throughout 1993–94; the financial downslide beginning with tr Uranus opposed Uranus, ruler of the 2nd in 1991.

82 Van Wolferen, 89. Note: Saturn opposed Mercury: "the Japanese education system, on the whole, is hostile to such a purpose: spontaneous reasoning, along with spontaneous behavior, is systematically suppressed in practically all schools ... the emphasis is on rote memorisation." Page 83.

83 McRae, 100. The reverse is occurring in Britain where, with France, it was the oldest of the industrial nations in 1960: it is now projected along with the United States in 2020 to be the youngest, even though the size of the aged sector continues to grow.

powers." Former Japan Prime Minister Morihiro Hosokawa observes similarly, "I frankly believe we face very serious crises; Japan is like a ship on the verge of sinking."[84]

Leadership

The horoscope of Sovereign Japan suggests that the country has a *perpetual* crisis in leadership, with fraud and resignations at the highest political levels occurring routinely. The "fiction of responsible central government," as van Wolferen sees it, emerges from the days of grand Japanese reform—which eliminated the feudal domains and revolutionized industry, beginning in 1868—that culminated in the Meiji Constitution in 1889. Leadership today can not re-create that era of greatness.[85*]

Japan's great leaders at the close of the nineteenth century did not prepare a government that was independently strong in its structure for the leaders to come in the future, and those new leaders were/are simply not like the old, not of the same mettle.

Leadership became a mist, a fiction: only *the semblance of structure*—the symbology of life that permeates the Japanese way—continued with the Japanese people holding their silence.[86*] An example often cited to illustrate this is the militarization of Japan in its defeat of Russia (1905), invasion of China (1937–1939), and then—in self-deceiving arrogance—declaration of war on the United States (December 7, 1941): the military blindly followed the will of the elites; there was no mainstream surge of national inspiration or support; expansionism was an illusory and shallow doctrine satisfying only the military hierarchy.[87]

---

84 *The New York Times*, July 30, 1995; see Nicholas D. Kristof article, page 5.

85 Mutsuhito Meiji (born November 3, 1852 in Kyoto; died July 30, 1912) was one of the most beloved and successful emperors in Japanese history. He brought Japan into the industrial age and opened the country to Western culture. He was formally crowned on January 9, 1867 at age 15. He converted the imperial government to a constitutional monarchy: The Meiji constitution is dated February 11, 1889 at 12:00 Noon (speculative time) in Tokyo; see Campion *World Horoscopes*, 215–216.

86 In the Meiji constitution horoscope, Mercury, ruler of the Ascendant is *squared by Neptune* in Taurus; Neptune also *squares the Sun in Aquarius*.

87 Elitist leadership equates with militarist action in the history of Japan; with nationalism, arrogance, self-absorption. The era of conquest in the late sixteenth century especially, in which the military dictator Hideyoshi projected conquest of the world, resembled the era of the Khans in China. (See "Conquest," page 56.) Hideyoshi sent demands for submission to the kings of Indochina and the Spanish governor of the Philippines, etc. After Hideyoshi was humiliated in sea battle with Korea, outside-world conquest became dormant for 300 years; but long civil wars militarized Japanese society with a caste of professional warriors. The samurai and feudal warlord system were finally eliminated in the Meiji era, *but elitism stands still in the wings, as nationalism,* even with the embarrassment of World War II. (See Fernandez-Armesto, 227–228.)

The Past Lives On

It is simply extraordinary that the horoscope of modern Japan and the horoscope of the Meiji Constitution share the same powerful Moon position (within one degree). This means unequivocally that modern Sovereign Japan has the echo of the past living within it and exposed to the world. Here is "great tension between the old way of thinking about things and a new way; anxiety about change of the status quo"; it is perpetuated in the modern sovereignty horoscope by the almost exactly similar Moon position and as well through a dominating planetary configuration. This characteristic of the old ways grappling with the new, with the population's weak contact with a still weaker government, will not change for a long time. Japan's Astro-profile states it unequivocally: the government will not change or improve until the Constitution is changed; it can not be done without social revolution.[88*]

The United Nations (see page 20) and the Vatican (see page 26) also have the Moon in the same sign as the Meiji and Japanese Moons, i.e., in Gemini (as do Rwanda and Burundi, the Iran Islamic Republic, and others). These national examples share the "separation dynamic," the *divisionism* symbolized by this particular Moon position: there is a scattering, diversifying, indecisive, and self-absorbed nature about the national character, which can be modified, of course, through other relationships within each individual sovereign horoscope. For the United Nations, it expresses itself through dilution of force among so many constituents, fronts, and projects; for the Vatican and for Japan, through the schism between tradition/nationalism and modernity/liberalism.

Additionally, there is (from the Gemini position in the Japanese horoscope) the fascination with communications, acquisitiveness, learning, and creative applications, with the debilitations of indecision, overextension, imitativeness, and the muting of emotionality; there is the need to interact through commerce in order to survive and yet there is the self-absorption with intellectual self-containment. This is the unsettling duality of Japan's national posture.

88 In the Meiji Constitution chart: note the Moon at 27 Gemini compared to Sovereign Japan's Moon at 28 Gemini; note Meiji Jupiter at 00 Capricorn precisely upon the Sovereign Japan Ascendant! In the Sovereign Japan horoscope: *Neptune conjunct the Midheaven* squared by Uranus; Moon in Gemini on the horizon sesquiquadrate Mars; Venus, ruler of the Midheaven opposed Neptune; Mars, ruler of the 4th, the opposite party, retrograde and opposed the Sun.

Imbalanced Trade Practices

In the mid-1990s, Japan's "predatory" export practices have raised warning flags practically everywhere. In the 1970s and 1980s, Japan would select a particular product-line from the world market—for example, small cars, motorcycles, personal computers—imitate it and improve it *in the home market of the product* and drive domestic producers out of that market (their own market).[89*] Japan's trade surplus is presently over $140 billion (1995); in other words, Japan takes in that much more from its export sales than it pays out for imports from other nations, and *half of that surplus is income from the United States* (from autos, auto parts, medical equipment and telecommunications equipment).

This means that access to Japan's own enormous auto market, for example, is selectively barred to foreign countries, while Japan goes on to buy up resources in *foreign* countries with its enormous surplus of savings (for example: motion picture studios, lavish resort hotels, entertainment facilities, insurance firms). The imbalance in this practice is a point of corrosion in relationships between the United States and Japan, and between Japan and other countries. This is again evidence of the clash between Japan's drive toward international commerce and its pull-back to national indulgence, self-protection, and loneness: there is the inexorable outer thrust of the Japanese national export need, for profits to subsidize natural resource imports; and the national protectionism, self-isolationism, and loneness established through thousands of years, with the people of the nation continually *accepting* all that happens, fatalistically, as they would an earthquake.

Ties with the United States

The Security Treaties between the U.S. and Japan are similarly lop-sided, with the United States taking on responsibility for full-scale defense of Japan and receiving in return a troop outpost from which to maintain surveillance of Russia, China, and North Korea. Former Prime Minister Yashuhiro Nakasone, a decade ago, called his country the [United States'] "unsinkable aircraft carrier in the Pacific."

---

89 McRae, 162; certainly a manifestation of the Japan Moon in Gemini on the Descendant and Uranus in the 7th. Mark Simon's editorial, *International Herald Tribune*, November 9, 1995, page 10, put it aptly: "East Asia's economic miracle is best summed up as the biggest price undercut in history. The region grew because it was the cheapest source for the low-technology consumer goods that the West craved."

Since the war, Japan has ridden the crested wave of United States support, not only in terms of military defense, but also in terms of international diplomacy. Van Wolferen refers to the treaties with the United States as the "shield" behind which Japan built up its formidable post-war economic machine.[90]

Does this let Japan get away with trade-murder, believing the United States can not, will not enforce sanctions on Japan—its security partner—for making U.S. products too expensive for the U.S. market? Does this force the United States to play its major defense and/or trade quota trump card to settle the world market down, i.e., establish stringent trade quotas against Japanese goods; withdraw its defense forces? This is especially critical with the advent of a market-mature China tipping the globe, as it were and will be, toward the East. What about the United States World War II memories still spinning without the closure of Japanese apology? Does the United States respect the Japanese nationalist isolationist theme—the past used as prestige and protection—pronounced by Dr. Eisuke Sakakibara, the newly appointed Director-General of the Finance Ministry's International Finance Bureau, *that Americans should stop trying to destroy traditions that Japan has built up over more than a millennium?*[91]

The ties between the United States and Sovereign Japan are extremely strong viewed astrologically; the interdependency, the trade and security relationship are clear, *but so are the mutual fear and antagonism.* In fact, many writers have pointed out that the Japanese are the people Americans most love to hate.[92*]

At the Crossroads

So the Japanese have reached a crossroads, and so have United States' relations with Japan: with the dissolution of the Soviet Union, the Japanese defense position for the United States is *greatly lessened in importance* and the public outcry in Japan to rid Japan of the American presence is an everyday concern, exacerbated by the

---

90 Van Wolferen, 41.

91 *The European* newspaper, July 7–13, 1995, Klaus Engelen column, "Economics." Sakakibara is the author of *Japan Surpasses Capitalism.*

92 U.S. Jupiter-Venus in Cancer conjunct Japan Descendant, U.S. Sun conjunct Japan Uranus in the 7th; Japan Saturn square U.S. Sun, but trine U.S. Ascendant and Uranus. *Japan Jupiter=U.S. Sun/Moon. Japan Pluto exactly opposed the U.S. Midheaven.*

crimes committed by the American military upon the citizens.[93] Aside from an extraordinary sequence of Japanese government scandals that have toppled many Liberal Democratic statesmen and businessmen of extraordinary power, long, long dependence on American direction has *undermined development of strong Japanese government leadership.* No governmental direction is established beyond mega-corporate plans for profits (van Wolferen's "fiction of responsible central government").

Ichiro Ozawa, longtime member of the Japanese Diet, author of *Blueprint for a New Japan,* Secretary-General of the opposition New Frontier Party and outspoken critic of Socialist Prime Minister Tomiichi Murayama, links Japan's rudderless postwar system to the way of ancient Carthage: "the belief that wealth alone could sustain a nation ultimately caused its demise." He refers to Japan's "politics of indecision" (another incisive description of the Japanese Moon in Gemini). He sees no imminent agenda for reform. He refers back to Japan's finest times in the Meiji era (the catchword was "Japanese spirit, Western knowledge") because these ancestors ventured into the world and adapted for Japan what they found in industry, education, the military, and politics. He laments Japan's "systemic senility."[94]

Japan is in deep crisis. Even Murayama must leave the picture abruptly, and his replacement thereafter.

---

93 In a *USA Today* poll (September 1995) conducted with Japan's *Sankei Shimbun* newspaper, Fuji TV, and Gallup, 43.5% of Japanese questioned said all 44,000 U.S. troops in Japan should be withdrawn; only 31% said they should stay; 45.8 % said they believe the defense arrangement benefits the United States more. In parallel polling of the United States, the percentages were reversed, Americans thinking Japan gains more and that Americans should stay.

94 *Foreign Affairs* magazine, September-October 1995, Edward W. Desmond (*TIME* magazine Bureau Chief in Tokyo), "Ichiro Ozawa: Reformer at Bay," 117–131. Even with his great popularity and political power, Ozawa himself has been criticized openly for being involved with corruption and for lacking the senses of obligation and human feeling that are cardinal virtues within Japanese culture.

Ozawa was born on May 24, 1942. His horoscope shows a powerful triple conjunction of Sun, Uranus, and Saturn in early Gemini! He will be an important catalyst for change in Japan in the immediate future, as tr Pluto opposes this power center for rebellion and departure from the past.

■ Prediction ...

Investments Returned to Asia—With the flood of its extraordinary, corporate-led rise to manufacturing prominence as a world power, Japan has mismanaged its investments throughout the world, over-investing for its growth rate, wasting much, with borrowers then unable to service their debts incurred—all on a mega-amount level. Japan's labyrinthine banking system— with corporations performing as banks (so complex are the investment strategies), repeated money scandals involving key cabinet members ("almost an everyday occurrence," according to Eisuke Sakakibara, Director-General of the International Finance Bureau of the Japanese Ministry of Finance) have created a financial mess, as we have seen. That mess will have peaked between July and September 1997. The opposition party will have its strongest entrance to center stage. More leadership scandals will occur in the Summer of 1998, and finally the Opposition Party will take over May–July 1999, with great prosperity stabilized in June–September.[95*]

Investments will be recalled strongly from throughout the world and reinvested into Asia itself, *the region that presents the highest growth market internationally.* Additionally, Japan will be building its financial bastions *against China;* eventually managing co-leadership of the Pacific Market with China. The new investment maneuvers will take place most strongly between March and September 1997 (with a singularly great misunderstanding and/or deception in August 1997, related to a trade agreement, perhaps to do with oil imports, contemporaneous upheaval in the Persian Gulf, and/or investments in the Middle East (see "Jordan," page 141); see Iraq, 142).[96*]

---

95 Tr Pluto opposed Sun/Moon (3 Sagittarius), February-April, December 1996, July–September 1997, with SA Saturn opposed Pluto/Node, tr Uranus square Sun, tr Neptune square Jupiter, tr Saturn conjunct the 4th cusp! Additionally, SA Moon squares Mars.

96 Tr Uranus enters the 2nd House; *SA Neptune=Sun/Moon.* Additionally: Jupiter–Saturn Conjunction Chart (May 29, 2000 at 00:59 A.M., JST at Tokyo) places Sun–Pluto opposition in the 3rd–9th axis, with Pluto ruling the 8th; Jupiter–Saturn in the 2nd, Jupiter ruling the 9th and the Midheaven, the conjunction squared by Uranus. The Moon is in Aries rising.

■ Prediction ...

Apology to the United States—In February–May 1999, Japan will apologize to the United States for its aggression in war in this century—formally, without linguistic hedging, complete-ly.[97] This will humanize the Japanese nation, establish a fresh relationship with the United States *vis a vis* its imminent withdrawal from Japan and ennoble the conviction of the Japanese people for their social revolution ahead. The words of its Nobel Prize-winning novelist, Kenzaburo Oe will be vindicated: "Japan's unwillingness to come to terms with its past is not just morally offensive. It prevents Japan from playing its proper role in Asia."[98]

■ Prediction ...

United States' Withdrawal from Japan—Presently Japan regards its tight involvement with the United States as a buttress against the rising, market threat of China. Within the upheaval outlined above, the United States will withdraw its on-site and stringent constitutional involvement with the Japanese and alter its defense commitment (Japan will have become a drain on U.S. attention elsewhere, specifically the Middle East; see Israel, 103). Japan will be forced (allowed) to mature on its own and reach out to China to share leadership of the burgeoning Pacific Market. The ostensibly full withdrawal of the United States from the Japanese picture will

---

97 Indeed, new (mid-1995) Japanese Prime Minister Tomiichi Murayama "broke ranks with the little minds in his government" and spoke out on Japan's wartime actions, with an unqualified repentance never heard from his predecessors, on the morning of the fiftieth anniversary of Japan's surrender.

  The language *did* include the word "apology," but references were still vague with regard to China, South Korea, the United States, the role of Emperor Hirohito, etc. Japan's right wing insists that Japan's guilt is a fiction created by Japan's conquerors. The majority of Japanese reportedly feel that Murayama did not go far enough. See *TIME* magazine, August 28, 1995, 47.

98 *The New York Times Magazine*, July 2, 1995, pages 28–29. The astrology: Accumulated semisquare Solar Arc February 1999, with tr Saturn conjunct the Sun in May. Indeed, there have been carefully worded apologies, generalized and non-specific, offered by high officials of the government; at the fiftieth anniversary of the Hiroshima bombing, August 6, 1995, for example, but they are not formal, specific, or direct as the United States needs.

coincide with Japan's social unrest, its building revolution, Summer–Fall 2006.[99*]

■ Prediction …

Religion to the Forefront—Van Wolferen develops the observation that what government there is in Japan has little legal, religious, or intellectual development through which to evaluate itself. The System judges *itself* and is therefore intrinsically virtuous. In this way, the System becomes a substitute for religion.[100*]

The structures of religious sects become *social havens* for people when times are stressed—a contrasting parallel in Japan to the highly developed corporately controlled life-situations—and the more radical religious sects focus a potential source of power, i.e., upsetting instability. With neither spirit nor conscience as we know it in the West, the sects can prey on frustration and economic problems. The growing sense in Japan that it is being deprived of its due opportunities and rewards, especially in 1997–1999, can easily ignite passionate and irrational movements, and will play a major role in the Social Revolution that is building.

This observation is eloquently corroborated in Japan's horoscope and, in modern Japan, it is important to note that socio-political events have *always* invited fanatical reactions. As occurred most recently March 19–20, 1995, in the gas attack on the Tokyo subway, the national religious fringe had its say.[101*] This followed the great January earthquake that toppled earthquake-proof bridges and killed over 6,000 people. These calamities occurred in the midst of record unemployment. To the Japanese, this cluster of hardship exceeds customary day-to-day discomfort (the sacrifice the Japanese make in terms of living space and Spartan ways, all in the name of communalism).

---

99 For the United States: beginning in 2004, with tr Neptune conjunct the Midheaven (an entire adjustment of ego presence), departure from Japan will be completed in late 2006 with tr Jupiter-Neptune conjunct Moon, tr Saturn conjunct the 4th cusp, and SA Uranus conjunct Pluto in the 9th House and SA MC square Venus.

100 Van Wolferen, 273. Note the Neptune prominence in the Japan horoscope, conjunct the Midheaven. It speaks continuously.

101 SP Moon square Neptune and Midheaven; tr Pluto stationary-retrograde, precisely semi-sextile Ascendant.

Now, approaching the close of the century of wars and pain, of loss and gain, of Winter and Summer, the Japanese people, to the highest degree, are vulnerable to a giant fall of spirit.[102]

There will be a great deal of frenetic excitement about all the pressures late in 1997; there will be intense fanatical uprising to protect the old ways, to revive them, as the break from them is pressed into the future. This upset will play directly into the Japanese masochistic way; it will recede after a few months, but then erupt again very powerfully in Summer 1998. Yet a new government (Congress and Prime Minister) will be installed by February 1999.[103]

■ Prediction ...

Social Revolution by 2008—Japan has had no reliable, consequential governmental leadership since World War II—due in part to the pervasive influence of the United States. Japan can not become a "normal" nation until there is new leadership, and this is not possible except through social revolution, i.e., a new constitution or a radical adjustment of it. This Social Revolution will take place in several stages: beginning in October-November 2002, with religious vanguard, becoming militaristic in April 2003; a moratorium will be called in which new directions will be formulated, ending in October-November 2004—a terribly crucial time, with the threat of militarism and social eruption everywhere.[104*]

---

102 There are over 300 religions organized in Japan; some are very large and powerful. For most Japanese, religion is a way to get somewhere, rather than something that defines or refines a core belief system. See Van Wolferen, 273–277: "In post-war Japan, after the lifting of all formal suppression, the new religions really began to proliferate. They included such esoteric specimens as 'Denshinkyo,' the 'electricity religion,' which worshipped Thomas Edison(!). In 1951, 720 new religions were registered, but a revision of the law to cope with widespread tax fraud has roughly halved their always fluctuating number."

103 Elections of the Prime Minister in Japan is accomplished by the Congress, which itself is voted in by the people, generally every two years or so. Elections are held for the Congress at the discretion of the Prime Minister, who can dissolve the Congress, depending on the political situation. There is no regular election process as is known in the United States.

104 2002: tr Jupiter-Neptune square Sun, tr Uranus conjunct the Node, tr Saturn conjunct the Moon, with SA Asc opposed Pluto; 2003, SA Mars conjunct the Ascendant with tr Saturn conjunct the Moon, ruler of the 7th; 2004, SA Moon conjunct Pluto, SA Sun conjunct Moon, SA Pluto conjunct Saturn.

At the same time, new trade agreements will be championed, probably with China, which will forestall (stabilize) the transition time of social upheaval, with true success focused clearly late in 2006 and extending for a full year. The Revolution to a new Japan should then be formally completed by the Spring of 2008.[105]*

Internationalism (not nationalism), trade and market share are the vital keys for modern Japan. Its huge population has simply nowhere to go but abroad. Japan is grievously lacking in natural resources and arable, livable land is drastically scarce. A smaller world means the abandonment of isolationist inclinations; and a bigger world for Japanese life.

■ Final Note ...

War with the United States?—George Friedman, a Professor of Political Science at Dickinson College, and Meredith LeBard, a writer, have collaborated on a book with an ominous title: *The Coming War with Japan.* The book received noteworthy acclaim in the United States and was the "#1 Bestseller in Japan." This latter credential calls for our notice here.

Friedman & LeBard exhaustively study Japan's need for access and power throughout the Pacific and Indian Oceans to keep their import supply lines open to the fullest. This position will also support their leadership of the Pacific Market, chiefly among Indonesia, China, Malaysia, the Philippines, and India, the markets that have enough raw materials—except oil—to supply Japan's needs. In turn, these markets can be cultivated to create a sufficient demand for Japanese products.

The converse position, having their sea outreach curtailed in any way, will threaten the life of Japan.

The researchers annotate the fears the United States takes on by giving Japan that power. Article 9 of the MacArthur Constitution reads as follows:

---

105 SA Mercury=Sun/Moon, SA Node=Sun Moon, *SA Pluto=MC/ASC*, SA Venus=Sun/MC in August-September 2005; SA Pluto square Uranus, ruler of the 2nd in December 2005; *SA Sun opposed Ascendant* in October 2006; SA Pluto opposed Mercury, August 2007, SA Saturn opposed Sun/Moon and transiting Pluto conjunct Ascendant in Spring 2008. Additionally, the Jupiter-Saturn chart [5/29/00 at 1:59 A.M. JST in Tokyo] is activated by tr Uranus through a square with the Jupiter–Saturn Sun, 2004-early 2006.

> Aspiring sincerely to an international peace based on jus-
> tice and order, the Japanese people forever renounce war
> as a sovereign right of the nation and the threat or use of
> force as means of settling international disputes.
>
> In order to accomplish the aim of the preceding para-
> graph, land, sea, and air forces as well as other war poten-
> tial will never be maintained. The right of belligerency of
> the state will not be recognized.[106]

The United States made exceptions to this in the cooperative defense plan mounted after World War II and increased then. Today, Japan spends *more money on defense than any country except the United States!* More than France, or Germany or Britain or ... [107]

Friedman & LeBard point out that economic self-confidence will inevitably lead to growing political self-confidence. Japan needs mineral supplies directly and reliably in order to be strong. Japan must control the Pacific. Might Japan drive the United States out of the Pacific Market, for personal hegemony, trade security ... and military dominance? Might this thwart the United States' demand for a Pacific presence to protect its western front?

The energies of unrest in Japan are so serious as to lead to conjecture of military confrontation between old friends/enemies. It is my opinion that such a confrontation will not take place; rather, the energies of unrest in Japan will be focused upon social upheaval and revolution, with the United States withdrawing national defense gradually but, in the spirit of continued reason and care, helping Japan become a "normal" nation: sharing responsible regional trade leadership of the Pacific, keeping it open to the other regions of the world, and maintaining Japanese subsistence through balanced trade with many countries. This is a chaotic and necessary time en route to the unity of world community early in the next century. It is a plight that haunts Japan not alone.

---

106 Friedman & LeBard, 102.
107 Ibid, 12.

China: Rising Star in the East

Time is regarded differently in the East than it is in the West. Patience is a dominant trait in China, a country that has been of giant size far longer than any country on earth. It is more isolated unto its own ways than any other country and it is decidedly antagonistic to foreign intervention.

As of 1750, for example, China had a population of *200 million* persons. Japan's population then probably numbered some 28 million, which itself was larger than France or Germany at that time! And India numbered perhaps 100 million. Europe was only a peninsula of the Eurasian land mass. The Americas were populated by perhaps 10 million Native Americans. A mere 250 years ago, world population was distributed much differently than today.[108]

China was mammoth, insulated, and defensive. Its history, in the main, was a record of *growth without development.* The world beyond its borders was irrelevant: China existed by god-mandate, as "indivisible as the sky itself." External relations were governed by the convenient fiction that China constituted all the world that counted, and the rest of mankind were barbarians clinging to its rim.

Oxford Historian Felipe Fernandez-Armesto, in his grand study *Millennium*, portrays the reality that, a thousand years ago, the balance of the world's resources was weighted heavily in favor of China. "The potential decisively to influence the rest of the world lay with the Chinese."[109]

The dynasty system of rule seems to have begun with the Hsia Dynasty around 1994 B.C.E., focused upon a semi-legendary Emperor Yu; then it settled into modern(!) form with Liu Pang in 206–195 B.C.E. (emerging from the collapse of the Ch'In dynasty, founding the Han era, consolidating power), which—after the internal upheaval of the Kahns in the thirteenth century C.E.—continued on through the Manchu Dynasties, in the main, from 1644 to 1912, an overall period of almost 4,000 years. Perhaps the most fundamental next bureaucratic mutation occurred only in 1949 with Mao Tse-Tung!

Within this Dynastic sweep of history, the prevailing isolationism, which the western mind tends to equate with peacefulness and order, shows a vitally significant catalytic theme of upheaval that is

---

108 Fairbank, 163–169. Additionally: a census in China in 1124 recorded twenty million households (Fernandez-Armesto, 128).

109 Fernandez-Armesto, 45.

in contradiction to the serene, stoic image. Two internal conquerors did much for China.

The Mongol Conquerors

Genghis Khan (b. 1155–67, d. 1227; given the name of Temujin) was a conqueror of the most barbaric order, beginning his meteoric rise to rulership from peasant status among ruthlessly warring clans in his native Mongolia. To avenge the murder of his father, Temujin assembled an army that eventually grew to colossal size (some 200,000) and systematically annihilated each enemy faction in turn, culminating with his total rout of the Eastern Mongol Tatars in 1201. Temujin systematically slaughtered every Tatar who was taller than the height of a cart axle, making certain that the next generation of Tatars would be loyal only to him. He then took on the name "Genghis Khan," which means "universal leader."[110]

Genghis Kahn's military genius with cavalry invasion and the tactics of siege led him to invasion and victory over the Ch'In dynasty centered in Peking. He conquered everything in his path, crossing China's borders—those borders that were protected by heaven—and conquering lands to the southwest, including Afghanistan and northwestern India, and southern Russia.

Kublai Khan (1215–1294) was the grandson of Genghis Khan and became famous through the writings of Venetian explorer Marco Polo who succeeded to integrate himself with the China court for an amazing fifteen years (1275–1290). Polo then returned to Italy with observations of China's life, scholarship, invention, and opulence that even today challenge credibility. Kublai exercised his times of conquest (attempting and failing to annex Japan in 1274 and 1281; see page 41) and finally opted for establishing peace throughout China, with himself as uncontested emperor. Kublai preserved the Chinese religious and intellectual ways and gradually sacrificed his Mongolian heritage (and Mongolia) to Chinese hegemony.

China's era of upheaval and conquest brought disdain into the concept of heavenly mandate: the barbarian rim of its world was to be despised as well as avoided; the outer others were not worthy even of conquest.

In the fifteenth century, the emperor Yung-Lo revived aggressive, expansionist ideas from Kublai Khan's early time. He invaded Vietnam

---

110 Axelrod & Phillips, 111–112.

and even drew isolated Japan into extensive trade activity. In 1403, he dispatched a Muslim eunuch of Mongol descent known as Cheng Ho, an extraordinary seaman,[111] on a series of seven voyage-expeditions over thirty years. The voyages involved sixty-two huge junks—the largest ever built—225 support vessels, and 27,870 men, ranging some 12,600 miles from home, visiting at least thirty countries.

Here was a seaborne empire decidedly ready to become an international political force, but a new emperor abruptly cancelled preparations and support for Cheng Ho's further projected voyages. The reasons for the cut-back were the embarrassing military losses in Vietnam and a change of court philosophy to Confucian ways: the moral and social philosophy and code of behavior based on peace, order, humanity, wisdom, and obedience. Renunciation of expansionism (shipbuilding) and the demotion of commercial values comprised the platform of the nationalistic scholar-elites of the new day. China would increasingly be governed by a code of scholars and gentlemen who were contemptuous of barbarism and indifferent to trade. Almost all of Cheng Ho's records—the wonders of navigational discovery and accomplishment—were obliterated from history.[112]

Internationalism and Change

The dynasty system began to break down with the introduction of trade contact with the western world and with missionaries of the Christian faith. Confusion and exploitation sparked the Opium War (1839–42; the war in China waged by the British "barbarians" there to gain tariff concessions, which shook Chinese imperial prestige severely); the horrific Taiping Rebellion (1851–1864; a civil war against the Manchu Emperor, in the name of Christianity, its leader claiming to be the second son of God, with 20 million peasants losing their lives[113*]); war with Japan (1894–95); and the Boxer Rebellion (1900–1901), the last-straw rebellion *against foreign intervention*,

---

111 The outreach of Islam by the tenth, eleventh, and twelfth centuries was enormous, transcending even the walls and cultural barriers of the Orient. It was carried back into the East through nomadic war hordes meeting up with the spiritual doctrine during their forays into the West. Islam was the most widely dispersed civilization the world had ever see until it was overtaken by the expansion of Latin Christendom in the sixteenth century.

112 Fernandez-Armesto, 147–149.

113 On June 26, 1850 at 2:40 A.M., UT, the signal of an age of rebellion formed in the sky: the conjunction of Uranus and Pluto in 29 Aries 40, with Saturn at 19 Aries. This phenomenological occurrence signalled much upheaval, including the United States Civil War which began with the first shot on April 12, 1861 at 4:30 A.M., LMT in Charleston, SC (rectification by Marc Penfield).

led by the secret society of "Harmonius Fists" (the Rebellion was defeated, and China was forced to indemnify United States and European powers for damages and assassinations). The last dynasty (Ch'Ing/Qing) was overthrown October 10, 1911, and, out of the Chinese nationalist movement, a Republic was formed.

Communism in China

In the twentieth century, during the 1930s and 1940s, communism was slowly adopted to curtail rampant inflation and organize an orderly agricultural and industrial economy. The People's Republic of Communist China formally came into being on October 1, 1949, with the completion of a constitution and installation of a government system with Mao Tse-Tung (Zedong) as Chairman.[114*]

China's Astro-profile shows a basic thrust of social sensitivity, people awareness, human rights, all the dimensions captured in its name, "The People's Republic." These dimensions are veiled, put under cover, and embraced with illusion (or vision). Pedantry, precise compliance, and an inquisitorial nature run away with national administration. There is a potential collision course mapped out for the people against the government, there is enormous energy devoted to international trade, nuclear energy, and education.[115*]

The initial years of Communist reconstruction were rewarding for China, but then there occurred an extraordinary period of failure, beginning with Mao's "Great Leap Forward," 1958–1960, a gargantuan mobilization of China's immense population to meet impossible quotas of industrial and agricultural progress. Some twenty to thirty million people lost their lives through malnutrition and famine due to the party policies imposed upon them.[116]

---

114 Famed British Astrologer Charles Carter, in his *Introduction to Political Astrology*, gives the time of 3:15 P.M. in Beijing (Peking), crediting the Astrological Magazine (Bangalore, India) issue of March 1950, page 213 as the reporting source, with no primary source noted. Yet, deep study of this horoscope against the timing of events and the nature of the nation attests to the extraordinary efficacy of 3:15 P.M. CCT.

115 Sun in Libra (conjoined with Mercury and Neptune in the 8th), Moon in Aquarius trine and in the 12th; Aquarius Ascendant, with Uranus square the Sun; Saturn peregrine in Virgo (note similarity of this Saturn position with that of Old Spain and the Inquisition (see "Spain," page 194), and Mars Pluto conjunction in Leo in the 7th square Venus in Scorpio in the 9th, ruled by Pluto. Saturn=Sun/Pluto.

116 From the very beginning, the Stalinist model of industrialization (primary emphasis on heavy industry at the expense of agriculture) was ill-suited to the Chinese because of the great preponderance of the countryside in the economy. Fairbank 357, 368–382.

The Great Leap Forward went against every known economic wisdom, especially against the gradualism that had been inculcated into the Chinese character out of the furious upheavals of internationalization at the turn of the century and before.[117*]

The second cataclysmic failure in twentieth century China was Mao's Cultural Revolution (early 1966–April 1969), a domestic political struggle which exploited the people in the name of its leader and party, and directly involved 100 million people. The movement was possible because of the Chinese people's deep past of Confucian teaching to reinforce social order through dutiful self-subordination. This philosophy made the people passive in politics and obedient to authority.

John King Fairbank, Harvard China historian, portrays Mao as a man with two careers: one as rebel leader, one as an updated emperor, the object of cult veneration, the acknowledged superior of the rest of mankind. Mao supplanted the local gods and other figures of the old peasant religion.[118*]

In *his* Revolution, Mao exploited the student-youth in particular: enforced doctrine was screamed to the world through the mouths of the nation's young, witch-hunts were instigated, "The Four Olds: old ideas, old culture, old customs, old habits" were attacked, and revolution was learned by *conducting* revolution. The Red Guards exerted brutal terror everywhere. With relentless purges, Mao dismantled the party structure that had framed his power. Only the Mao ego could endure, and "It has been estimated that 400,000 people died as a result of maltreatment."

In their eventual trial in 1977 (eight years after the virtual collapse of the Revolution in 1969), the Gang of Four, consisting of Mao's wife Jiang Qing and three of her colleagues in the Central Cultural Revolution Group, were charged with having framed and

---

117 The astrology is extraordinarily clear: the excellent reconstruction era culminating in the Summer of 1957 saw SA Venus conjunct the Communist China Midheaven, with tr Uranus conjunct the Descendant, tr Neptune square the Ascendant-Descendant axis (the dream, the illusion). Mao's first program disaster focuses two years later on July 01 1959: *SA Pluto precisely square the Midheaven*, SA Uranus precisely square Neptune, with tr Saturn opposed Uranus, ruler of the Ascendant. The SA of Jupiter conjunct the Moon represents the spiritual and doctrinaire mobilization of the people by Mao.

118 Fairbank, 383–405.

　Mao Tse-Tung was born December 26, 1893 probably at 8:00 A.M. at Shao Shan in Hunan province [113E30, 27N36]. It is extremely important to note that Mao's powerful *Moon at 14 Leo was exactly conjunct Communist China's Mars (conjunct Pluto) in 14 Leo in the national 7th House.* Mao was another of the "peasant-emperors," grand figures risen up from the fields, who punctuate Chinese history.

persecuted more than 700,000 people, of whom some 35,000 were pushed to death. Many more were physically and mentally crippled, and a great number committed suicide.[119]

The astrology of this time is eloquent indeed, showing the superficial euphoria of the big break, the optimism, the doctrine strength of the movement according to Mao; the enormous reinforcement of Mao's ego position but, at the same time, the irreconcilable break-up of everything China stood for, a tragic collapse of national structure; a deep deception of the people.[120*]

The new but crippled government began reconstruction, under leadership by Zhou Enlai, with Mao as a figurehead. Zhou's death in 1973 opened the way for Zhou's named successor, Deng Xiaoping, to carve out the security of his leadership position.

Nature helped: on July 28, 1976, the great Tangshan earthquake east of Peking (Beijing) suddenly killed nearly 750,000 people. Fairbank points out that "every peasant believed in the umbilical relationship between man and nature, and therefore between natural disasters and human calamities. After such an overwhelming portent, Mao could only die. He did so on September 9, 1976."[121*]

With the death of the Cultural Revolution and with the death of Mao, patience and gradualism clearly emerged from the violent past of accelerated demagoguery. China reformed itself under the leadership of Deng Xiaoping. In echo of its most enduring profile from the past, the nation became cautious, private, withdrawn; this is the real China in terms of its history and in terms of its modern horoscope.[122*]

---

119 Fairbank, 387.

120 Using August 1, 1967, as a midpoint of the Cultural Revolution (January 1966 -April 1969): SA Pluto=China Sun/Moon, SA MC squares Saturn, SA Neptune squares Moon, and deceptively, positively SA Uranus opposes Jupiter (the big break, optimism); with tr Jupiter on China's Mars, which is Mao's Moon and, sadly, transiting Saturn opposing the national Sun throughout the period.

121 Fairbank, 405. SA Pluto exactly conjunct China's Saturn, and much more; tr Uranus square the national Ascendant and tr Saturn exactly conjunct China's Mars, Mao's Moon!

122 The China Saturn in Virgo is peregrine (not making a Ptolemaic aspect with any other body) and will run away with the thrust of national identity: punctilious care, arch-discrimination, strategic delay. Additionally, this very powerful Saturn is "oriental," rising last before the Sun longitudinally (clock-wise), introducing extreme patience into the identity. As well, though, the Saturn=Sun/Pluto picture shows a deep capacity for ruthless (internal) power struggle. See Tyl, Synthesis, 155, 497. It is fascinating to see this modern horoscope for China echoing its past so strongly; just as we have seen the modern horoscope for Japan echoing key national identity dimensions of the preceding Meiji reign. (See page 45.)

The Deng regime reestablished its right to rule by acknowledging its errors.[123]* Education and agriculture, and industry (70% and 20%, respectively, doing away with collectives to encourage enterprise) were developed carefully.[124]* Deng's most spectacular reversal of economic policy was his "opening" to foreign trade, technology, and investment, a "swing of the pendulum" indeed, cites Fairbank.[125] It is not surprising: in astrology, foreign trade and education (as well as law, philosophy, ideology, propaganda, and travel) share the same basic symbolism; i.e., when one of these dimensions is emphasized an emphasis in one or more of the other dimensions is expected. For example, with the rededication to education, China had to find a way to reconcile this with its ideological commitment to Communism; it had to find a way to link education to management reform.[126]

The New China

Now with a population of some 1.2 billion people discovering the pleasure of buying for their own comfort, with double-digit growth rates, and with a world-recognized mandate to fulfill market potentials, China is cautiously watching the world anticipate its progress. Bolstered by surging exports, China's foreign exchange reserves (savings) have climbed to $70 billion, a jump from eleventh place to a virtual tie for fifth in the world, a doubling in the past year alone (1993 to 1994). This reflects the Communist government's conservative approach to finance and a hedge against the nation's $100 billion foreign debt, the potential increase in specific import prices (oil and grain, especially), and the transition costs involving Hong Kong

---

123 A fascinating emergence of the Libra Sun/Aquarius Moon blend of the "People's Republic," in the 8th and 12th Houses, respectively.

124 Education is a key index to a nation's future. Repressed under Mao, who cut out intellectuals from the mainstream of party planning, education made a powerful comeback under Deng: proficiency test scores in mathematics and science for thirteen-year-old pupils in twenty countries for 1991, from the International Assessment of Education Progress, cited in MacRae page 78, ranks China number 1 in average days of instruction per year, over 80% correct in test scores in mathematics and fourteenth in Science, tied with the United States (with Korea number 1). Again, this surge is the astrologically correct China; Pluto, ruler of the education 9th, is strongly reinforced by Mars; Jupiter is sextiled by Venus in the 9th.

125 Fairbank, 413, 416.

126 McRae, 79. It is obvious that with the increase of internationalism there is an increase of learning.

due to come. With increasing security, China will start investing this store of funds and affect the world.[127]*

If China's pace of momentum is maintained, it will have a larger Gross Domestic Product (GDP) than the United States by 2003. Even if its 1980s growth rate halved, China would pass the United States in 2014.[128]

In its growth that now occurs *with* development, China sees the collapse of the USSR, its communist patron, as a result of sudden, radical change encouraged by the United States zeal for immediate reform.[129] China also sees the enormous difficulties caused by the sudden reforms in Germany, the reunification of East and West. (See Germany, 152.)

■ Prediction ...

New Leadership—China's leadership is old. Chief among them, Deng Xiaoping, is ninety-one as of August 1995. He will be dead very soon.[130]* Astrologically, if his birth data is correct, there is a great pressure exerted upon his life-system between March and July 1996. That is the time that could introduce behind the scenes the first new wave of leadership for China.[131]*

It is important to note that Mao and Deng were powerful, charismatic leaders cast in the mold of historic Chinese emperors. Their successor(s) will not ascend from that mold. The

---

127 Reported by International Monetary Fund; see *New York Times*, November 10, 1995, page 1. Astrologically, note that the financial rulers (2nd and 8th Houses), Neptune and Mercury, respectively, are conjunct in the 8th, sextile Mars and Pluto (ruler of the 9th) in the 7th. The 8th House, other countries' monies, represents savings. And further, capturing an important dimension of the Neptune: a study released by the United Nations, conducted by Transparency International of Berlin, ranked nations on a survey supported "Corruption Index." The lowest scores—most corrupt—were Indonesia, China, Pakistan, Venezuela, Brazil, Philippines, India, Thailand, and Italy (*New York Times*, August 13, 1995). It is noteworthy indeed that five of those countries are immediately involved with the Pacific market.

128 Paper by Larry Summers, then chief economic advisor at the World Bank, 1993: *International Economic Insights May/June 1992.*

129 *The Washington Post*, January 30, 1994, page H5.

130 Deng Xiaoping, born August 22, 1904 at 11:20 A.M. in Gung'an; 30N28, 106E39 (12 Scorpio 57 Ascendant), according to Chinese sources, through American astrologer Bill Watson. Deng's Mars at 4 Leo is conjunct the national horizon.

131 Deng: SA Saturn square MC; tr Uranus opposed Mars; tr Mars square Mars late in May 1996; the national horoscope has tr Uranus conjunct Moon and Ascendant (Deng Xiaoping's Mars).

world is different, and so are the Chinese people: some forty million are unemployed, some 100 million are underemployed; there is disgruntlement about the 1989 suppression of the pro-democracy movement (Tiananmen Square); some 100 million people have moved away from the fields and into the coastal cities to pursue the way of life seen on television, and this number is expected to double by 2000. The next leaders will be politicians forced into social change by the demands to fulfill economic potential.[132]

China faces an extraordinary challenge: rise up to be the greatest market in the world, galvanizing the entire Pacific bloc (Hong Kong, Singapore, Japan, Taiwan, the Koreas, Indonesia, New Zealand, and Australia) and be able *to control the process.*

First, Hong Kong: Hong Kong has been a British crown colony on the South China coast since it was ceded to the British after the Opium War on August 29, 1842 (see Opium War, page 57). It was then leased to Britain in 1898 for ninety-nine years. Hong Kong will be turned over to China at midnight of the day July 1, 1997.[133]*

McRae calls Hong Kong "the most completely *laissez-faire* [do what you will] economy on earth—there is in effect no government influence at all." Since the 1980s, Hong Kong has become the communications and trading center through which mainland China sells its goods to the world. In Hong Kong in July 1995, a two-bedroom *pied-a-terre* rented for $7,200 per month, in contrast with similar quarters in New York renting at $2,150 or in Sydney at $1,100.[134] This free-wheeling, internationally connected, burgeoning economic center of Hong Kong now enters a mainland vista with extraordinary promise, a present viable consumer buying market of 300 million (still the

132 Statistics from overview presented in *TIME* magazine, November 6, 1995, 44–46.

133 On December 19, 1984, China and Great Britain signed an accord *confirming* the transfer of Hong Kong's sovereignty to China, and China in turn guaranteed that Hong Kong's capitalist system would continue unchanged for fifty more years, i.e., from 1997 to 2047. China has adopted a "One Country, Two Systems" doctrine with regard to Hong Kong. Additionally: September 1995 elections in Hong Kong gave 12 of the 20 directly elected seats in the sixty-member Legislative Council to the Democratic Party, a group founded in the wake of the Tiananmen Square massacre in 1989 to challenge China's plans for controlling Hong Kong. Transiting Pluto will be 3–5 Sagittarius square China's sensitive Sun/Moon midpoint (1997–98); tr Uranus will square the horizon.

134 Associates for International Research, Inc., cited in *The New York Times*, July 9, 1995, page 4.

largest opportunity in the world today) with a per capita buying power of $380 a year that can only grow.

Can China—with its central government in so vast a land, with millions leaving the farmlands to resettle in urban areas to be closer to higher wages—control its explosive growth? Can the tarnished communist philosophy take the light of the capitalist star represented by Hong Kong?[135]

The pressure is great. National economic reform and growth mask international reluctance. Among the old leaders, there is the residual fear of education, which translates into a fear of informed youth exposed to the rest of the world and its thoughts. Yet history reminds us that inspired leaders die, that success does not support radicalism, and that change occurs inexorably. Learning and economics will break loose from political anchor.

China has not only seen abrupt change destroy the USSR and deplete Germany but, at the same time, it has witnessed the gradual and sustained success built up by Hong Kong, Taiwan, and Singapore. This has been accomplished without extreme reliance upon Japan and its technology. With Japan's role diminishing within its extreme national problems (See "Japan's Problems," page 42), China will seize leadership of the Pacific Market and affect the world trade balance considerably: they will eschew the Japanese way of catch-up through imitation and place major emphasis on innovation and creativity.

Is the central control of the government in China prepared to accomplish what is needed to realize its extraordinary potential? It must look to its youth. As Japan has become the oldest nation, China is becoming very young again (see Japan: "Social Resources," page 43).

■ Prediction ...

Communist Government Breakup—In short, within gradualism, China's old leadership is holding on to the death throes of communism. Soon the infrastructure will be dead. China will modernize government in several stages; it will subdivide somehow; it will release control from the central anchor of

---

135 *The Washington Post*, January 30, 1994, page H5.

Communist government and spread it throughout its 3.7 million square miles in the spirit of democratic enterprise. China is dedicated to doing this gradually.

United States Ambassador J. Stapleton Roy also sees China in a crucial state of transition: "poised awkwardly" between a Marxist centrally planned economy and the "socialist market economy" that Deng has set as a national goal.[136] In this awkward position, China has pulled back in 1995, withdrawing its ambassador from Washington.

A coolness between the United States and China has been built up since the Tiananmen Square massacre in the Summer of 1989.[137*] International horror greeted China's old guard's ruthless disregard for human rights. China's horoscopic signature for ruthlessness was activated; it is always there, even within reform, even during the best of days.[138*]

So, there is a suspended moment in time now, 1995–97: world market potential beckons, the leaders exit, the past dies, and the *human* potentials to fulfill the promise are strongly re-illuminated by the lights of Hong Kong. The people are demanding recognition. The government makes new plans.

A hold-over of the tyrannical, military approach may surface in March-April 1996.[139*] The tension here may be to depress the continued rise of Taiwan, for example, China's renegade state co-existing in a "One China" policy since 1949. Hong Kong is returning to China, but Taiwan is not. Might Taiwan upstage China as the front-runner toward capitalistic marketing stardom and in attracting the African market, upon which Taiwan is focusing strongly with enormous investments there? China could assert itself strongly, militaristically, but it would lose much emerging good will and unity with the rest of the world. China simply does not want to lose face as transition begins.

Profit potential should overcome principle here and pave the way even more for greater changes in China's leadership and national philosophy. The death of Deng may divert tensions

---

136 *The New York Times*, International Section, June 18, 1995, page 7.

137 SA Uranus exactly conjunct Mars in the 7th, with tr Pluto exactly square Mars, and more.

138 Natal: Saturn=Sun/Pluto; the Tiananmen incident saw SA Moon opposed China's Saturn, i.e., SA Moon=Sun/Pluto, with concomitant measurements that signified force (see preceding footnote).

139 Tr Uranus conjoining the national Ascendant.

from Taiwan's vociferous trade program and open a negotiation window between mainland China and the island.[140]

■ Prediction ...

China Abandons Communism—The Communist philosophy of China will soon be discarded.

There are two phases to this monumental change, concomitant with China's fulfillment of market promise. First, there is the beginning of the leadership deaths of the old guard in Spring 1997; the student population will mobilize once again and create a powerful international/free trade movement around the Hong Kong "acquisition," especially in February, April–May, and November 1997. This will be a loud, dangerous time.[141*]

China will make a major Millennium public relations event out of its plans to begin phasing out communist rule at the turn of the century, between April 1999 and January 2000.[142*]

Should the government *not* make its decision for change at this time, it will be like a woman resisting the birthing process. The astrological measurements will correspond to the people's eruption out of disillusionment to topple the vestiges of the communist regime and improve their standards of living. This scenario then could be violent social upheaval.[143*]

There is every indication of enormous change and success here—a great Summer shining out from a long Winter, with what cells remain of the old guard disappearing rapidly. Gradu-

---

140 For example, Beijing has been suspending relations with countries that open embassies in Taipei, Taiwan's capital.

141 *Tr Uranus conjunct Ascendant; tr Pluto = Sun/Moon;* tr Saturn opposed Sun; tr Jupiter conjunct Moon.

142 SA Sun conjunct Midheaven and then SA Pluto conjunct Sun! Additionally, tr Saturn conjunct the 4th cusp, opposed the Midheaven in July, 2000 and March 2001, with tr Uranus opposed Pluto October–December 2000, and tr Neptune conjunct Ascendant, March 2000–January 2002.

  Also active, exact in September 2000 is the difficult SA Neptune=Sun/Moon, connoting deception, discontent, and—with Neptune's rulership of the national 2nd House— financial loss. This could correspond to hard-core communist factions being disillusioned.

143 Jupiter-Saturn Conjunction Chart (May 28, 2000, 11:59 P.M. at Peking) Pluto at the Midheaven (party in power) opposed the Sun in the 4th (party not in power; other political platform); Jupiter-Saturn in the 3rd, Jupiter ruling the Midheaven, squared by Uranus (ruling the Ascendant) at the Ascendant. This Mundane Chart definitely shows the breakdown of Communism.

alism will be the key for this transition. For China, its rising Sun—its Millennium claim to fame—shines on the plan to accomplish epic rebirth.

Korea: Toward One Soul

Arnold Toynbee has written that cultures at the edge of a central, dominant civilization eventually acquire capacities, energies, and distinctions *that the central core culture lacks.* This is the case certainly for Japan and Korea dominated for so much of history by the behemoth presence of China. With the industrial revolution, with the revolutions of political manifestos, with the requirements and backlashes of wars, and the concomitant modernized, industrial ascendancy of Japan and South Korea especially, the national profiles of these "peripheral" countries have pulled away from that of still centralized, still agrarian Communist China.[144]

When the world became urbanized as never before after World War II, some 42% of the world population was urban (but for the weight of enormous rural populations in China and India, the percentage would have been well over fifty), but China lagged behind in its isolation, in political dogma that reinforced a different way of life (the cult of Mao). The peripheral nations forged ahead.

William Pfaff points out this phenomenon and notes that, "because they were apart from the imperial civilization and politically endangered by it, they [the peripheral countries] were from the start forced into a certain 'national' mobilization to assert and defend their particularity."

With urbanization's demands for services and greater productivity in industry, there was also an enormous rise in the number of occupations requiring secondary and higher education. Literacy and education became extremely important; education was/is another defining characteristic of Japan's and Korea's (and the other peripheral nations) developmental contrast with China.

South Korea is cited as a marvel in educational rise. In just eight years—from 1975 to 1983—(South) Korean students rose from 0.8 percent to almost 3% of the population. The great world boom made it possible for modest families to send their children to school full-time. By 1991, Korea's students ranked internationally first in

---

144 See Pfaff, 152.

performance aptitude in science (United States ranked fourteenth) and second in mathematics (United States is fifteenth).

But China, from its fall-back during the Mao regime, has worked hard to catch up with the peripheral nations. China has worked particularly hard to improve educationally, since learning is antithetical to communist ideology, unless that learning is involved with reforms linked to management of collective enterprise. And China has made its marks: first in mathematics and fourteenth in science (though test scores were scanty in the survey).[145]

Similarly, the gaps of urbanization, industrial productivity, and international marketing are closing fast. As the world implodes, it is clear that the central dominant nation is once again enfolding the peripheral nations. Beyond China becoming modern, a Pacific Market is forming, the biggest market of cultural uniformity (intermix) and population that the world has ever known.

Korea—North and South—lives on a 600-mile-long, mineral-rich peninsula in the Southwest Japan Sea, approximately 200 miles at its tip from the Southwestern islands of Japan, across the Korean Strait. Korea's northern border abuts China. With Japan and China, the three cultures unify a geographic and marketing presence in the Pacific that requires and commands access to the sea for trade to the southwest, to the Philippines, Indonesia, Vietnam, Australia, New Zealand, and on to India.

Korea's early history was similar to that of Japan and China, except for the absence of conquest. Korea was the victim: in the early thirteenth century, the Mongol invasions came from China and, then again, invasion and occupation by China in the early seventeenth century. Thereafter, Korea worked toward isolationism, becoming known as the "Hermit Kingdom."

But when the Japanese moved through Korea to get at Manchuria during Japan's war with China in 1904, its troops stationed in Korea never left that country. The annexation of Korea by Japan lasted until 1945, until the end of World War II. During that time, enormous reforms were instituted in Korea industrially and culturally.[146]

---

145 Hobsbawm, 297; McRae, 78: proficiency scores noted for 13-year-olds in 20 countries, 1991.

146 Sporadic attempts to overthrow the Japanese were unsuccessful; a provisional Korean government was established in Shanghai under Syngman Rhee.

During World War II, in 1943, at a conference held in Cairo, the United States, Britain, and China promised Korea that, at the end of the war, Korea would have its independence.[147]

At the end of the war, Korea was divided into two zones as a temporary expedient; Soviet troops were North and American troops were South of a line drawn at 38 degrees Northern Latitude. The Soviet Union thwarted all United Nations efforts to hold country-wide general elections and unite the country. With Cold War tensions building between the USSR and the United States, trade between mineral-rich North and agrarian-strong South Korea ceased. Great hardship followed.

In 1948, two separate regimes were established: the Republic of Korea to the South and the Democratic People's Republic to the North, under communist rule.[148*]

The Korean War

On June 25, 1950, the North launched an attack upon the South, initiating the Korean War.[149*] China entered the war for the North in November 1950. Severe hardship, devastation, and some three and one-half million casualties were incurred (half-million dead) before an Armistice was signed on July 27, 1953. To date, a Peace Treaty has not been signed.[150]

It is not clear to historians or military analysts why the North invaded the South. Friedman and LeBard and others suggest that

---

147 The conference took place November 22–26, 1943, with Churchill, Roosevelt, and Chiang Kai-Shek in attendance. The Cairo Declaration of December 1, 1943 asserted that, upon Japan's defeat, Japan's boundaries would revert to what they were before the late nineteenth-century conquests of Chinese territory.

148 South Korea: August 15, 1948, at noon in Seoul, South Korea (no exact time known). North Korea: September 10, 1948, at noon in P'yongyang, North Korea (no exact time known). See Campion, *World Horoscopes*. Note that the South is defined by a Leo Sun conjunct Pluto and Saturn and Mercury, trine Jupiter in Sagittarius (remember the Olympics) with a Capricorn Moon opposed Uranus; the North is defined by a Virgo Sun (ideology) square Jupiter in Sagittarius (dogma), with *Mercury-Neptune* square the Capricorn Moon, also opposed Uranus (broadly).
   The North has a powerful national focus in the picture: Pluto=Sun/Moon (suggesting the potential of atomic energy within its national image, and, of course, brutal force). The South has a dominant picture: Jupiter=Sun/Mars (optimism, success, international promotion). Both countries have a Scorpio Ascendant.

149 At 4:00 P.M., troops crossed the 38th parallel at eleven points to invade the South; cited by Campion, *World Horoscopes*, footnote 1463.

150 The Civil War in Spain, led by Francesco Franco (1936–39) lasted the same length of time as the Korean War but with twice as many killed, i.e., one million. (See "Franco," page 202.)

Stalin wanted to test the limits of United States commitment in Asia. The fall of Korea was of no concern to him: the long debilitating war and the "mutual loathing" of China (backing the North) and America that would result would be strategically important to him.

From the United States perspective, the Soviet threat was again testing United States defenses (as was being done in Europe at the same time). The United States had to respond in order to stand strong with its post-World War II power position; and, specifically, the United States had to defend the crucial position of the Sea of Japan (and access to the Pacific) from Soviet intrusion.[151]

The United States was not prepared for war in this region. It had to reach out for supplies and reinforcements from within General MacArthur's Far Eastern Command. The United States was pressed to protect Japan (by treaty/constitution), needed to control the Pacific access region, and had to keep South Korea from falling to the communist regime. Japan had to cooperate in the effort as well; South Korea could not be defeated; Japan could never be secure if an enemy power were sitting across the straits of its sea in Korea.

Japan Prospering from the Korean War

The defense of South Korea immediately set up a great infusion of capital into the Japanese economy. Export orders in Japan to sustain the United States Korean War effort rose by a factor of seven, with total "new" income of some $3.5 billion accruing to Japan in four years.

The Korean War started Japan's post-World War II boom. Stalin's warring posture sustained the Cold War and was the catalyst for Japan's industrial boom—birthing the corporations Mitsubishi, Hitachi, and Kawasaki through shipbuilding; Toyota and Nissan in truck manufacture, etc. "The threat of peace terrified the Japanese investor."[152]

A special note: Astrologers know the dates for the formations of the Koreas, but not the exact time. However, there are response profiles to the noon-mark time reference (which astrology uses in

---

151 Friedman & LeBard, 112–118.

152 Later, when Stalin died March 5, 1953, *two months before the Korean Armistice was signed*, the Tokyo Stock Exchange plummeted!

place of the actual time) that do command attention and reinforce predictive security.

For example, both Koreas were admitted to the United Nations in September 1991 and the astrology corroborates that national recognition.[153*]

Specifically for South Korea, there was an attempt to assassinate General Park Chung Hee, South Korea's President (1963-1979) in August 1974 (his wife was murdered), and then he was killed in a second assassination attempt on October 26, 1979. These two events show strongly in the astrological profile of the country.[154*]

Additionally, South Korea was awarded the Summer Olympics, the games taking place September 17–October 2, 1988. This grand event also has strong astrological corroboration.[155*]

North Korea's Point with "The Bomb"

The world fanfare about the discovery of atomic energy capacity in North Korea late in 1994 *was seen ahead of time* in North Korea's horoscope, relating to a measurement justifying the noon-mark birth.[156*] From this strong base, it is significant to note that this measurement point, the Ascendant (the Sign degree coming over the horizon at the moment of birth), *is the same as the Midheaven* (the ego culmination point) *of the People's Republic of China*, 27 Scorpio 09). North Korea anticipates China's colossal rise in the world market and is eager to attract attention, to identify itself with world power, and be taken along for the profitable adventure: the peripheral nation rejoins the central colossus.

---

153 For the North: tr Uranus conjunct the Moon, tr Jupiter conjunct Saturn; for the South: tr Pluto approaching square to the Sun, tr Jupiter conjunct Sun. And especially for the South, a major angular contact: SA Moon precisely conjunct the 4th, opposed the Midheaven.

154 August 1974: SA Neptune exactly conjunct the Ascendant; SA Mars exactly square the Midheaven! October 26, 1979: SA Neptune applying to square the Midheaven, tr Uranus square the Sun in the 10th, tr Mars conjunct the Sun in the 10th; SP Mars exactly conjunct the Ascendant; SP Moon=Sun/Pluto in the 10th.

155 SA Uranus and Venus at the Midheaven, squaring the Ascendant, with tr Pluto squaring the Midheaven.

156 Tr Pluto conjunct the Ascendant; success with the gambit: SA Venus conjunct Sun and SA Sun semisquare Jupiter, Nov 1994-May 1995. The Ascendant established at 27 Scorpio 19 received the transit of Pluto in January, May, and November of 1994, corroborating the profile of Atomic Energy inquiry and discovery in North Korea, as well as *the death of leader Kim Il Sung* (see next footnote).

Leadership Crisis

Kim Il Sung, the "Great Leader" of North Korea, died July 8, 1994. He was revered by his people as the man who solely defeated Japan in World War II and liberated Korea from Japanese control.[157]

The son of the "Great Leader," Kim Jong Il was expected to succeed his father, but to date (late 1995), no succession has been announced. Kim Jong Il, fifty-three years old, has never been known to speak in public and, according to United States officials, has "evidently never met an American."

■ Prediction ...

Kim Jong Il will not Lead—The succession of leadership in North Korea should have been announced in October 1994— at the latest December 1994. A deception definitely took place in terms of a coalition of people inside the government out-side Kim Il Sung's extended family circle. The plans of this coalition gathered strength over the first six months of 1995 and faced no opposition after that time. Kim Jong Il is out of the picture.[158*]

The rule of North Korea now by committee may not be formalized in public awareness until January or August 1997. This sham is a very important early first step to the breakdown of communist leadership structure, great public suffering, and the rise of national awareness of the necessity for change.[159*]

---

157 In an interview with Kim Dal Hyun, a nephew of the "Great Leader" and a senior mem-ber of the national hierarchy, the question was asked why the dictator was so revered. Kim: "He is the man who defeated Japan in World War II and liberated Korea from Japanese control." Kim was then asked about the U.S. role in defeating Japan and about the 100,000-plus Americans who died fighting in the Pacific. He replied, "This is the first time anyone ever suggested to me that America helped defeat Japan in World War II. History shows us that it was Kim Il Sung who defeated the Japanese." T. R. Reid, *Washington Post*, October 22, 1994, A26.

158 SP Moon conjunct the Midheaven; simultaneously, SA Neptune conjunct the Ascendant!

159 SA MC=Moon/Pluto (national consciousness) with tr Saturn square Moon and Nep-tune, tr Uranus square Mars; SA Sun=Node, SA Saturn=Sun/Pluto with tr Uranus square Mars, and more.

■ Prediction ...

North and South Korea Unified—With China's decentralization, modernization, and shift away from Communism beginning strongly in late 1999 (see page 66), North Korea will have to follow.

Korea's time for reunification will be accomplished between April 2003 and September 2004, motivated by grand prosperity throughout the Pacific Market, with student unrest (the expanding younger population segments of both countries) demanding change.[160*]

Key Countries in the Extended Pacific Market
The Philippines — Pacific Sentinel

To reach India and then Japan! For centuries, that was the romantic voyage, inspired, confused, and dangerous for so many explorers. Sailing eastward through the Indian Ocean, searching for the expanse of the Pacific, these explorers encountered a maze through which passage was bewildering but necessary: the vast archipelago of the 13,000 islands of Indonesia and the 7,000 islands and rocks of the Philippines. These lands define the crescent-shaped sentinel line between the Near East and Far East.

The Spanish Beginning

It is easy to see on maps—as if uncovering a secret of Nature's history—that the Philippines separated themselves eons ago from the present coastline of Vietnam, as if on their own voyage further east toward Japan, to the Orient. The around-the-world Spanish expedition admiralled by the Portuguese Ferdinand Magellan "discovered" the mineral, agricultural, and forest-rich lands of the Philippines in 1521. Over the next five years, other Spanish expeditions followed. One of the later ones was led by Admiral Miguel

---

160 North Korea (where the move for reunification will start): SA MC semisquare Sun, April 2003, and then SA Mars opposed Uranus and SA Pluto square Moon in December 2003–January 2004, with tr Jupiter conjunct the Sun and tr Pluto conjunct Jupiter; SA Jupiter opposed Pluto, September 2004. South Korea: SA Jupiter opposed Midheaven in November–December 2003; SA MC semisquare Sun and SA Ascendant conjunct Moon in May 2004, with tr Pluto conjunct Jupiter and tr Neptune opposed MC.

Lopez de Legazpi; he was under orders from King Philip II to annex the islands peacefully and without bloodshed. This completed the Spanish king's chain of communication around the world. Philip then possessed an empire upon which indeed the sun never set.[161]

Religion was the prod of these expeditions, the rationalization of outright annexation. The Philippines became the farthest outreach of Eurocentric Christianity and, as distance seems to encourage distinctiveness and intensify belonging, Catholicism became a powerful cultural attraction and force in the Philippines. Some 288,000 people were converted to the faith in just twenty-five years. Today, the Philippines is extrovertedly 84% Roman Catholic.

Before the Spanish arrived, the Chinese had traded constantly with the Philippines. The Spanish hacked down this Oriental "intrusion," and the Chinese were converted to a feared and hated working class in the Philippines.

United States Possession

When the Spanish-American War erupted in 1898, a major United States victory took place in the Philippines on May 1. The Americans arrived with great naval might and promised the Philippinos the reward of independence if they would rally together and fight *against* the Spanish. This independence was then framed within the first democratic constitution ever known in Asia.

But, at the Treaty of Paris (August 9, 1898; with the Treaty signed on December 10), which closed out the Spanish-American War, the United States paid $20 million to Spain "to possess" the Philippines. The Islands did not receive their reward of national autonomy after all.[162]

The United States then faced a mammoth project to subdue guerilla warfare conducted by the Philippine rebels. These battles cost more money and took far more lives than the actual Spanish-American War had. The opposition was finally quelled through trade—a formidable weapon to stop war and keep peace. Affluence defused

---

161 Parker, 115, 146. The name "Philippines" does not come from King Philip II of Spain, however. It comes from a group of early settlers from the Malay peninsula (to the southwest, below Vietnam) called the Filipino; the native language is called Pilipino.

162 In that Treaty as well, the United States acquired Guam and Puerto Rico; Cuba became a free Republic. The treaty was signed at 8:45 P.M., LMT in Paris. (See Campion, *World Horoscopes*, 281.)

radical doctrine, and thereafter, the Philippines became almost entirely dependent upon the American market for their new way of life.

World War II

During World War II, the Philippines were a natural frontier and springboard for United States control of the Pacific and for battle encounters with the Japanese. The greatest naval engagement in history took place there, in Leyte gulf, October 23–26, 1944. It was an epic United States victory over the Japanese. At war's end in July 1945, General MacArthur announced "All the Philippines are now liberated"; independence was finally granted to the Philippines on July 4, 1946. *A military assistance pact* was signed the next year, which—as with Japan—afforded the United States key outposts in the Philippine Pacific from which to monitor the Soviet Union during the Cold War.[163*]

Marcos Mayhem

The Astro-profile of the Philippines is demoralizing: it portrays a nation of power struggles, clashes for control, internal warring activities and financial corruption.[164*] And history has borne this out: World War II reconstruction was complicated by communist guerillas (Huks) using terror and violence to gain political power; the Huks were brought under temporary control in 1954 with a

---

163 The independence of the Philippines is specifically timed to the lowering of the United States flag and the raising of the Philippine flag. Campion's news report research (the National Historical Institute) sets the time at 9:15 A.M.

My rectification study adjusts this time to 9:26 A.M., CCT (-8 hours): perhaps the time element of lowering one flag, folding it ceremoniously, retiring it and raising the new flag, slowly, with fanfare.

Rectification proofs: *In social chaos, Marcos imposes martial law on September 23, 1972* (to last for many years): SA Pluto conjunct Ascendant, SP Moon conjunct Ascendant, and tr Neptune exactly opposite the Midheaven. *Opposition leader Benigno Aquino assassinated, August 21, 1983:* tr Uranus precisely opposed Midheaven in the fourth (the opposition party); *Marcos flees the Philippines, February 25, 1986:* SA Saturn exactly conjunct the Ascendant with tr Saturn precisely opposed the Midheaven.

It is important to note that the Philippines horoscope is dominated by an exact Uranus-Node conjunction in the 10th House, square the Moon: strong indication of the influence of females in the government. Witness to date: Imelda Marcos and Corazon Acquino (b. January 25, 1933, wife of the assassinated leader). Aquino was proclaimed president on February 15, 1986.

164 Saturn=Sun/Pluto, Uranus/Ascendant; Pluto=Sun/Mars; Pluto conjunct Mercury, ruler of the Ascendant (the people) and the Midheaven (the government) in the 12th House; Neptune in the 2nd square the Sun; Saturn in Cancer and without aspect (insecurity and domestic upset) rampant; defensive eastern orientation guarding the Ascendant; Mars rising in Virgo (dogma enforcement).

firm anti-communist policy adopted by the government; Ferdinand Marcos was elected in January 1965 and faced a revived Huk uprising rife with assassinations and terror; by August 1969, civil war threatened, there were riots, and martial law was instituted in September 1972, to last nine years until 1981.[165*]

Out of the Marcos time, an immensely popular opposition leader emerged: Benigno Aquino. He was assassinated August 21, 1983, at Manila airport. One million Philippinos marched in Aquino's funeral procession, and his widow, Corazon Aquino, took over her husband's political position and ran against Ferdinand Marcos in an election February 7, 1986. Marcos engineered a fraudulent declaration of himself as winner; this maneuver was exposed; and Aquino became president.[166*]

President Marcos fled the Philippines on February 25, 1986 amid the charges of colossal financial deception (estimated at $10 billion). He died in Hawaii on September 28, 1989.[167*]

Aquino then faced the defection of her vice-president (Salvadore Laurel) who formed an opposition party against her; there was a coup attempt led by the military and remaining Marcos adherents. The platform was again to gain independence, to rid the Philippines of the United States presence. Aquino declined reelection, and designated her former Defense Secretary as the next president, a former General, Fidel Ramos. Ramos was elected by a million-vote margin on May 11, 1992.[168]

Such is the eruptive profile of the Philippines, a rich country curiously separated from the Asia mainland, vital to Japan for its mineral wealth and ocean position, and strategically important to the United States for its location as a defensive front in the Pacific. This latter defense position from the United States perspective includes the stratagem of *containing* the Japanese, according to the

---

165 Another indication of deep unrest: when Pope Paul VI visited Manila in November 1970, there was an assassination attempt made on his life.

166 Corazon Aquino was born January 25, 1933. Her Saturn tightly opposes the Philippine Mercury, ruler of its Ascendant and Midheaven.

167 At his death, he was also under United States indictment for having stolen at least $100 million from his country and using it to buy real estate and art in the United States. His widow, Imelda, was acquitted of similar charges on July 2, 1990 in New York City. Marcos was born September 11, 1917. His Saturn-Neptune conjunction in Leo conjoins the Philippines Mercury-Pluto conjunction in the 12th, with Mercury ruling the national Ascendant and Midheaven!

168 Ramos was educated at Illinois University and West Point Military Academy in the United States; he is a veteran of the Korean and Vietnam wars. He led the mutiny that forced the deposition of President Ferdinand Marcos (1986), his second cousin(!).

hard-look views of Friedman & LeBard (See "War with the United States?" page 53).

Japanese investment in the Philippines has been strong for 15 years and is increasing, specifically in oil exploration, in order to have a source nearer to hand than the Persian Gulf (along with Indonesia). The Philippines, Indonesia, China, Malaysia, and India have enough raw materials to export to supply Japan's needs— excepting possibly oil, and these countries' markets can be developed further to create a sufficient demand for Japanese products. Increased investment in Asia is part of Japan's future. Keeping the Philippines open to Japan is critical for Japan's trade and freedom upon the Pacific and within the burgeoning market there. Friedman & LeBard suggest that Japan will go to the extent of war to protect the open Philippine and Pacific positions.[169]

■ Prediction ...

Ramos Defeated—There is no doubt that the Philippines want to be left alone, without excessive dependence on any other country. The United States represents a confinement. With the end of the Cold War, the pressure to oust the United States from its bases in the Philippines prevailed, and those bases were evacuated in 1992.[170*]

At the same time, Japanese power threatens the Philippines. The memories of World War II are still very much alive. And the Philippines know that China will not think twice about fracturing the islands' autonomy.

The Millennium issue for the Philippines will be its precarious, essentially strategic geographic position; again the Philippines will be the card being passed back and forth in an international gambit to position Japan and the United States as strategically as possible within the Pacific Market.

Additionally, twenty-five to thirty typhoons threaten the islands each year, with 25% of them depleting the rice crop: the

---

169 Friedman & LeBard; 387.

170 While the United States and Philippines Suns conjoin, the U.S. (July 4, 1776, 2:13 A.M. LMT, in Philadelphia) Pluto in the 9th is opposed the Philippine Saturn, which makes no aspect and is dominant in its self-absorption. That Saturn conjoins the U.S. Mercury, the Ascendant ruler (the United States people will give no support to a renewed military presence in the Philippines). U.S. Uranus squares Philippines Mars, etc.

Philippines must now import food (increasing their vulnerability to embargo, political manipulation, and exploitation) against the rise in population and these natural disasters; politics is still threatened by growing unemployment and restless Muslim rebels; the need for land is increasing as population growth within prosperity uses up arable land.

Times of crisis for the Ramos government begin in October 1996 and develop strongly to February–March 1997, with citizen uprisings about unemployment, trade practices, and national autonomy (the opposition parties in the main are the People's Reform Party, the Nationalist Party, and the Filipino Democratic Party, all nationalist in orientation). Then, public dissent will rise in October 1997 and May–November 1998, surrounding the presidential election (every six years). General Ramos will not be reelected.[171*]

The height of all tension in the Philippines as the world changes—as the social revolution grows in Japan, as China makes its move away from Communism—will be in February 1999 and April 2000. There is dramatic promise of enormous government upheaval, even assassination(s) that will develop over international trade, treaties, and hidden enemies within the nation.[172*]

With maturation of the Pacific Market, between January 2002 and April 2003, the Philippines will prosper as never before in their history.[173*]

Indonesia — Sprawling Gateway

Just below the "left hip" of the Philippines, in the South China Sea, are the more than 13,000 rich volcanic islands of Indonesia. This is the fifth most populous nation in the world, with more than 300 languages spoken throughout the extraordinary expanse of space, as sprawling in area as the United States is wide. It is the natural barrier between the Indian Ocean and the Pacific.

---

171 SA Uranus conjunct Mercury; tr Pluto conjunct the fourth cusp, tr Saturn square the Sun, tr Uranus opposed Pluto.

172 Jupiter-Saturn conjunction chart (May 28, 2000 at 11:59 P.M. CCT at Manila): Jupiter-Saturn Chart Pluto at Midheaven opposed Sun-Venus, Pluto ruling the 9th; Jupiter and Saturn in the 3rd, squared by Uranus in the 12th.

173 SA Sun conjunct Ascendant and then square Midheaven.

Early Arab traders brought Islam to Indonesia, and today 87% of the population is Muslim. This represents the largest Muslim (Moslem) population under one government in the world.[174] With its lava-rich soil, the country is strong in agriculture, minerals, crude oil and natural gas. Indonesia is also one of the world's major rubber producers. It is one of the wealthiest countries in the world.

What Indonesia has in common with China, with Korea, and with the Philippines is invasion by Japan. As Fernandez-Armesto observes, being invaded is not always a testament about aggression but often it is a compliment of the victim's strategic position or wealth in resources. Japan desperately needs resources in order to survive; its success and continued growth demand more and more imports, more fuel for its production and human systems. Japan invaded Indonesia for its oil and, in the process, took on the United States in World War II.

Japan's fears of its natural resource poverty and its vulnerability to embargoes by enemies shape its entire international policy. And always, there is the press for more living space: late in the nineteenth century, as Japan *promoted* population growth to create more and more manpower for industrialization, this drive for living space became dominant. Expansionism led international aggression.[175]

Indonesia's long struggle and wait for independence after being under Dutch mastery for over 300 years came to an end on December 27, 1949, when Queen Juliana signed the Act of Transfer in Amsterdam.[176*]

The Astro-profile of Indonesia shows tremendous tension—a far cry from the romantic visions conjured up by just the mention of "Bali"; for example, the Indonesian province imaged in the song "Bali Hai" from Rogers and Hammerstein's *South Pacific*.

---

174 Roberts, 837. "Muslim" is a variation of "Moslem" (lit., one who renders to God). These terms are used interchangeably to connote a follower of Islam.

175 Fernandez-Armesto, 620. And further: the carving up of the world by white imperialism barred Japanese immigration.

176 The Act occurred at 9:22 A.M. GMT (10:22 A.M. in Amsterdam) *(5:22 P.M. CCT in/for Jakarta, Indonesia)* according to Campion's research, with an alternate time given as 10:17 A.M. in Amsterdam. See Campion, *World Horoscopes*, page 202 and footnote 263.

However, the time *10:01 A.M. in Amsterdam* (5:01 P.M. CCT in/for Jakarta) correlates much better with major events in Indonesia's history (without logical explanation): namely, withdrawal from the United Nations, the Communist coup attempt and subsequent execution of thousands, inciting public riots and chaos, beginning September 30, 1965, and lasting until March 12, 1967: SA Pluto conjunct the fourth cusp and more. The subsequent great prosperity 1969–1972: SA Venus conjunct Midheaven.

Here is driving force, militancy, the hard bargain, a temperamental retaliatory national personality. There are grand riches and extremely profitable international trade. There is the constant threat of upheaval from within, from the party out of power, from battles of doctrine.[177]*

The Indonesian Nationalist Party arose under the leadership of a politician named Sukarno during the Japanese occupation. Immediately after the Japanese surrender, Sukarno proclaimed the Independent Republic of Indonesia and was elected president. His rule was inefficient and corrupt. Public unrest led to even more authoritarian rule.

Sukarno began to cultivate the friendship of Communist China. In 1965, he withdrew Indonesia from the United Nations. Food shortages occurred and inflation got out of control; a coup (believed to be Communist-inspired) was struck against Sukarno's presidency. The coup was thwarted by the military under the leadership of General Suharto, who then gradually assumed power for himself.

While the military stood back ostentatiously, thousands of alleged Communists were executed by the outraged population, and people everywhere took the law into their own hands. A widespread massacre ensued throughout the nation, with perhaps 750,000 people murdered. Entire villages were eradicated.

General Suharto brought an end to the chaos late in 1966, broke off relations with China (renewed only in 1990), reestablished good relations with the United States, and reentered the United Nations. On March 12, 1967, the Indonesian National Assembly voted Sukarno out of power and named General Suharto acting president and then president.[178]

Export programs flourished and prosperity followed.

But pockets of civil unrest, feelings of annexation (fact or fiction) continue on many of the islands. The army under President General Suharto is the nation's dominant political institution. Indonesia is a pressure cooker steaming at the gateway to the biggest market of the world.

---

177 Working with a 6 Gemini Ascendant (5:01 P.M. in Jakarta), there is a dominant cardinal angular Grand Cross; Venus and Jupiter opposed by Pluto in the international trade 3rd-9th axis; Saturn=Moon/Midheaven; Jupiter=Sun/Midheaven. Note the congruence between the Ascendant of Indonesia and the Ascendant-Uranus of the United States.

178 Some of the losers of the 1965 revolt are incarcerated to this day (1995). A few are taken out from time to time to be hanged as evidence of resolute prosecution of the struggle against Communism and an example to any future resistance. Roberts, 838.

■ Prediction ...

Technology Drives Trade—With the formalized assembly of the Pacific Market—China, Japan, Korea, the Philippines, Indonesia, and Vietnam at the core—there are clearly two focal points: China, for its great size and the effects that will be created by its full entrance into world activity, and Japan, for its survival-need of imports and history of annexation. Indonesia is/will be tenaciously eager to be part of the leadership of all trade activities; to be a first-rung power as well.

Tying all the Pacific Market countries together with the future is the "soft" product of technology. Japan has already experienced the tremendous manufacturing and marketing backlash from the United States after years of stealing, imitating, and improving American technological advances: when information flow was restricted, competition was aroused, and politics were engaged. The Americans caught up and clamped down. Japan does not want such competition from the Pacific Market. Japan is paying extreme attention to the control of its technology export.

To this end, Japan coordinates its foreign aid and foreign investment programs in other countries *to support penetration of other countries' local markets*. (See "Imbalanced Trade Practices," page 46.) This is similar to the United States proffering its foreign aid and investment in return not only for market share but also for strategic defense positions, especially in the Pacific area (witness Japan itself, Korea, and the Philippines).

Already in Southeast Asia, Japanese firms dominate local economies through strategic control of manufacturing and cybernetic technology. In Thailand, for example, Japanese manufacturers already control 90% of the automobile market; in Malaysia, Matsushita's operations alone account for about 4% of the Gross Domestic Product and employ over 17,000 Malaysians. In Indonesia—which is at the top of Japan's list for Foreign Aid (because of the oil sources and more)—the capitalization by Japanese firms dominates the local financial markets. In the last decade, Japan has sent these three countries alone tens of billions of dollars of foreign aid. This

Japanese investment dwarfs United States investment in the area: some $3 billion to $900 million.[179]

As a powerful investment commodity and market lever, technology will become the reigning political gambit of the Millennium transition period. Japan barters its technology to preserve its import security. The protection of this information and deployment of its power work to keep Japan at the leadership position of the Pacific Market.[180*]

■ Prediction …

Indonesia Will Fight for Trade Leadership—Indonesia will build a command position to consolidate its assets and share leadership of the Pacific Market with Japan—and China. The first headlines about its push should start in the Summer of 1996 and extend into March–April 1997. (It is a push for recognition similar to that made by North Korea through "the bomb." See "The Bomb," page 71.)[181*]

[Indonesia dislikes being treated insignificantly. This deeply entrenched feeling was voiced in brilliant oratory by its first president Sukarno: "Americans are under the impression they're saying to us, 'Here poor, dear, poverty-stricken brother … have some money … here, poor little underdeveloped Indonesia, we are going to give aid because we love Indonesia.' This is hypocrisy. America tolerates underdeveloped Asian countries for two reasons. One, we're a good market. We pay back with interest. And two, she worries we'll turn communist. She tries to buy our loyalties. She gives bounty and plenty only because she's afraid. then, if we don't act the way she wants, she yanks back her

---

179 *Foreign Affairs* magazine, November/December 1995; "Dominance through Technology," 14–20. And Friedman & LeBard, 284.

180 This technology barter and transfer are symbolized by Uranus in the Jupiter-Saturn Great Conjunction chart (May 28, 2000, 3:59 P.M., GMT). Uranus squares the Great conjunction in Earth, and, throughout the Pacific area, the Conjunction Chart drawn for the capital cities accentuates the 3-9 and 4–10 axes predominantly, i.e., trade and government. Additionally, technology manipulation is part of the symbolism of transiting Pluto in Sagittarius; information, education, internationalism, export-import trade doctrines, etc.

181*SA Mars square Pluto in August 1996; SA Uranus=Sun/Moon with tr Pluto square Midheaven, conjunct the 7th cusp, March 1997; SA Neptune square the Midheaven in September 1997.

credit and warns, "No more unless you behave yourself!' Manuel Quezon of the Philippines once said, 'It is better to go to hell without America than to go to heaven with her!'" This sentiment—with the Communist threat excised from the text and Japan substituted for the United States—lives still.][182]

Both China and Japan will resist Suharto's bid for prominence; there will be extreme upset with Japan in Indonesia, specifically in relation to oil trade; there will be threats, discord, uprisings. But Indonesia will be forced back into its already comfortable position, September 1997, the year of general elections in Indonesia (the People's Consultive Assembly selecting the President). Suharto appears secure for another term, with emphatic suppression of dissident voices.

This will not sit well with Indonesia, and another push will be tried in Spring 1999, taking advantage of Japan's building social unrest and China's steps toward non-communist organization (see "Japanese Social Revolution," page 52, and "China Abandons Communism," page 66). In this period, culminating in Summer 2000 for Indonesia, the country will have grown into the Pacific Market with maturity and solidity.[183]*

Vietnam — The Lone Struggle

Migrants from China settled in Vietnam in earliest history. China later followed the migrants and conquered them there in the second century B.C.E. Seven hundred years later, Vietnam grew strong enough to oust the Chinese. The country was then divided up into smaller states and factions.

The French unified Vietnam late in the nineteenth century, grouping Vietnam, Laos, and Cambodia to form the Indochina Union. Then—Japan again—Japan occupied the entire Indochina area during World War II. Afterwards, the Viet Minh guerillas declared Vietnam independent, but the French refused to accept the claim; they assumed and enforced colonial rule. Fighting went

---

182 Quoted in *The People's Almanac*, Wallechinsky and Wallace; New York: Doubleday, 1975, page 406.

183 SA Mars=Sun/Moon in July 1998, SA MC=Sun/Pluto December 1999. SA Venus conjunct Moon, July 2000.

on for some eight years until the Geneva Accord, the peace Treaty signed April 26–July 1, 1954. This Treaty divided Vietnam into two zones.

Further fighting began between North and South in 1960, and the United States became involved through a treaty of amity and economic assistance with South Vietnam on July 13, 1961. Then, on November 13, President John F. Kennedy started escalation of United States presence in Vietnam to help the South against the Viet Cong guerillas from the North. The conflict escalated greatly, with some 550,000 U.S. military troops eventually involved.

At the end of the Vietnam War, April 30, 1975, when Saigon surrendered to the North's National Liberation Front, the country was in ruins, victim of history's most intense bombing expeditions.

The Socialist Republic of Vietnam—the united country—came into existence at the time of proclamation on Hanoi Radio at 8:30 A.M. on July 2, 1976.[184*]

The Astro-profile of Vietnam is dismal: it suggests a country covered with problems, chief of which are/will continue to be financial. The horoscope shows a propensity of alienating all allies, of being chained to old ways of doing things, of actually resisting modernization and recovery. The most positive thrust, if the government can get out from under in terms of debt and aloneness, is through education so that the next generation can take its place in the great Asian market growth ahead.[185*]

In true national character, immediately after unification, Vietnam expanded its control of Southeast Asia by invading Cambodia and strengthening its military presence in Laos. This attack alienated Vietnam from China, its longtime ally, and worsened its international relationships generally.[186*]

Vietnam is mineral- and timber-rich, especially in the north. Mining and sea products provide the major items for export, but industrial productivity is woefully behind the rest of the Pacific

---

184 See Campion, *World Horoscopes*, 435-336.

185 The Sun square Pluto in the 2nd, Mercury ruling the 2nd is quindecile (165 degrees: upheaval) Neptune, ruling the 8th; Saturn precisely square Uranus, ruler of the 7th; eastern protective, self-isolating orientation; Moon=Saturn/Pluto. The positive hope: Jupiter on the Midheaven squared by Mars, ruler of the 9th. In the Jupiter-Saturn conjunction chart (January 1, 1981 at 4:23 A.M. at Hanoi) the Sun is in the 2nd, receiving the Jupiter-Saturn square, Jupiter ruling the Ascendant.

186 Out of the precise Saturn-Uranus natal square, Uranus transited to exact opposition of the Midheaven, conjunct the fourth cusp, January 7, 1979, when Cambodia fell to Vietnam's attack. Uranus rules the 7th. SP Moon was conjunct Pluto, ruler of the 4th, land acquired.

world, due to the interruptions of the long war period. Food processing and textile manufacturing are large and growing economic activities.

History shows that a good performance in one country in any life dimension stimulates similar activity in its neighbor(s). This is a sympathetic vibration phenomenon where a success theme can reverberate throughout an entire market. Specialized technology, for example, can leap across boundaries, out-and-out imitation of products can quickly affect approximate market parity between two countries, investment in one country can invite a similar deal-offer from the neighbor. The market homogenizes itself. This is competition.

As countries develop, their economic structure changes: agriculture plays less and less a part in national output, and industry takes up the banner; then, when industry starts to decline—reaching capacity in terms of innovation and lowest expense in production—a variety of "service industries" comes to the foreground (health care, promotion and marketing, information services, banking and investment, design, consultancies, construction, tourism, etc.). A rise in living standard seems to parallel this developmental trend.

Vietnam is years behind in such a development scenario. While it is on the rim of a sophisticated and exploding market, while it has the example of its neighbors growing faster than surveys can record, it is anchored to the exhaustion and tether of old ways, old concepts, and old wounds.

■ Prediction ...

Vietnam Needs Time and Fresh Government—It is entirely possible that, in the Spring–Summer of 1996, Vietnam will complete a trade agreement of high potential. Part of its reward will be industrial education, the incorporation of technology through the trading partner, to begin the growth pattern the Pacific Market demands.[187]*

---

187 SA Uranus square Ascendant; SA Saturn conjunct Ascendant (major new start; sober learning, working situation; new ally), with Uranus ruling the 7th and Saturn ruling the 6th. At the same time: SA Mercury conjunct Venus, ruler of the Midheaven. In September: SA Saturn square Jupiter, proving a point about its dedication to long term planning for success.

A second step of development, similar in excitement to the Spring–Summer of 1996, will take place between February and July 1997, obviously successful in October–December 1997.[188*]

But then, in Spring 2000, Vietnam presses clumsily, suddenly to expand beyond its right. Vietnam loses ground, alienating what few allies it will have once again. On the one hand, there is greater prosperity than has been known for two generations, but there is a fall, and more time is needed to rebuild yet again.[189*]

Analyst Hamish McRae sees Vietnam's great "human potential," due to "take off" late in the 1990s. But it is a long pull from extreme poverty, and so much is dependent on the rich market of North America. But this time, Vietnam is basically alone. The rise will be there; but the flight will be aborted until there are grand government changes perhaps beginning in Spring 2000.

Australia and New Zealand — Looking Up

The Commonwealth of Australia was proclaimed on January 1, 1901, in Melbourne.[190*] The British monarch is head of state and appoints a Governor General.

The Astro-profile of Australia without question portrays a country of extraordinary energy, adventurism, and bombast of character. It is totally tied to international commerce and legalism for its identity and development. And therein lies the seed for dramatic

---

188 Tr Uranus=Sun/Moon, with SA Sun=Pluto/Midheaven (2/97) and SA Sun=Jupiter/Pluto in October 1997, with SA Uranus semisquare Pluto.

189 Tr Saturn crosses the Midheaven in Spring 2000 with SA Sun conjunct Saturn; tr Uranus crosses the seventh cusp. In December 2000: SA Jupiter=Sun/MC, but in Spring 2001, lasting until early 2001, tr Uranus will have lodged itself in the 7th and *SA Uranus=Mars, SA Pluto=Saturn; tr Pluto conjunct Neptune* (deception; financial loss; the rise of the opposition to the government).

190 Proclaimed at a ceremony at precisely 1:25 P.M. See Campion, *World Horoscopes,* 81 and footnote 22. The horoscope is an extraordinary portrait of the country that has developed an image complex about identification between Europe and Asia: tremendous emphasis of the 3rd–9th axis, with Jupiter in Sagittarius in the 9th, a final dispositor, opposed Neptune(!). The signature picture is Mars=Uranus-Pluto, promising enormous energy in trade and international banking (as well as great development in the services "industry": health care, information supply, finance, etc.). The energy is not frenetic: there is the anchor of Sun conjunct Saturn, also in Capricorn.

The Moon in Taurus (set in its ways; resisting change) is without aspect and dominating; interestingly, as one of its first acts, the Parliament passed a law (in May, 1901!) granting voting rights to women.

change and development: intensification of nationalism and the separation from England for its own national perspectives.[191]*

England's Captain James Cook (1728–1779) led three celebrated expeditions onto Pacific. He brought the Pacific Ocean out of mythical legend and into commercial feasibility. Cook landed at Botany Bay on April 29, 1770 in Australia.[192]

The Continent's originating population were the aborigines, migrating there from somewhere some 40,000 years ago. Indeed, the continent was first sighted by the Dutch in the early 17th Century and noted as "New Holland," but there was little interest in this faraway place. Cook's arrival at the east coast disclosed extraordinarily fertile soil—thus, "Botany" Bay. He claimed the coast for Great Britain.

The first settlements followed in 1788—supporting a penal colony where Sydney now is—and by 1829, the entire continent was a British dependency.

Gold was discovered in 1851 and the population tripled in ten years. Gold was discovered in a new region in 1857, and the population there doubled in one year. Gold was yet again discovered in June of 1893, and the "Golden Mile" was established around Kalgoorlie in southwestern Western Australia.

The gold rush demanded cheap labor—coolie laborers from China. Some 60,000 Chinese entered the country, and loyalists were up in arms since the first act of the Australian Parliament in May 1901 was to proclaim a "White Only" national policy. Rampant race riots began in 1857. By 1884, a Cardinal Moran suggested that oriental languages should be taught in Australian universities! Already, Australia was assimilating the East.[193]

In the second half of the twentieth century, the racial immigration barriers were relaxed. By the late 1980s, Vietnam, the Philippines, Malaysia, and Hong Kong together accounted for more than one-fifth of settler arrivals, and the total they supplied outnumbered that from the United Kingdom. Tourism and trade and all the new arrivals helped defuse the outrage, but the split between mercantile identity and political and patriotic allegiance had begun.

---

191 Uranus and Pluto=Sun/Moon!

192 The name "Australia" is derived from the Medieval English and earlier Latin roots referring to the south wind, with a touch of the "east" in it through the Latin *aurora*, dawn. "Alia," is "other one."

193 Fernandez-Armesto, 670–671.

Australian prosperity depended on Asia. From down under, Australia had to look up to the North, the Northeast.

New Zealand

As Australia had been, the islands of New Zealand were first sighted by the Dutch in 1642. They named the sighting "new" Zealand, after a Dutch province at home. Captain Cook then visited New Zealand—discovered the Polynesian Maoris who had settled the islands in about 1000 C.E.—and claimed the land for England.[194]

Maori chiefs acknowledged British sovereignty in exchange for recognition of their territorial rights by the Treaty of Waitangi in 1840. Systematic colonization began. The Treaty was broken often by white settlers who fought the Maoris for their land.

Secure government was established in 1852, a gold rush began in 1861, similar to that in Australia, and then, in 1907, New Zealand became a dominion under the British crown.[195*]

The Astro-profile of New Zealand is quite different from that of Australia: New Zealand is shown as reserved, consistent, socially aware in human interest terms. There is a spiritual and even paranormal sensitivity throughout the portrait. A strongly stated reserve overcomes an aggressive underpinning, and there is a notable resistance to change. New Zealand lives quite unto itself.[196*]

While not an active mixer nation, New Zealand is dominantly aware of social welfare and human rights. Even before becoming a dominion of Great Britain, New Zealand enacted a series of measures that were uniquely comprehensive in their time (1890–1903): a social welfare system, aid to workers, old-age pensions, and government insurance plans.[197]

Most recently, New Zealand's resolute social welfare posture expressed itself *vis a vis* the United States: on February 4, 1985, the Prime Minister of New Zealand refused to allow a U.S. Navy

---

194 Some 320,000 Maoris still live on New Zealand, to the north.

195 Proclaimed at 11:00 A.M. on September 26, 1907, in Wellington. See citation in Campion, *World Horoscopes*, 265; also note chart—and typographical error in the text date of "1906"—in Baigent, Campion, Harvey, 461.

196 Sun in Libra-Moon in Taurus blend, highlighting Venus, in Libra conjunct the Sun in the 10th. Key signature: Mercury=Mars/Neptune. Aries Point=Moon/Jupiter, Jupiter ruling the 12th. Saturn, ruler of the Ascendant, is retrograde and square Pluto (separatist loner). Moon stolid in Taurus.

197 These programs and the overlap of their enactment with the establishment of dominion status reflect in the founding chart through the Sun-Venus conjunction in the 10th in Libra, square Uranus rising.

destroyer to dock in New Zealand unless it stated that it was not carrying nuclear weapons. The United States refused, and this led to the collapse of the defense treaty among the United States and Australia and New Zealand.[198]*

■ Prediction ...

Australia and New Zealand Gain Independence from England—The two "Anglo" societies of the Asia/Pacific region potentially link East Asia into the rest of the world. Their natural resources are extraordinary and could feed most of the entire region. For example, Australia supplies Japan with nearly half its coal imports and nearly 40% of its iron ore. There is important Rest and Recreation space in Australia for wealthy other-country executives and families—and the Japanese have invested in a string of hotel chains there. At the same time, Australia and New Zealand have had to face up to the gradual closing of their access to the United Kingdom market, with the latter's involvement in the European Union.

New Zealand's public support programs (professional services), according to analyst Hamish MacRae, will probably become the social care-models for much of the industrial world.

In turn, Australia is acquiring keen entrepreneurial skills from the new immigrants from East Asia, particularly from Hong Kong. Some sixty percent of the immigrants come from the Philippines, Vietnam, and Hong Kong. As these new arrivals assimilate themselves into Australian society and prosper, they provide a cultural and economic link between Australia and the East Asian countries.[199]

The commercial redirection inclines Australia and New Zealand more and more away from their British heritage and the western economic system. McRae observes, "For Australia and New Zealand, the combination of their location and their ability to absorb immigrants is enormously advantageous, for it helps bolt their economies on to what will eventually become the world's largest economic region." To top it all off, these two countries have a history of political stability.[200]

---

198 SA Neptune=Sun/Venus (deception in relationship), with tr Neptune square Sun and tr Saturn opposing Moon.
199 McRae, 88–89.
200 Ibid, 260.

Analyst William Pfaff points out that Australia and New Zealand and Canada have no *ideological* foundation. In other words, they exist as nations because *they were made to exist.* In contrast, the United States has an ideological base, and its early Revolutionary War—as an act of principle—had great influence upon the French Revolution which followed, which in turn influenced the Latin revolution of the nineteenth century.[201]

Australia (the Australian Republican Movement) is in strong debate nationwide with regard to succeeding from British dominion and becoming independent under an Australian head of state. Australia has now developed principle and an ideology of its own, and this ideology is tied to its success in the Pacific Market, its thorough assimilation of and into the East. It is emphatically shown in the astrology of Australia that it will effect independence based upon trade considerations and its rise as the Anglo-Asian power of the Pacific, of the world.[202*]

Australia will finally achieve independent status in November–December 2001.[203*] Naturally, this transition requires time for extended debate, the management of two Federal elections (before May in 1996 and three years later in 1999), and the difficult rewriting of the formal Constitution and the "informal" unwritten Constitution that pervades Australian government, a hold over from the old frontier days. The beginnings have already taken place with the ruling Australian Labor Party and will gather great strength in the Spring of 1997. There may be a setback in Spring of 1998, quite possibly a political scandal, that suspends debate until after elections in Spring 1999.[204*]

Then, the movement takes off on its final flight in Spring 2000, grows through the "Summer Olympics" which will be held in Sydney

---

201 Pfaff, 162.

202 Jupiter-Saturn Conjunction chart (May 29, 2000 at 1:59 A.M. at Canberra) is extraordinarily focused in the 3rd–9th axis; Jupiter rules the 9th and Saturn rules the 10th, the conjunction squared by Uranus in the 11th and ruling the 11th (new goals, economics of the government action, the second of the 10th); and the Moon is in Aries precisely upon the Ascendant!

203 An extraordinary focus of measurements: SA Sun conjunct Ascendant in November 2001, with SA Midheaven conjunct Moon/Ascendant; tr Pluto conjunct Uranus, tr Uranus square Moon, tr Saturn conjunct Pluto and opposed Uranus (the old giving up to the new), and tr Jupiter opposed the Sun. Applying within 10 minutes of arc: SA Pluto square Mercury, in the 9th, new international perspectives of power.

204 SA Midheaven semisquare Pluto in April 1997 with tr Saturn square Sun; tr Saturn conjunct the Ascendant with SA Neptune=Pluto/Midheaven.

in September 2000 (the Australian Spring), and climax on Australia's 100th birthday celebration in January 2001.

New Zealand, more conservative, more set in its ways, will have to follow Australia's move. Sharing so much of the Asian market, New Zealand will not be able to afford isolation or extension of its ties to England. The movement in New Zealand—based upon sound economics, the import investment potential and the trade with the East—will begin in powerful earnest in late Spring 1997, concretize in its projection by October 1998, and be fulfilled by January 1, 2002.[205]*

Out of the Pacific and on to India

The grand Pacific Ocean is approximately seventy million square miles (181,300,000 square kilometers) in size and occupies one-third of the surface of the Earth. It is connected with the Arctic Ocean as well as with the Indian Ocean (and the Atlantic, through the straits of Magellan). It touches shore at land masses at the North and South Poles, California and Japan.

Two powerful wind systems divide the ocean at the equator. Sailing East to West required different routes than sailing West to East, and early on in maritime history, the prevailing wind routes linked only lands of low population and low productivity. Nature was not helpful where secure, direct travel was specifically needed.

For example, a direct crossing between Mexico and the Philippines was comparatively easy with the northeast trades and the north equatorial current, but, to get back, a long detour to the north, through belts of stormy and unpredictable winds, was demanded, before turning south with the currents that gird California. Timing was essential so as to avoid seasonal typhoons, i.e., the wind system around the Philippines, for example; in the tropical and subtropical zones, there were some 130 cyclones annually with winds of at least 150 miles per hour (not to mention the 400 mile per hour Tsunami tidal wave). Loading and unloading in Asian ports often had to be transacted in a few days or some six months

---

205 First: the Jupiter–Saturn Conjunction chart (May 29, 2000 at 3:59 A.M. at Wellington) emphasizes the 2nd–8th House axis powerfully. In the national horoscope, there is the accumulated 90-degree Solar Arc in June 1997, with tr Saturn opposed Mercury, ruler of the 10th. SA Neptune conjunct the important Mercury and SA Saturn conjunct Pluto and more, with tr Saturn conjunct the fourth cusp in the Fall of 1998. [SA Sun square Venus in Spring 2000 with tr Uranus square Moon, tr Saturn-Jupiter conjunct Moon in May 2000. *SA Midheaven opposed Pluto with tr Uranus square Moon in January 2002.*

could be lost. Historian Fernandez-Armesto calls the Pacific at that time the "one-way ocean."[206]

The first circumnavigation of the earth was made between 1519 and 1521 by the Portuguese navigator Ferdinand Magellan. It was an accomplishment of extraordinary endurance and leadership and navigational skills. It was he who named the ocean the "Pacific."[207*]

The search for a two-way route between America and Asia rivalled the earlier European search for a passage to the Orient. It took until 1565 when Spaniard Andres de Urdaneta travelled 11,600 miles (the longest sea voyage so far recorded without a landfall) in five months and eight days on a curling arc across the north Pacific and charted the courses that guided the remaining era of sailing.

Captain James Cook was the seaman cartographer who went as far as man could go, charting the extremes of the Ocean: in three voyages of the Pacific he charted Australia and New Zealand as well as the west coast of Alaska. He was the catalyst of enormous scientific invasion of the Pacific by expeditions from England, France, Spain, and Russia in the late eighteenth century and early nineteenth century. The professional explorer—from the time of Columbus just a generation earlier, now with Magellan, Cook, and others—became the figure of the Age.

The Atlantic was open to Portuguese and Spanish exploration for commerce, with other European nations to follow. Magellan showed that the oceans of the world were linked together. The Pacific touched on lands beyond earlier imagination. And Europeans began to see their relationship with the world in a new way. World historian J. M. Roberts summarized the great significance of this time of new trade vistas: "Jerusalem ceased to be centre of the world; the maps men began to draw, for all their crudity, are maps which show the basic structure of the real globe."[208]

---

206 Fernandez-Armesto, 559–661.

207 It is curious that Magellan chose such a serene name for the threatening body of water dominating the earth. He did not know the expanse of the ocean at the outset, of course, and his expedition was an intrepid thrust of visionary proportions; the voyage began on September 20, 1519. The horoscope was dominated by Neptune (vision, water, deception): Neptune opposed Moon, Neptune trine Mercury-Mars-Jupiter conjunction (passionate idealism) in Libra; Neptune=Sun/Saturn (aloneness in his quest), Jupiter=Sun/Uranus and Sun=Uranus/Neptune (innovation, creativity, success). Magellan was killed in skirmishes with the natives in the Philippines on April 27, 1521. One ship of the original five returned to Spain, mission accomplished.

208 Roberts, 426.

In the nineteenth century, the steamship reduced the Pacific frontier to a maritime market: routes became more direct, weather less of an enemy, and commerce was able to accompany migration and development. The importation of Chinese labor (coolie) to the west coast of North and South America (from Alaska to Peru) and to Australia became an enormous business, with tremendous ships, costing a million dollars to build with federal subsidies, plowing the waters in thirty-three days, often with death rates among the 1200 passengers reaching forty percent.[209]

Even in those times, the world expanding to its limits was also getting smaller as those limits were brought closer to civilization. The earth took on life, exhaling to its fullest and inhaling new energies. This rhythm, this pulse, defines time, and the peopled cells, the nations, subdivide and create growth and history. The fevers and illnesses of war introduce dominating traits of spirit and behavior. The new blood of immigration and the aid of shared and bartered resources keep life going. The body earth defines itself.

Conversion of war technologies gave rise to the economic boom after 1945. Leadership by the United States, its reconstruction aid, and its market consumption powered the manufacturing and supply explosion throughout Asia. The circulatory systems of trade and communications multiplied and strengthened.

Intercontinental travel technology now brings exceedingly long voyages down to a matter of hours; telecommunications link the events of world life into everyone's present. Exposure of government activity and business development expresses the power of political intent and national resources; exposure minimalizes political surprise and improves international security, and the winds of nature inhibit the deployment of megapowerful nuclear weapons by threatening the spread of fall-out to non-target areas, eventually to the earth itself to end its life.

Just as the Atlantic Ocean defines the European market in terms of United States participation and well-developed trade, the Pacific Ocean defines the newest, biggest market complex on earth: the Asian Market to be headed by China and Japan, with Korea, the Philippines, and Indonesia defining its nucleus, with Hong Kong, Singapore, and Malaysia (including Vietnam) swarming

---

209 Fernandez-Armesto, 659–660.

together in interdependence on natural resources, and all interacting with Australia and New Zealand to the South on the border with yet another ocean.

The Indian Ocean—the third largest at 28,350,000 square miles (73,427,000 square kilometers)—is bordered by Malaysia, Indonesia and Australia to the East and Africa to the West. The ocean is dominated by India, the world's second most populous country, with close to 900,000,000 people.

India — 5,000 Years in the Making

For a period of some 5,000 years, India has worked for assimilation of the diverse ethnic and cultural streams that have flowed constantly through its land. Even before organized, substantive settlement of the Levant (the fertile crescent of the East Mediterranean, including Israel, Syria, Lebanon), a sophisticated civilization flourished at Harappa and Mohenjo-Daro, now in Pakistan. These origins were first discovered in 1826 by a British Army deserter and wanderer known as Charles Masson. His record intrigued archaeologist Sir Alexander Cunningham, who then explored the region formally in 1873. Cunningham observed that, with its centralized planning, precision of two-story houses on substantial foundations, communal wells and remarkable sanitation system, etc., "Mohenjo-daro exhibited a degree of urban planning virtually unheard of in the third millennium B.C."[210]

Continuous exploration has gradually pushed the dawn of Indian civilization deep, deep into the past, back to the remote Neolithic Age of 7000 B.C.E.[211] Successive invasions of migrant Aryan people from a region in the Caucasus (the region above Turkey and Iran) brought philosophies and religion that were organized as the Vedanta, an assertion—known intellectually and experienced in meditation—that all life is unified within an all-pervasive cosmic

---

210 *Lost Civilizations: Ancient India - Land of Mystery*, Alexandria, Virginia: Time-Life, 1994, 13.

211 Indeed, in the Levant, there were settlements as well, but of the outpost nature, guarding access to water and trade route crossings leading North to Anatolia, South to Egypt, and West to the Mediterranean. The ruins of successive walled "cities" at Jericho, for example, on the Dead Sea, are dated back to 9000 B.C.E. See Ruby.

system. The individual is part of a cosmic whole rather than a separate fragment.[212]

Aryan priests were called Brahmins, *and they gave divine sanction to a social caste system*. This stringent social stratification actually went against the Vedic philosophy; in practice, the *spiritual* idea was not translated into a completely homogenous and internally mobile society. This flaw has been the major weakness of the Indian system, according to Columbia University historian Arthur Lall. It has undermined an overall national civic consciousness and thus accounts for India's retarded growth into modern times.[213]

The way things were is the way things are in many villages of modern India. Ways of gathering and milling food today are identical with the ways of long, long ago. Gods and goddesses, whose cults can be traced to the Stone Age, are still worshipped at village shrines. And the caste system regulates it all, and the lives of millions.[214]

The Brahmins proclaimed Buddha as avatar of Vishnu—a reincarnation of the Preserver, in the Hindu Trinity of Brahma, Vishnu, and Shiva. Buddhism was thus assimilated into the Indian Religion. And then this capacity to synthesize and assimilate the different ethnic and spiritual streams of life in developing India received the Muslim "invaders" from the Arabian Sea region in the West. Islam would tolerate no compromise with its singular book of law written by God himself and given to the final prophet, Mohammad. There could be no synthesis.

Indian society closed ranks, and the caste system became more rigid as a defense against these confrontations, including those with the influx of Turks and Mongols who arrived with philosophies of their own. "Anyone opting out of the Indian system would become a *malaiche*, which is the name for those who are beneath contempt and are total outcasts. The result was that those converted to Islam were, most frequently, those who were already outcastes in Hindu

---

212 The term "Aryan" is Sanskrit for "noble." It was/is a term used in Semantics usually for the family of languages now known as Indo-European. However, the word acquired political connotations in Nazi Germany, being interpreted as "Nordic" or non-Jewish, and has been discredited in modern usage.

Additionally: it is interesting to note here the modern neo-classical existential theology of German-born Protestant Paul Tillich (1886–1995), for whom God is presented as "the all-pervasive creative principle."

213 Lall, 3.

214 Roberts, 95.

society and who could improve their status in the more egalitarian Muslim society."[215]

The instability prevailed for centuries, until, in the last half of the eighteenth century—when India was the world's most productive state—a full-fledged synthesis did seem possible. The Muslim element had become Indianized by cohabitation, intermarriage, and cultural sharing.

It was at this point that the British arrived, attracted by the fabled wealth of India. Lall observes that the "British became a truly massive impediment to the process that would certainly have brought into being an Indian confederation embracing at least the entire subcontinent." Historians agree that it is with the India experience that the British developed their national identity beyond entrepreneurial traders to that of empire builders.[216]

India had been visited by European explorers first in 1498 (the Portuguese, Vasco da Gama), and the British, Dutch, and French followed for trade. In the mid-eighteenth century, India was absorbed with religio-cultural assimilation, sorting out princely dynasties, and thwarting an Afghan invasion. The country—even then old and underdeveloped—was open to exploitation by a mighty power. The British swooped in in 1747 and, for seventeen years, fought the French furiously for control of the expansive country.

Lall observes that the Indians for 4000 years had become accustomed to visitors settling in and eventually becoming part of the country's process of assimilation and synthesis. The British would soon enough learn the ways of India, and the lives of the Indians would be enriched by the infusion of British identity. "The Indians therefore looked forward to a process of sociological and political integration with the British." The British were unwilling. No integration was possible.[217]

British Rule

British dominance flourished. By 1905–06, with the growth of India having made conspicuous progress under British leadership, it became clear that some of the power had to be shared. The population was gigantic, figuring one-quarter of the world's people; there

---

215 Lall, 6.
216 Ibid, 8.
217 Ibid, 10.

had been the Indian Mutiny of 1857, Hindu soldiers rebelling against innovation and modernization on religious grounds, which rebellion lived on as inspiration to other rebellions. British central rule was hard pressed to keep everything together. Giving the Indians some control would lead to self-government. The handwriting was on the wall.[218]

Japan's war with Russia in 1904–05 showed India that a small country could achieve international prominence; India, so very much larger, could also play a significant role on its own.

Shortly after the outbreak of World War I, Indian soldiers were rushed to the French front to join with the British against Germany. This bolstered the concept of Indian equality with Britain. A common purpose pressed in war should similarly be pressed in peace, and Mohanda K. (later Mahatma) Gandhi—soon to become a great hero of modern India—appeared on the scene, a loyalist to the British Empire.[219]

Britain made a gesture to India in 1917, but, as a hedge, included a set of legal stipulations (the Rowlatt Acts) that allowed British judges to try cases of Indian agitators without juries, without due process of law. It was against this civil slap that Gandhi began his national campaign for India's independence, with passive resistance (orderly civil disobedience), which in turn led to massacres by the British in coercion and punishment.

Eventually, Gandhi and the congressional leader Jawaharla Nehru prevailed and formed governments in seven of India's eleven provinces. The British continued to crack down—even in the face of an Indian National Army—and jailed Gandhi and other leaders.

At the same time with this nationalist rebellion, the Muslim movement was growing as well, occupying twenty-five percent of the seats in Gandhi's Congress.

Finally in May 1946, while India was torn with Hindu-Moslem rioting and its politicians squabbling over the future, Britain's Labour government offered self-government to India, projecting a date for Independence not later than June 1948. Also stipulated was that there would have to be *two new Dominions* established: Pakistan,

---

218 The Indian Mutiny specifically was a mutiny of Hindu soldiers who feared the polluting effect of using a new type of cartridge, greased with animal fat. This *is* significant: much of the rebellion was the response of traditional society to innovation and modernization. The Mutiny became an important myth and inspiration. Roberts, 652–53.

219 Lall, 34.

at the extreme north of India, predominantly Moslem, and India, officially secular but overwhelmingly Hindu in every way.[220]

Independence was achieved in fact at 00 hours on August 15, 1947 in Delhi. For his part in the grand achievement and his sympathy to Muslims, Gandhi was killed by a Hindu fanatic on January 30, 1948. Nehru became Prime Minister.[221*]

But an emphatic proclamation of the republic occurred on January 26, 1950 at 10:15 A.M. in New Delhi.[222*]

The Astro-profile of India is depressed. Enormous problems abound, the bureaucratic system is weak, and the country is torn by factionalism (not homogenized by assimilation as old conventional wisdoms would have had it). India is a loner country, with a curiously depressed level (manifestation) of ambition. There is a conversion of uniqueness, if you will, into eccentricity, not in tune with the times. High mineral resources are indicated, as well as iron and steel.[223*]

Trade Profile

Japan's suppliers of its major mineral needs can be organized into three market groups: the Eastern Pacific (United States, Canada, Chile, Peru), the overwhelmingly important Pacific Market (Aus-

---

220 See Roberts especially, 787.

221 Gandhi had eschewed wealth; he had refused to own property; he dressed in a simple loincloth and shawl and lived the simple life. He was viewed as a holy man. Gandhi was born October 2, 1869 at 7:33 A.M., LMT in Borbandar, India. See Tyl ed., *Sexuality in the Horoscope*, Llewellyn Publications, 1995, page 260–262: "Freeing the Spirit" by Ted Sharp for his sensitive analysis of Gandhi.

222 Campion, *World Horoscopes*, 201. Campion suggests that this time of 10:15 A.M. was selected astrologically. Rectification tests by Tyl agree: Nehru (b. November 11, 1889) died May 27, 1964: SA Saturn exactly square the India Midheaven, tr Neptune square Pluto; India became a nuclear power on May 18, 1974: tr Pluto conjunct the 7th (square the Midheaven), tr Saturn conjunct the 4th, opposed the Midheaven; Prime Minister Indira Gandhi (Nehru's daughter) assassinated on October 31, 1984 and Union Carbide gas-leak catastrophe December 4, 1984 (2,000 killed, 200,000 affected): tr Neptune applying to conjunction with Midheaven; Indian troops withdrawn from Sri Lanka (9/18/89), Rajiv Gandhi lost election and resigned from government (11/22,29/89): tr Uranus exactly conjunct the Midheaven, tr Pluto square Pluto (R. Gandhi assassinated in May 1950).

223 Dominant signature: Saturn retrograde=Sun/Moon; AP=Saturn/Node (loner); MC=Saturn/Neptune (loss of ambition); *peregrine Uranus on the fourth cusp* (Quindecile Mercury in 10), divided lands, border upsets, nuclear power (with Pluto opposed Jupiter, semisquare Uranus)), and technology (runaway world center for software development). Sun-Moon exact square (upheaval at time of origination). Moon in Taurus: resistance to change. Saturn=Iron; Uranus accentuation of the 4th: mineral discoveries; Mars, ruling the Ascendant trine Venus-Jupiter, is steel (and spices).

tralia, Indonesia, the Philippines, China, etc.), and the Indian Ocean Basin (the Persian Gulf, India, South Africa, etc.). Above all, Australia leads in import importance; Indonesia follows, and then there is India.[224]

Of all this activity, 47.13% comes from the Indian Ocean Basin. As the heading nation of the Indian Ocean, India is emerging as an extraordinarily important source for Japan's needs. Indeed, the Indian Ocean Basin easily appears as an extension of the Pacific Market.[225]

India is crucial to Japan.

■ Prediction ...

India Rescued by Japan—From the Japanese point of view, an agreement of trade and technology exchange and domestic reconstruction (a "Revival Program") can be realized in India through massive investments and co-production agreements; a transfer of technology, particularly the manufacture of mid-technology products being phased out in Japan suited well to India's low-ware environment; and the underwriting of Indian Navy support (to command the Indian Ocean as an extension of the Pacific Market).

India would give Japan favored treatment with regard to raw materials; favor Japanese products in world trade; and the Indian Navy would guarantee the flow of raw materials to Japan. Friedman & LeBard see such a potential alliance as so large that other countries could be involved as well, namely Indonesia and China.[226]

The alliance could very well be under formulation at this time in late 1995. It could be brought to light between March

---

224 Friedman & LeBard, Table, page 172–173.

225 Freidman & LeBard point out that of the thirteen nations in the Indian Ocean area (counting the Persian Gulf Oil suppliers as one entity), eight are important mineral fuel and metallic ore suppliers to Japan. This compares significantly to ten Pacific nations out of 23 [13:8 vs 23:10].

   The shortest route between the Indian Ocean and the Pacific Ocean is through the Straits of Malacca and past Singapore. About 140 to 150 ships pass through the straits daily, and 44% of the ships larger than 30,000 tons are Japanese, as is 74% of the oil passing through the straits.

226 Friedman & LeBard, 315–316.

and July 1996, coincident with the new elections, and/or gain major exposure in the Spring of 1997.[227]*

The first major successes from the alliance will be obvious in late 1998, and again in late 1999.[228]*

The alliance would fit Japan's presumed plans to reinvest heavily in the extended Pacific Market. It keys into India's history of cultural assimilation, and, it will go far to solve India's extraordinary domestic problems of urban decay, of extraordinary overpopulation, of public servicing crises—tens of thousands on apartment waiting lists for more than fifteen years, the waiting list for telephones numbering 343,600, etc.; of traffic, squalor, water, electricity. "By 2001," says the Voluntary Health Association of India, "the city (New Delhi) will be the biggest slum in the world."

The cities of the country *will* decay if such an infusion of investment is not achieved at this time. India would topple back into the ages of long ago.

India will not be rescued by the United States, either directly by the government or through corporate investment. The nationalist movement in India has developed an anti-foreign furor that is in the main specifically anti-American. While technology companies from the United States, Germany and other countries are prospering there still, United States fast-food companies are being used as scapegoats for the still-present fears of exploitation and control by outsiders.

Overseas firms spent only $1 billion in India in 1994, whereas China attracted $34 billion in direct foreign investment.[229]

The potential for Japanese investment in a grand alliance is less threatening to the nationalists because, with the Japanese, there is no cultural similarity to the British and there is a decided kinship within the extended Pacific market.

---

227 Tr Uranus conjunct the Sun, tr Saturn conjunct the Ascendant with SA Saturn square the Sun in July 1996; tr Jupiter and Uranus conjunct the Sun with SA Pluto conjunct the 7th cusp (Pluto ruling the 8th, investments in India). When transiting Pluto came to the seventh cusp, India became a nuclear power, May 18, 1974, certainly a change of international image.

228 SA Venus square Midheaven, SA Jupiter square Uranus, with tr Uranus conjunct Venus-Jupiter and tr Saturn square Sun. The India-Japan synastry shows Japan's Ascendant conjunct India's Midheaven, its Mercury conjunct India's Nodal Axis, its Sun conjunct India's Moon, and its Saturn conjunct India's Mars (robbing India of its own initiative, part of the partnership/leadership profile).

229 *TIME* magazine, September 18, 1995, 91–92.

■ Final Note ...

As the world grows smaller, as the major countries on earth come closer together through trade bloc organization, commerce, and communications, the regionalized world could see India as the key power in Southeast Asia, especially if it can improve its relations with China.[230] India's navy, already one of the largest in the world (with two aircraft carriers), could clearly challenge American control of the Indian Ocean.[231]

This idea is included in Friedman & LeBard's scenario of a revival of war tension between Japan and the United States (See page 50). The analysts see Japan retreating and being pushed back from the Far West market and the European Union—to protect its cohesion—and creating the colossal regional market in the Pacific and Indian Oceans. This would be too much for the United States, i.e., its "primordial" fear of being physically forced out of the Pacific being intensely exacerbated—all the more so should Communism regain its hold in Russia.

230 The tense relationship began October 20, 1962, when China launched a massive offensive in Kashmir in Northeast India.
231 Friedman & LeBard, 389.

4

THE MIDDLE EAST

Israel: Keystone East and West

A major rift runs throughout the length of Israel and southward through the Red Sea. It branches as well into Africa. This "rift valley" is an elongated depression or trough in the earth's crust, bounded by other faults and normal terrain. The flat rock of the trough area has dropped down below the adjacent land, as a keystone would leave its crown position within an arch.

A rift valley is the precursor to a breakup of a land mass, a tearing away. In every sense of the word, Israel has spent its eternity in such unsettledness.

The land now called Israel is indeed at a keystone position: trade routes north and south, between ancient Syria and the land of the Pharaohs, east to west by invading hordes from above, below, and beyond the Tigris and Euphrates rivers (now in Iraq) to the Mediterranean Sea. Israel has always been the gateway of Europe, Asia, and Africa. From the first outposts at Jericho, some 9,000 years ago, through the nomadic migrations from Syria through Canaan to Egypt and back, so many times, through conquests by Egypt, Syria, and Iraq, in the main, and countless tribal states and papal Crusades, doing battle on its severe hills and plains, to the birth and enshrinement of three world religions (Judaism, Christianity, and Islam), this land—and namely, the city of Jerusalem—became the central focus of the world.

Three eras in ancient Jewish history are extremely important for our understanding of modern Israel: its historical enmity with the Arab world; its self-belief as a chosen people; and its aged rifts with Syria and Iraq and the Israeli sense of "return."

The Seed of Abraham

In the history of the Jews as recounted in the Old Testament of the Bible (the early books prepared during Babylonian Exile early in the sixth century B.C.E.; see below), the world was implicitly divided into two spheres, the Jews (Hebrews) and the rest of the world. The presumption was that the Jews were the chosen, the promised people, because they issued from Jacob, renamed Israel *(contender with God)* after he had wrestled with the angel of the Lord (Genesis 32:28). Jacob was the son of Isaac, the (second) son of Abraham, through his wife Sarah—*after Abraham had had a son, Ishmael, through Hagar, Sarah's Egyptian servant.*

Abraham was the patriarch founder of the Hebrew people. He was chosen by God to establish a new nation. Leaving Ur (now in southwest Iraq), Abraham and his wife and nephew (Lot) traveled to Canaan (now Israel). Sarah was old and infertile. With Sarah's permission, Abraham begat a son with Hagar. This first son in the new land was Ishmael.

After the birth of Ishmael, Sarah miraculously became fertile at age ninety. She gave birth to Abraham's son Isaac.

At this point, Sarah became jealous on behalf of the son Isaac, and Hagar and Ishmael, who was being groomed to succeed Abraham as leader, were sent off into the desert toward Egypt. An angel of the Lord protected Hagar and Ishmael. Ishmael married and begat twelve sons, *from whom the Arab people trace their spiritual lineage.*[232]

There is an interesting prediction in Genesis 16:12 that Ishmael "will be a wild man; his hand will be against every man, and every man's hand against him." Was this written into the tale (history) so long after in order to establish the line of Isaac over that of Ishmael?

---

232 In the Quran (Koran), major emphasis is placed upon Abraham, and indeed, Muhammad identified himself closely with the patriarch. The angel Gabriel directs Abraham to take Ishmael up and guides them to Mecca, where they build the Ka'ba (a fifty-foot cubic structure around a holy rock and beside Hagar's holy well), the most sacred building in the Islamic world, the center of Islamic worship. (At Abraham's death, Ishmael becomes sole master of the Ka'ba and himself dies at age 130, leaving twelve sons. (Roberts, 2–8.) There are different readings of these histories: in one, the Quran regards Isaac and Jacob also as Abraham's sons, and they become Prophets also. (Roberts, 119.)

Meanwhile, back in Canaan, Abraham's faith was tested when God ordered him (through the visitation by three angels) to sacrifice Isaac upon an altar. An angel intervened at the last moment when Isaac was upon the stone. Canaan became the "promised land" because God then promised that the land indeed would belong to the descendants of Abraham, Isaac, and Isaac's son, Jacob (Genesis 12:7; 26:3; 28:13). Jacob, who was renamed Israel, as we have seen, also begat twelve sons, *who were the founders of the twelve tribes of Israel.*

This fascinating story from ancient times lives still in the present spirit of the Middle East, throughout the extraordinary tensions between Jews and Arabs, between Judaism and Islam. The people of Israel were chosen and the land promised to them; the people of Ishmael were chosen and the land promised to them.[233]*

The Moslems (the descendants of Ishmael, called Saracens by the Medieval Christians) invaded Jerusalem in 638 C.E. The forces were led by 'Umar (in power 634–644), second successor of Muhammad, the holy prophet of Islam. There was nothing on the holy Jewish Temple site since the Roman Vespasian had overthrown Jerusalem on July 1, 70, and razed Herod's expansion of the remains (the rebuilding by Zerubbabel, c. 530 B.C.E. after Babylonian Exile) of Solomon's original Temple, c. 1000 B.C.E.). By the early thirteenth century, some six *mosques* had been built and rebuilt on the Temple Mount.

From 1095 to 1291 throughout Europe, the Crusades, under papal inspiration (See "The Crusades," page 138), were planned repeatedly to attack and recover for the Christians this holy place in Jerusalem, this keystone of cultures, religions, and lands. "The Dome of the Rock," one of Islam's holiest shrines

233 See the Grand Mutation Conjunction Chart for Jupiter-Saturn, December 31, 1980 at 9:23 P.M. GMT, drawn for Mecca (10 Libra 15 Ascendant), the capital city of Islam (along with Medina). *This chart is the signature for the modern Middle-East crisis period:* the Conjunction was rising at Mecca, resurrecting and reflecting the grand issues of Israel/Ishmael, the identity of the "chosen." It could be seen that God's will would aggressively develop Arab (Islamic) dominance of the Middle East and, quite possibly, through strategies tied to oil, exert a major influence upon the rest of the world. There would be aggression from other nations, through the Mars ruling the 7th square to the Moon, ruling the Midheaven; and also: trouble at home, through the 4th House emphasis, the Sun-Mercury squares to the Conjunction, with Saturn ruling the 4th. It is definitely an indication of an internecine struggle, Arabs warring with Arabs.

built over the rock from which Muhammad ascended to heaven, still dominates Jerusalem. This is also the location of Mount Moriah (Zion), the place where Abraham, in greatest faith, began the sacrifice of Isaac. And it is the site of Solomon's Temple. The rift between Jew and Arab is profound.[234]

The Exodus

The Exodus of the Jews out of Egypt has become the greatest event in the whole of world history, the most inspiring event for a people. It signifies the personal meeting of a *nation* with its god.

Historians and archaeologists have speculatively placed the Exodus in 1205 B.C.E. in the reign of the Pharaoh Ramesses II. (See "Bronze Age," page 10.) It is unfortunate and, at the same time, alarming, that there is not one shred of evidence to confirm or even suggest that the spectacularly important Exodus occurred at this time—or ever occurred at all.[235]

Yet there is strong *astrological* evidence and, indeed, emerging archaeological evidence that the Exodus[236]—surely in less populous numbers than the Bible suggests—i.e., a most significant migration, did occur in the mid-1400s, *at a time of great cataclysm*, for which there are correspondences to the plagues rained upon Egypt at the time (See the *Bible*, Exodus: 7:14, 12–32).

---

234 Medieval Muslims knew much about the end of the world, anticipated by a dark sun rising in the west [perhaps a recall from the collective unconscious of a part of the cataclysm of the fifteenth century B.C.E. when the earth did change its rotation and the sun was darkened; see Velikovsky in text], the barbarous hordes of Gog and Magog [from the North, thought in modern days to be Russia; Moscow shares the same longitudinal axis as Jerusalem], the one-eyed anti-Christ (Dajjal) who would mock the miracles of Jesus before a procession of 70,000 Jews, and forty days later, the descent of Jesus from the heavens, slaying the anti-Christ, calling all people to follow Islam, and destroying the cross. The sun would shift to the east, all living things would die and, at the second call of the trumpet, every man and woman who had ever lived would be resurrected and brought to Jerusalem to be judged. (See Riley-Smith, Chapter 10.)

235 There is a fragment of text on the so-called Merneptha stele (thirteenth son of and successor to Ramesses II; c. 1224–1211 B.C.E.) a record of an alleged military victory to the North that announces "Israel is laid waste; its [grain] seed is not." Grant (*The History of Ancient Israel*, page 37) explains that the word "Israel" here is written with an inflection indicative of "people," *not of "country"* like other names mentioned in the same inscription, so that the term may, perhaps, not be describing a community already settled in Israel, but a party of wanderers in that country, without a permanent home. This is the prevailing thought among scholars: see Thompson, 274–275; Redford, 408–429; *TIME* magazine, December 18, 1995, 62–71.

236 See Ruby, the archaeological digs of Kathleen Mary Kenyon at Jericho, pages 106, 116, 142.

Scientist, researcher, historian Immanuel Velikovsky created a sensation around the world in 1950 with his extraordinarily annotated presentation of cataclysmic theory depicting the earth literally shocked on its axis by changes in our Solar system. His book *Worlds in Collision* still has classic proportions in the interest it commands. Forty of his findings were later corroborated by a French commission and were backed up by outerspace findings.

Astrology suggests the time of that cataclysm, when, researched by Velikovsky, a comet came so very close to Mars that it exchanged an electrical shock with Mars that altered its orbit and in turn altered the earth's orbit around the sun. Then, forty-nine years later, the comet and earth interacted again; the earth was jarred again and regained its original motion, and the comet became a planet: Venus—the new "comer" to the Solar system.[237]*

The cataclysm put fear into the memories of all people on earth; passing so close to the earth, the comet's tail deposited showers of burning oil, dust, and meteorites over most of the globe; which caused vast tidal waves, earthquakes, hurricanes, and volcanic activity, and an actual shifting of the earth's crust on its molten core as well as a reversal of the electro-magnetic polarity of the globe, which altered the earth orbit and the lengths of days, months, and years, for which there is abundant evidence.

Here was an act of God of cataclysmic proportion. Here was God's work, the god of divine rage, exceeding moral provocation, the near-daemonic god written into the Old Testament manifesting in the greatest upheaval the world has ever known. The migrating people *personalized this phenomenon;* it was the crisis that originated and confirmed their faith and brought them to the promised land.

---

237 My discovery of the astrology of this time dates the cataclysm in relation to the exceedingly rare triple conjunction of Saturn, Uranus, and Pluto on April 3, 1462 B.C.E. Fascinatingly—independently—this date is the Exodus date determined by Bible chronologist E. W. Faulstich of Spencer, Iowa. It is corroborated to the year by *The Jerusalem Report* magazine. It is a contemporaneous echo as well of Velikovsky's findings.

The triple conjunction in this momentous chart *defines the Ascendant of modern Israel at 23 Libra!* Arcing the Sun in this Exodus chart forward, 3,410 years and one month to May 14, 1948, the birth date of modern Israel (at 4:00 P.M. EET in Tel Aviv), the SA Sun came to 26 Cancer 01, *within 59' of the Midheaven of modern Israel!*

Syria's Invasion of Israel

The Exodus is regarded as a return of the people to the promised land.[238] The concept of return is terribly important in the history of Israel.

In 722–701 B.C.E., the Assyrians (Sargon II and then his son Sennacherib; Assyria, a sprawling, relatively short-lived kingdom with borders beginning in Iraq and ending in modern Syria) took over Israel, deported and scattered the people.[239] The invasions were violent affairs, but a miracle outbreak of the plague preserved Jerusalem during one attack in the reign of Hezekiah (a brilliant engineering king of Israel), until other attacks a few years later completed the siege.

The end of the northern kingdom of Israel at that time concluded a tragic history of little more than two centuries. Twenty kings, each ruling an average of ten and one-half years, had been on the throne, and seven of them had murdered their predecessors! Idolatrous cults abounded. All leaders were in "sin," and this shameful demeanor was blamed by the Prophets of the time (Elijah and Elisha) for the near elimination of the people. The Assyrians were the punishers for those sins. Assyrian settlers took over the land of Israel.[240]

The second kingdom, Judah—in the south of the land—met its downfall to the Babylonians some 120 years later. In 597 B.C.E., Nebuchadnezzar conquered Judah and the reemerging Israel and

---

238 The naming of the people of this land is difficult during the chronology of its emergence: from the death of Solomon (son of David, 965–927, builder of the Temple) onwards, for some centuries, Israel was simply one of the two kingdoms into which the territory was divided, the other being Judah, but this reference is then popularized for the period after Exodus.

During the late Greek and Hasmonaean periods, there are the terms of Judaean and Samarians. Even later is the reference "Palestinians," the Roman name for the Philistines (the Sea People marauders who settled in Canaan around 1205) and has little to do with the Israelites.

The term "Canaanites" refers to a land area that includes parts of Syria and Phoenicia (Lebanon) to the north and predates David and Solomon. And the earliest reference to the time of Exodus is to "the people of Yahweh," the name of God given to himself during the Exodus in pronouncement to Moses. The word "Jew" comes originally from the descendants of Jacob's son Judah, and the term "Hebrew" quite possibly comes from the ancient reference to nomads called the "Apiru" or "Habiru," related to the remote times before Abraham (pre 3,000).

239 Some 27,290 captives were deported from Israel, according to Sargon II (early in his reign or as his predecessor Shalmaneser's army commander). See Shanks, 131. The deported people from Israel became the Lost Ten Tribes (Grant, 163).

240 Shanks, 131, 134–137.

deported almost all the people back to Babylon, where they would remain for two generations. Only a small group of farm people were left behind to care for the land.

With the population of Israel and Judah dispersed by the Assyrian invasion and then by the Babylonian invasion (Iraq) and the people held captive in Babylon, the concept of the Dispersion, the Diaspora, the Exile was born to describe the Jewish settlements living in Babylon. It was later extended to Jewish settlements anywhere outside of the Holy Land.

Some historians see the Diaspora as an enrichment of the Jewish faith through the influence of other cultures (namely the monotheism of Zoroastrianism, through Cyrus, the Persian liberator, see below); other historians see the Dispersion as a historical continuity of persecution.

The Jews in Babylon held themselves together: the concept of the synagogue was born to maintain tradition and education and preserve ordered society. During the Exile, sometime after 600 B.C.E., the early books of the Bible were written. Bringing this information together kept the people together. Yahwism—meeting the god of Abraham, the god of the people—preserved the memory of the long distant past, including memory of the legendary cataclysm postulated by Velikovsky, linking the Exodus story and the first appearance of God to this upheaval. The Bible beautifully and dramatically focused the spirit of the people.

To identify with the true Israel was to assert one's roots in exile. Looking back became vital as foundation: there was the empire of David *for the sense of grandeur;* the extraordinary military conquests of Joshua for strength (which sieges archeology has proved did not happen; for example, Joshua's early conquest at Ai could not have happened since Ai was a ruin for 1,000 years before Joshua arrived; see Ruby, 142); the dramatic wilderness journey with Moses (the introduction of Yahweh at the Exodus) *for faith,* and the beginning of it all with Abraham as the chosen People, *for dignity.*[241]

In 539 B.C.E., Cyrus the Great of Persia invaded Babylonia to the West and defeated Nebuchadnezzar. Cyrus freed the people of Israel and, again, as a second Exodus, they jubilantly returned to the Promised Land and rebuilt the Temple of Solomon.

---

241 See Thompson 422. This source in its entirety is a most complete academic source overview of the emergence of the Israelite People.

This movement to establish a Jewish national home in Palestine, ever since the destruction of the land in 70 C.E. by the Romans, came to be called Zionism, after the citadel (Mount of Zion) established by the great king David (1000–965 B.C.E.) on the southeast hill of Jerusalem. It is on this Mount that now stands the Dome of the Rock, one of the holiest shrines of Islam (see "Temple Mount," page 105).

Why Israel is So Complicated in World Affairs

The deepest conviction of being chosen by God—as a people, a nation—is unshakable in the Jewish spirit. It is the foundation of the nation's political tenacity. The passion of returning to the land, to achieving permanence, dominates the spiritual and political life of Israel.

The Astro-profile of modern Israel shows extreme tenacity and monarchical pride, and a national stance empowered through suffering for renewal (martyr complex). There are indications of pervasive inspiration and/or self-deception or internal duplicity.[242*]

Jews in Israel are differentiated by how they relate to the land of Israel and to the state. Multiple Pulitzer Prize-winning analyst and scholar Thomas L. Friedman portrays the set of options that define the Jew:

First, there are the Secular Zionists—like Yitzhak Shamir who built Israel and Shimon Peres, a protégé of David Ben Gurion and Prime Minister under Shamir, who came to Israel in rebellion against their grandfathers and the Orthodox synagogue-oriented ghetto Judaism of Eastern Europe. The state, the army, and observing all the holidays become a substitute for religious observance and faith. This is the largest sector of Jewish demarcation, perhaps forty percent of the population.

---

242 Israel born on May 14, 1948, at 4:00 P.M., EET in Tel Aviv. It was Standard Time. I emphatically endorse and reinforce this time through the deepest of study over seventeen years. Transits and Arcs in relation to the angles provide incontrovertible confirmation; see most recently the assassination of Prime Minister Yitzhak Rabin, discussed below in the text. This time is corroborated by the research of Campion as well, *World Horoscopes*, 209–210.

Note: the Taurus Sun squared by Mars and Saturn; the Leo Moon peregrine. Sun/Moon=29 Gemini=Aries Point (public thrust). Key midpoint pictures: Saturn= Moon/Uranus (struggle between past and future); MC=Venus/Saturn (never important, successful enough); Neptune=Sun/Mars (progress undermined). The counterpoint of religious propaganda and rebellion seen within the Jupiter-Uranus opposition shows a profoundly compelling point of view; and the continuous influence of Neptune square Venus, ruler of the Ascendant, suggests a disturbance, a confusion among the people in terms of religion, spirit, self-projection, and the sense of sacrifice.

Second, there are the Religious Zionists [about thirty percent of the population] who see the creation of Israel as a *religious* event, with synagogue and state side by side.

Third, the Religious Zionists with a messianic bent who see the state as necessary to help bring the Messiah back for the 1,000 years of peace and glory.[243] [About 5%.]

And Fourth, the Ultra-Orthodox, non-Zionist (not political) Jews, the "Haredim," who are "those filled with the awe of God." This sector of perhaps 15% of the population is content to live in modern Israel, waiting for the conditions that will welcome the Messiah, recreating in relative separatism the pinnacle of the Jewish life, living-by-the-code as they did long ago in Eastern Europe. This group speaks Yiddish.[244]

Friedman observes that each of these four main schools in the great Israeli identity debate was so convinced that the others would wither away that, as a group, they were never willing to convene and achieve some consensus about the meaning of the state of Israel and the land of Israel for the Israeli people. As a consequence, these different visions grew side by side. "Israel became more secular and more Orthodox, more mundane and more messianic, all at the same time. Israel seems to have brought out of the basement of Jewish history every Jewish spiritual option from the past three thousand years."

Out of this confusion is there support for the statement by Orthodox rabbi Benjamin Blech, referring to the late Yitzhak Rabin, "He's too religious ... I simply can no longer abide the super-piety of the prime minister since the signing of the Oslo agreement"? Blech can not tolerate the implicit forgiveness manifested, through (Yitzhak) Rabin of Israel for Yasser Arafat, *without* the PLO leader's acknowledgment of guilt, expression of regret, and commitment to refrain from any repetition of the same crime in the future, i.e., the National Covenant to destroy Israel.[245]

---

243 Reference to this sector taps into the worldwide movement of Millennialism that has endured from earliest Christian times: the destruction of the world—when all enemies of the faith are conquered—will bring the (return of) Messiah. It is apocalyptic thinking (unveiling that which is hidden, esoteric), tied to cryptic keys in the Book of Revelations and in the Book of Ezekiel (see Boyer, especially chapters 1 and 5). The Jews and, now their nation, are the focal point of this final, ecstatic development in world history, with the Armageddon to take place at Migiddo in Israel. The Jews are "indestructible": the barometer of history, the "index finger of God," the people for whom history is *already* written. Believers—those who are "saved"—according to religious leaders like Jerry Falwell, will not go through "one moment of Tribulation."

244 Friedman, 284–288.

245 *The Jerusalem Report* magazine, issue dated October 19, 1995, page 56; published sixteen days before Rabin was assassinated, November 4, 1995.

Out of this confusion is there support for the report beginning, "Yitzhak Rabin does not have long to live ..." suffering and death await the prime minister, or so say the kabbalists who have cursed him with the *pulsa denura* (Aramaic for "lashes of fire") for his 'heretical' policies? "He's inciting against Judaism," according to the Jerusalem rabbi, who read out the most terrifying of curses in the tradition of Jewish mysticism, opposite Rabin's residence on the eve (October 3) of Yom Kippur, one month before Rabin was assassinated.[246]

Prime Minister Yitzhak Rabin was assassinated on November 4, 1995 by a young law student, Yigal Amir.[247*] Amir had had debate with fellow students about the reasonings of Moses Maimonides (1135–1204), the foremost medieval Jewish philosopher (author of the *Mishneh Torah*, a codification of Jewish doctrine). Maimonides attempted to interpret Jewish tradition in Aristotelian terms. The point at issue was Rabin's qualification for *din rodef*, the "judgment of the pursuer," i.e., a pursuer could be killed by a righteous man before the pursuer killed. Rabin, according to Amir, was poised to spill the blood of other Jews, and so must die. In his act, Amir believed he was serving the holy cause of Israel—and he is not in the minority.[248]

The passion and conviction of 3000 years live every day in Israel, at the center of the world's strongest religions, past and future.

Israel's Importance to the United States

In the 1950s, the new nation of Israel felt particularly vulnerable. The United States had just concluded an arms delivery agreement with Iraq in April 1954, and the Israelis saw the potential of this relationship development extending to Egypt as well. The govern-

---

246 *The Jerusalem Report* magazine, November 16, 1965, page 17. The article lists previous recent curses and the demise of public figures, with the possible failure so far of those directed against Saddam Hussein of Iraq.

247 Rabin was born March 1, 1922 at 3:50 P.M., EET in Jerusalem [source: Israeli astrologer Maurice Fernandez to me personally, from Israeli compendia of data]. At the moment of his assassination, November 4, 1995 at or very near 9:30 P.M., his SA Mars was conjoining his seventh cusp, opposing his Ascendant (47' orb). Tr *Neptune* was at 23 Capricorn 02, *precisely* opposed the Ascendant of the assassination moment *and* square the Ascendant of Israel at 23 Libra 02. In the Jupiter-Saturn Conjunction chart of 1980 (December 31, 1980 at 11:23 PM at Tel Aviv), valid for the assassination, there are many contacts made by assassination event transits. The Tertiary Progression chart of Israel for the assassination moment is a study of exactness, especially TP Pluto conjunct Saturn in the 10th, *TP Mars conjunct Israel's Neptune in the 12th(!), and more.*

248 *International Herald Tribune*, November 13, 1995, pages 1, 6; *The Jerusalem Report* magazine, November 30, 1995, page 5: "Rabin wasn't my prime minister," said Amir.

ment resolved to explore the possibility of obtaining from Washington a security guarantee, i.e., American "protection."

The United States made any such guarantee conditional to progress in the Israeli-Arab conflict. The dealings were most complicated and protracted, and indeed, never formally resolved. But the key understanding dates to a message by John Foster Dulles to the Israeli Foreign Ministry that "Even without a formal link, which we will reach when the time comes, Israel should trust that the U.S.A. will not abandon her."[249]

Israel's insecurities in the U.S. eyes were adjusted strongly when Israel achieved a rapid and crushing victory over Egypt, Syria, and Jordan in the surprise attack Six-Day War (June 5–10, 1967), in which Israel seized the Gaza Strip (the coastline in southwest Israel) from Egypt, the Golan Heights (the border area with Syria to the north) from Syria, and the West Bank of the Jordan River from Jordan. Israel was now an undisputed regional power defying all the Arab countries together. This exposed the fact that Soviet arms and Soviet prestige had not provided effective support for the Arabs.[250]

President Johnson publicly assured Israel that "Israel will not be alone." Israel was now a strategic keystone for the United States, a staging base for defense of American interests in the Persian Gulf, in the Soviet Union, Eastern Europe, and Africa—a definite asset for international American might.[251]

Annual Foreign Aid to Israel from the United States (after an initial $100 million in 1949, its first year) has grown from $35 million in 1951 to $126 million in 1966, to $4,913 million in 1979, and $3,428 million in 1990. It continues. There has been $49,312,000,000 of Foreign Aid given to Israel by the United States from 1949 to 1990, including military and economic loans and grants.[252] Additionally, U.S. investment in Israel is recorded at $1350 million in 1994.[253]

---

249 Mansour, 39, 74-75, 84-85.

250 In the Six-Day War, Israel recovered the lands that had been annexed from them in the war waged at the time of its formation as a nation. See "Relationship with the Palestinians."

251 The logistics of distance across the Atlantic are key here, just as are distances from the United States across the Pacific to Japan, the former Soviet Union, Korea, the Philippines, etc. Staging bases are need to store food, materiel, fuel, and personnel.

252 Mansour, 191, compiled from Congressional Research Service, Washington, D.C., Library of Congress, January 5, 1993.

253 World Almanac 1996 (Funk and Wagnalls, New York), 128, compiled from Bureau of Economic Analysis, U.S. Department of Commerce.

Israel is seen worldwide as a surrogate for America in the Middle East. To some analysts, this image is a burden to the United States world position in that the relationship with Israel undercuts close U.S. relations with friendly Arab states and inhibits the U.S. ability to respond to opportunities for improved relations with other Arab countries, such as Syria (and Iraq).[254]

The United States lives in Israel. Israel's international policies and action—especially those with countries of the Middle East—explicitly involve U.S. positions as well.[255*]

Relations with the Palestine Liberation Organization

After World War I, Great Britain received Palestine as a mandate from the League of Nations. Zionism had actively been striving for an independent Jewish state since late in the nineteenth century. The militant opposition of the Arabs to such a state and Britain's inability to settle the dispute eventually led to a session of the United Nations General Assembly in 1947. (See "Balfour," page 137.)

A special United Nations committee created a plan to divide Palestine into a Jewish state, an Arab state, and a small internationally administered zone, which included Jerusalem. The plan was passed; the Jews accepted it; the Arabs did not.

As the British prepared to leave Palestine, to give over their mandate rule formally at midnight at the end of the day May 14, 1948, Jews and Arabs prepared for war. Under the leadership of David Ben-Gurion (1886–1973), the leader of the World Zionist Organization after World War II, resistance fighter against the British, founder of Israel and its first prime minister, impelled Israel into being eight hours before the end of the British mandate. The rush was to focus national energies in the face of actual attacks beginning by Arab forces. On the same date, May 14, Israel received recognition from the United States.

---

254 Mansour, 37, quoting a report by Henry Shaw, former head of the military assistance branch of the Office of Management and Budget (1985/1986).

255 Israel-United States synastry reveals twelve clear-cut, strong bonds. Key among them is the Israel Sun completing an Earth Grand Trine with the U.S. Neptune and Pluto, closing a circuit of practical support from the United States; the Israel Mercury conjunct the key U.S. Uranus, ruler of its Midheaven (Israel's strategies invigorated by the United States); Israel's Venus conjunct the U.S. Jupiter (financial endorsement bond); Israel's Pluto opposed the U.S. Midheaven; Israel's Neptune square the U.S. Sun (Israel taking advantage of U.S. largesse), etc. See further: Tyl, *Synthesis & Counseling*, 414–415.

The forces of Lebanon, Syria, Jordan, Egypt, and Iraq invaded Israel on that day of founding. Two weeks later, Israel surrendered the Old City of Jerusalem to the Arab Legion of Jordan but held on in the New City.

An Armistice was declared late in January 1949. Israel had increased its allotted land holding by one-half. Additionally, Jordan had annexed the area adjoining its territory (the West Bank) and Egypt was occupying the southwest coastal area (the Gaza Strip). The Palestinians had nowhere to be.

On May 11, 1949, Israel was admitted to the United Nations, and Israel strengthened its claim on Jerusalem by moving their capital seat there.[256*]

Then the government developed a worldwide program to offer automatic citizenship to all Jews who migrated to Israel. The Law enacted in 1950 was called the *Law of the Return*, a clear echo of the Jews' exiles in history and the cohesion within the diaspora.[257]

In the elections in Israel on June 23, 1992, the Israeli Labor party, led by Yitzhak Rabin, defeated the incumbent conservative Likud party.[258*] Conciliation was brought into Israel politics. Secret meetings held in Oslo, Norway, about the Palestinians led to a land-for-peace accord (not a final Treaty), signed September 13, 1993, in Washington, D.C. (at 11:43 A.M., EDT). The Palestinians returned.[259*]

---

256 Yet another reinforcement of the 4:00 P.M. birth time: on May 11, 1949, Tertiary Progressed (the most sensitive measurements we have) brought the Ascendant to exact square with the Moon in the 10th; the TP Moon opposite the natal Moon, and TP Mercury exactly conjunct the Israel Sun/Moon midpoint at 29 Gemini 00 in the 9th House!

257 The Law of Return is debated strongly, ideologically in 1995-96: one side affirms that the Law of Return is fundamental to the State of Israel and Zionism, and the ultra-Orthodox want an ingathering of people who meet certain religious prescriptions. There is the premise that the age of ideology has passed, that Israel must be a "normal" country without belonging to all the world's Jews or providing for their national survival. For the post-Zionists, the Law of Return is seen as a major obstacle on the way to becoming a liberal democratic country. See *The Jerusalem Report* magazine, October 19, 1995, 57.

258 Tr Pluto exactly opposite the Israel Sun.

259 Note the Uranus-Neptune Conjunction, generation-signal chart drawn for Tel Aviv, the epic symbolization for overturning the status quo, repealing injustices, revolutionizing movements: February 2, 1993, at 2:51 P.M. EET in Tel Aviv. Uranus-Neptune is precisely on the Descendant (public show of a revolutionary new image, post election). This is magnified by a square from Jupiter in the 4th and is reiterated by much more in the chart. Note the dramatic Venus in 00 Aries (conjunct the Aries Point, public display) precisely upon the Midheaven and peregrine (peace running away with everything as the government's new image). The people won't necessarily like the peace: the Moon ruling the Ascendant is in the 12th; Mercury ruling the 12th is conjoined by Saturn; Mars retrograde is rising, ruling the Midheaven (reluctance).

All these things considered and more enabled my prediction published eighteen months before the fact: "There is considerable pressure on Israel to alter its position on

The Peace Accord called for Israeli withdrawal from much of the Gaza Strip and Jericho in return for an end to the Palestinian armed struggle. Powerful right wing movements within the Palestinian authority, namely the Hamas activists (the Islamic Resistance Movement) and the much smaller Islamic Jihad (literally, "striving," i.e., striving to advance Islam; popularized now as "holy war" with the sense of vendetta), are using terrorism to retrieve *all* lands lost in the war in 1948 and 1967 (see the birth of Israel, page 115, and the "Six-Day War," page 113).

The decision for the Peace Accord was not overwhelmingly popular in Israel—and this is a very important observation in the light of the religious fractures in Israel, the relationship between religion and politics, the extremist militant movements, and the witness of Rabin's assassination (see above). [And further: the Knesset approved the action of Oslo II (see below), by the slimmest margin: 61 to 59.][260]

The Peace Accord was not overwhelmingly popular within the Palestinian Authority. The terrorist Hamas faction argues violently that, by settling for a practical solution of the land issue, the Palestine Liberation Organization had sold Palestine (which for the Islamic militants includes all of present-day Israel as well) down the river. Hamas said it would treat Arafat and his police force as proxies of the Israeli army, as collaborators with the enemy.[261]

Arafat has stated that these groups "have some importance." He sees coordination between these Israeli fanatic groups and some of the fanatic Palestinian groups, both working to destroy the Oslo agreement(s).[262]

Oslo II was signed in Washington, D.C., on September 28, 1995.[263*] The massive agreement is "perhaps the most important

---

the land-for-peace issue. With its new political leadership in place in the Fall of 1992, there is strong indication that Israel will yield on its position, either in February 1993 [when the Oslo talks began] or around the second week of September 1993 [when an Accord was indeed signed]." Llewellyn Publications, *1993 Moon Sign Book*, page 283, published in the Fall of 1992, written in March 1992.

260 *The Jerusalem Report* magazine, November 2, 1995, 15.

261 Ibid, July 27, 1995, 32; interview with Hamas leader Imad Falluji. The parallel with right wing accusations of Yitzhak Rabin in Israel is clear. To many, the road to peace through negotiation is unacceptable, even perfidious; peace is total victory only.

262 Interview with Arafat, *TIME* magazine, November 20, 1995, 81.

263 Yet another reinforcement of Israel's 4:00 P.M. birth time: the signing occurred with SP Moon exactly upon the Israel Descendant of 23 Aries, with Jupiter precisely sesquiquadrate the Midheaven and opposed Mercury; for Yasser Arafat (born August 27, 1929, at 2:00 A.M. EET in Cairo; manifesting the PLO chart), SP Moon exactly sextile Sun, tr Saturn exactly sextile Moon, with tr Jupiter applying to opposition with Jupiter.

treaty Israel has ever signed, and is worthy of the world's attention." Its implementation will in effect bring to an end almost three decades of Israeli occupation in much of the territory it conquered in the 1967 war (see "Six-Day War," page 113), i.e., Israel pulling out of all West Bank cities (with the exception of Hebron) and handing over civil control of 450 Palestinian towns and villages to the Palestinian authority. It details the foundations for Palestinian democracy, demands that both sides work to adjust the mindset of their people, sets up priorities for economic cooperation, and establishes a joint Israeli-Palestinian security mechanism.

With the establishment of a new eighty-two-member Governing Council early in 1996, *the PLO is obliged to excise anti-Israel clauses from its covenant.*[264]

[While the Knesset debated the Oslo accord, an estimated 30-40,000 Israeli demonstrators voiced their disapproval outside the parliament building.]

■ Prediction ...

The Oslo Agreements Will Prevail—The latest completion date for permanent status talks, beginning early in May 1996, i.e., after additional areas of the West Bank will be handed over to Palestinian jurisdiction and completion of the Hebron redeployment accomplished in the Spring of 1996, is May 4, 1999. There is high probability that that time period will see completion of the Palestine liberation accords, with the final status set.

■ Prediction ...

Great Upheaval Accompanies Peace Process—There has been a steady, dramatic drop-off of Israeli endorsement of the "gamble" for peace with the Palestinians, from almost two-thirds to below 50% pre-Rabin assassination (blamed on continued Palestinian violence and apparent self-rule incompetence). This drop reversed itself in the aftermath of the assassination.

Violent attacks on Israelis by Israelis and by the Palestinian Hamas and Islamic Jihad groups have increased; Prime Minister Rabin ("The blood of martyrs has fertilized political

---

264 *The Jerusalem Report* magazine, October 19, 1995, 58; October 19, 1995, 4.

and religious causes for thousands of years.") has been eliminated. The benchmark of pre-1967, Six-Day War boundaries
frames nationalistic fervor on both sides. The people see developments (the return of lands) as a threat to Israel's very existence (it is land "God gave to the Jews").

All this considered, we can expect continued upheaval,
enormous pressure upon the leaders, and violence that will
again become part of the history of this tortured region.

A profile of violence emerges astrologically throughout the
past three years, and so much of it (including Rabin's fall) was
predicted accurately in earlier writings. It continues. For Israel,
the period January 7, 1996, through May 8 will have been particularly dangerous; August, 1996 through October 1997, similarly, a protracted period of seditious upheaval from within
Israel itself, directed at now-acting Prime Minister Shimon
Peres and the government, with elections supposed to take
place early in that period, October 1996.

These calamities will be painfully publicized to the world
for they will occur and threaten to mar the nation's "Jerusalem
3000" celebration September 1995–December 1996, marking
the trimillennial anniversary of King David's conquest of the
city. Already, the European Union of nations has boycotted the
celebration because Christianity and Islam have allegedly not
been given equal time. The city is yet claimed by the Palestinians: it is the city of greatest importance to Islam for Muhammad's ascent into heaven from the Rock upon Mt. Zion; it is the
city that saw the life and death of Jesus and the birth of Christianity; it is throughout history the most important of all cities.

New Party in Power

The election in Israel, October 1996, will unseat the liberal Labor
Party (Rabin's party; led by Peres), and the conservative Likud will
take over the government once again. If the election is moved up to
an earlier date—as is allowed by Prime Minister decree—the Labor
Party (Peres) can improve its chances for a strong showing, but the
turnabout astrology should prevail.[265*]

---

265 Tr Neptune upon the fourth cusp opposing the Midheaven (the party in power); SP
Moon (ruling the 10th) squares Pluto in the 10th; tr Uranus opposed the Moon (July-
August pre-election attacks); *SA Pluto square Sun/Moon*, SA Neptune=Mercury/Node.

Following the Rabin assassination, there will have been a backlash of new support for the peace negotiations and a clamp-down and clam-up with regard to the right-wing sectors, but the decorous backlash will dim, and the religion-supported, often Rabbi-led rhetoric will return. Hamas violence and internal right-wing violence will occur again and again (150 Israelis have been killed by terrorists since Oslo I, September 1993). The return of fearful voices and heinous acts will begin early in 1996 and build as the election nears.

If the elections are moved up to an earlier time, the Labor party can benefit more from this post-Rabin assassination backlash support and may hold more strongly to its incumbent position. If the elections remain as scheduled—October 1996—resistance to the Labor party becomes considerable again. Benjamin Netanyahu (the Likud leader, running against Peres) gains his strength in the Summer of 1996. It will be a very, very close election.

The contemporaneous negotiations with Syria—and their success, see below, signifying *still another* return of land to others, giving up the Golan Heights in the border area with Syria, represents a move that is massively unpopular in Israel. This will be the core issue of the elections.[266*]

Shimon Peres has never won an election in Israel (he has tried three times). He lacks Rabin's towering persona as a tough war hero. He has a reputation for missing opportunities, of not being able to persuade the Israeli public, of even undermining Rabin when they were in opposite parties.[267*]

Peres' Labor Party will be unseated, unless the United States supports him mightily and secures his image as an instrument of American power, beyond the gloss of diplomacy, but this should not affect the peace process, theoretically. The agreements are international agreements with co-signatures from Egypt, Jordan, the United

---

266 *The Jerusalem Report* magazine, 78–82. "Peres thinks the opponents [to the Syria negotiations] will change their mind if they are presented with not a proposal but an actual peace treaty." Additionally, there are observations that Syrian officials prefer dealing with Peres (rather than the "flinty" Rabin). Similarly, Mubarak of Egypt has counseled Arafat that Peres is easier to deal with than the Likud party.

267 According to his son, told to my colleague in Israel, Peres was born August 16, 1923 (not August 21 as is sometimes published) in Visnevo, Russia (USSR2), "as night turned to day," the statement in his biography. My rectification study suggests strongly the time of 5:51 A.M. (26E14, 54N08): Sun-Mars-Neptune-Venus conjunction in Leo in the 12th, Venus ruling the Midheaven, the stellium trined by Jupiter in Scorpio in the 3rd. Mercury conjunct the nodal axis, rising in Virgo, is opposed by Uranus, which is in the 7th at the midpoint of Sun/Moon. The Moon is in Libra conjunct Saturn and squared by Pluto. This is an eloquent rebel, depressed, driven, privately ego-absorbed and proud, a promoter of a cause, forced to adjust his position to please others.

States, Russia, and Spain in the name of the European Union, but the change in party leadership will have been the result of and catalyst for enormous upheaval in Israel.

Increased Violence Brings in the United States

Beginning in March 1998, progress of Oslo II negotiations will achieve a milestone for the Palestinians, for Arafat, and escalate public fear and violent response in Israel. This will be a seven-month period of upheaval and pain in Israel.[268*]

The peace process itself will then appear to be threatened. The negotiations will prevail throughout the harshest of uproar but meet the deadline May 4, 1999. The United States will be called into Israel to establish presence and maintain peace. [This will be a smooth entry from United States peace maintenance presence already in Israel, in the Golan Heights, tied to the peace negotiations with Syria, see below.][269*]

Should the United States not "enter" Israel, there will be civil war there March-October 2000.[270*]

It is important to note that the Jewish nation historically has so often been torn apart by vicious in-fighting. There are classic examples framed in the period of destruction of the First Temple, at the beginning of Babylonian captivity, and then in the first century when the Romans destroyed Jerusalem (and the Second Temple). These times are recorded in the Talmud (the ancient record of Jewish oral law and rabbinical teaching and wisdom, second only to the Bible in prestige), and so is the warning "Jerusalem was destroyed because her people did not reprimand one another."[271]

---

268 Tr Mars-Saturn conjunction (April 2, 1998 at 5:29 A.M. GMT at 21 Aries 56) applies to Israel's seventh cusp *square the Midheaven.* Saturn rules the 4th (the party out of power) and Mars rules the 7th (the public reaction, militancy from the outside as well as inside Israel, attacking the government position). Additionally, tr Uranus conj Pluto , SP Moon (ruling the 10th) squared by Mars. SA Neptune square Mars (change of course due to dissatisfaction). While Arafat has SA MC conjunct Jupiter. In the chart for the Signing of the Peace Accord, Sept. 13, 1993 at 11:43 A.M. EDT in Washington, DC: *SA Saturn conjunct the fourth cusp.*

269 Israel: SA Pluto semisquare Saturn, SA Jupiter opposed Saturn, tr Neptune opposed Moon, etc.

270 Israel: SA Uranus=Sun/Moon, SA Uranus=Saturn/Pluto, with tr Jupiter-Saturn (May 28, 2000 at 03:59 P.M. GMT at 22 Taurus 43) conjunct Israel's Sun and Arafat's Moon. The Jupiter-Saturn Great Conjunction chart (5:59 P.M. EET at Tel Aviv) shows the Sun at the Descendant Opposed by Pluto, ruler of the Ascendant (the people); Uranus is square the Jupiter-Saturn conjunction. The United States: tr Saturn square U.S. Moon and Midheaven; tr Uranus conjunct US Midheaven and Moon.

271 Talmud, Tractate Shabbat.

Relations with Syria

Like Israel, Syria, just to the north, is placed on trade and military routes vital to all of eastern Mediterranean history. Arcane, Biblical names of the earliest conquerors include the Amorites (ancient settlers of Canaan) and the Hittites (ancient settlers of Anatolia, now Turkey), the Egyptians. The city of Ugarit *(yoo'-gah-rit)* on the Syrian coast was extraordinarily well developed in 1500–1300 B.C.E., as an administrative center and religious center dedicated to the important god Baal *(bahl)*.

Thereafter, this land (with the region that is now Lebanon) became Phoenicia *(foh-nee'-shee-uh)* in the very late Bronze Age and early Iron. These people achieved fame as long-distance navigators of the sea, and as craftsmen, brought to Jerusalem to assist Solomon in the building of the great Temple around 1000 B.C.E.

Syria suffered long invasions thereafter by the Assyrians (ancient Iraq), Parthia (ancient Iran), and Alexander the Great who stabilized the area in 331 B.C.E. Hellenism (Greek influence) revived the country until the Romans under Pompey invaded it in 63.

In the fourth century C.E., when Rome divided into the Eastern and Western empires, Syria came under Byzantine rule (Byzantium: Constantinople). Then, in the period 633–640 C.E., Muslim Arabs conquered Syria and the country adopted Islam as its religion.

Invasions and controls by outsiders continued, even as the French, after World War I, took the mandate from the League of Nations to govern Syria. By 1926, religious nationalist uprisings brought about the formation of a separate country called Lebanon, sharing Syria's western border, and touching the Mediterranean. In 1941, the French proclaimed Syria and Lebanon independent Republics.

In 1945, Syria joined the United Nations and three years later joined the Arab states in the unsuccessful war against the new Israel. The defeat undermined Syria's national confidence. A series of coups followed.

Similarly, losing to Israel once again in the Six-Day War (see "Six-Day War," page 113), losing the Golan Heights territory on its southern border above Israel, hurt the national identity deeply. From early 1958 to late September 1961, Syria was part of the United Arab Republic. Finally, General Hafez al-Assad, spearheading the Baath, radical nationalist party which stood for the need to defeat Israel, improve relations with the Arab states, and lessen Syria's economic and military dependence on the Soviet Union, stormed Damascus. In the successful coup, Assad ousted president al-Attassi. Several months later Assad was elected overwhelmingly to the presidency for his first term of seven years.

Assad's coup took place on November 13, 1970 "at dawn."[272]*

The Astro-profile of Syria shows a severe, private, stubborn identity. It is under wraps, secret, hidden from view as to its true goals and mission; it does the unpredictable and inconsistent as a matter of course. It resists change. Perfectly consonant with this portrait is that, for two decades, Syria has been implicated in sponsoring international terrorism, especially in support of Iranian, Palestinian, and Libyan causes. And yet, Syria was the first Arab country to condemn Iraq for its invasion of Kuwait and sent 20,000 troops to serve in the Gulf War coalition.[273]*

Since 1974, oil has become Syria's major export.

Arab Syria and Jewish Israel are bitter enemies. Although in May 1974 the two countries signed a cease-fire agreement,[274]* they have clashed repeatedly in neighboring Lebanon. The *cause celebre* is continuously the Golan Heights won by Israel in the Six-Day War in 1967 and formally annexed by Prime Minister Menachem Begin in 1982.

President Assad, a former air force officer, was Syria's defense minister in 1967 when Syria lost the Golan Heights and most of its air force to Israeli forces. Assad's career has been defined by confrontation with Israel. Assad has built a 400,000-man army and equipped it with modern Soviet arms; he has suppressed religious and political dissent in Syria, and created a grand personality cult about himself with the people, building everything upon the confrontation and stand-off with the enemy Israel.

The pressure has been building on Assad to make peace with Israel since 1978 when the peace accord between Israel and Egypt shattered any dream of a united Arab front. Actual negotiations for a Treaty with Israel have been going on for several years. President

---

272 No exact time is known. My study of Syria and my tests with time suggest strongly that the time of 7:06 A.M. EET (Ascendant 2 Sagittarius 21) is a good base for the portrait of the country and its leader. Further adjustments will be revealed by events to come.

273 Venus-Jupiter-Sun in Scorpio in the 12th with precise Neptune-Mercury conjunction, Mercury ruling the Midheaven. Saturn opposes this cluster, and is exactly conjunct the *Moon in Taurus*. The major mid-point picture is MC=Pluto/Node, the need for association with others for success. When Libya and Russia made a trade alliance in 1980, Syria benefitted; but Syria turned away from Russia when the Soviet Union began to falter.

274 Syria: SA Jupiter conjunct Sun, tr Jupiter exactly opposed Midheaven.

Assad is ultra patient, steadfast, constant. He is called ruthless and inaccessible, with extraordinarily centralized power in his hands only. He is thought to be impenetrable, suspicious. He is also diabetic and has a history of heart problems. His health is deteriorating. He has waited "half a lifetime" for the return of the Golan Heights and manifests a highly visible paranoia on the issue with regard to Israel.[275]

Assad's regime is infamous for his eradication of a mere hint of Islamic rebellion in February 1982: he sent troops to slaughter some 20,000 of his own people, an entire area of Muslim radicals in the city of Hama. As well, he has left members of the former leadership which he ousted to rot in jail for twenty-five years. All this is also seen as evidence of Assad's "decisiveness."[276*]

With the break-up of long-time ally, the Soviet Union, Assad has lost a major backer and key arms supplier (i.e., sophisticated technological support). He has become aware that he never can achieve military parity with Israel and can only retrieve the Golan Heights through negotiation. Assad has made it known he wants investment from the United States and high technology as well.

This enemy of Israel awakens Israel's extreme fears of being destroyed insidiously, little by little, giving away land to the Palestinians and, as well, to the Syrians. It is almost too much for a large sector of the Israeli population to countenance, especially those living in settlements on the West Bank and on the Golan Heights, those areas now under occupation by the Palestinians and occupying center stage in the negotiations with Syria.

Assad—true to his country's astro-portrait—strongly needs to westernize his country, to ally it with the United States. His people see the freedoms of the West through their television windows to the other world. For his regime "to survive" a Treaty with Israel, Assad must reverse the years of brainwashing of his citizenry, that Israel is the most hated enemy, a threat to Syria, that the modern West is Satan's domain, so that his people will continue to support him when he does make peace with Israel and draw vast Western

---

275 *The Jerusalem Report* magazine, "Portrait of the Enemy," July 27, 1995, 24–30.

Assad was born October 6, 1930 in Qerdaha in northwest Syria: he is a student of human nature (Libra Sun, Pisces Moon), a patient administrator (Saturn in Capricorn trine Neptune, square Sun). His powerfully resourceful Mars-Jupiter-Pluto conjunction in Cancer trines Syria's Jupiter-Sun conjunction, his Sun conjoins Syria's Uranus, and his Moon probably opposes Syria's Pluto.

276 At the time of the massacre in February 1982, tr Saturn was exactly square Assad's Mars.

investment into Syria. Also, the potential peace threatens the military elite stratum of Syria's rulership. *The Jerusalem Report* on Assad points out that he modeled his regime on Nicolae Ceaucescu's Romania and does not want to incur the Romanian leader's fate at the hands of his own people.[277]

■ Prediction ...

Syria Signs Peace Treaty with Israel—There is a "rush to peace" being staged by Israel, the United States, and Syria. Working with the "trial" birth charts for Syria, President Assad should complete the Peace Treaty with Israel in July 1996. [278*]

The persuasive key and the infrastructure of such dramatic change of the status between these two nations will be the United States' involvement: military installation in the Golan Heights region to keep the peace. Yet, it is important to note that the Israel elections, if moved forward in time from October 1996, may upset this "rush to peace" and delay it. But the fact remains: the Syria-Israel Peace is near.

Relations with Iraq

The rise of Babylon, the city, occurred around 2200 B.C.E., a thousand years after the advent of writing, after the rise of great city cultures throughout Mesopotamia in the land of Sumer some 3,000 years earlier. As Babylon began, Abraham was reputedly born in Ur (in southwestern Iraq) and was led by an angel on a migration to the northeast and then south, to the land called Canaan.

Babylon became the greatest city of its world time by virtue of its geography: the two great rivers, the Tigris and Euphrates, come close together there and gave great control of irrigation to nourish the land; two major roads of trade terminate naturally in Babylon,

---

277 *The Jerusalem Report* magazine, July 27, 1995, 30. Assad well remembers "the 'Assadescu' graffiti that appeared in Damascus at the time of the [Romanian dictator's] fall."

278 SA Saturn square Syria's Midheaven, SA Jupiter exactly square Midheaven, SA Ascendant square Pluto, with tr Pluto exactly conjunct the Ascendant. The Tertiary test of Syria's horoscope for this time reveals TP Moon conjunct Mercury and Ascendant; TP Venus and TP Ascendant conjunct Venus.

For Israel: SA Pluto sesquiquadrate Node (a life-significant relationship); SA Jupiter square Node; tr Uranus opposed Moon, ruler of the Midheaven.

For Assad: SA Jupiter exactly conjunct Mercury.

roads from the West and East. Anatolia (Turkey) and Assyria were to the east and Parthia (Persia, Iran) to the West. Babylon, agriculturally, commercially, and military was dominant.[279*]

And so were its great rulers, issuing from the rulers of Sumeria, who issued from heaven before the Flood. There was Sargon I perhaps just before the time of Abraham; there was Hammurabi about 800 years later (Hammurabi, 1792–1728) who united Mesopotamia and is famous today for the Code of Hammurabi, a compilation and expansion of laws before and during his time.

And then a thousand years later, Sargon II (722–705), Sennacherib (705–681), Assurbanipal (668–626), and Nebuchadnezzar (also "Nebuchadrezzar," 604–562), one of the most celebrated figures in ancient history. He was a statesman of exceptional talents, a master-builder with great imagination, whose creations had no rival anywhere. His vicious campaigns of war against Jerusalem were of only minor importance in the wider arena of his Middle Eastern affairs, including major campaigns against Egypt, but it is the rape of Jerusalem and the captivity of the Jews that haunts the conflicts of modern history still.

Neubchadnezzar's campaign against Israel lasted about 18 months and ended with Solomon's Temple completely demolished, and almost the entire Jewish population deported to Babylonia (see page 109).

And 2,000 years later, there is Saddam Hussein. Saddam took over control of the government of Iraq upon the resignation of President Ahmad Hassan al-Bakr, July 16, 1979.[280*]

The kingdom of present-day Iraq, with Baghdad as the reiteration of ancient Babylon, was formed on August 23, 1921. Britain had invaded Iraq during World War I, in its front against the Ottoman Empire, an ancient grandiose empire of Turkish power (once comprising all of Palestine, Syria, Jordan, and Lebanon, parts of western Iraq, and northern Saudi Arabia, formerly known as "Syria") that began to die in its last-ditch alliance with the Germans during the Great War. After the war, the British received Iraq from the League of Nations and turned it over to King Faisal I, by proclamation of King George.

---

279 Oates, 9–10, 27, 32, 128–130.

280 Beginning that day, Saddam's rule by decree took on the signature of his Moon in Aries (conjunct Iraq's Moon) opposed by Pluto; Mars square Saturn in Virgo (inquisitional).

The Astro-profile of Iraq is dramatic indeed: arrogance, confidence, and "rightness" dominate. There is secrecy, which is quite similar as a public image and strategy to that of Communist China. All of this works to weaken the overall system of government.[281*]

Immediately upon taking power, Saddam Hussein purged the Ba'ath political party (a socialist group working for Arab unity) of its liberal members. In the next year, he directed a war against Iran, which lasted eight years—the fight was over the rights to a water way, but one can suspect revival of animosity from ancient times when Cyrus the Great of Persia (Iran) conquered the great Nebuchadnezzar.

At the same time, Kurds (some eight million Iraqis in the north—Kurdistan—fighting for a very long time for national autonomy) were rebelling against the regime of Iraq and siding with Iran in the war. When the war ended, Saddam quelled the Kurds with poison gas. Thousands were killed and many survivors sought refuge in Turkey.[282*]

Saddam Hussein has fashioned himself as a new Nebuchadnezzar, minting commemorative coins with the profile of the ancient king and his own side by side, building fifty new palaces or luxury residences at a cost of $1.5 billion, with one complex at Lake Tharthar five times the size of the White House and fifty percent bigger than Versailles.[283]

---

281 Associated Press report in the August 24, 1921, edition of the *New York Times*, sets the time at 6:00 A.M. on August 23, 1921; a great gathering had assembled to hear the proclamation read by Sir Percy Cox. Sunrise that day was at 5:34 A.M., but British civility prevailed for 6:00 A.M.

Sun in Leo, Moon in Aries, 12th and 8th Houses respectively. Fixed star Regulus conjunct Sun-Mercury, ruler of the Ascendant and Midheaven. Jupiter-Saturn Great Conjunctions rising in Virgo. Saturn=Sun/Moon.

Indeed, there are subsequent horoscopes to consider as well; see Campion, *World Horoscopes*. The "kingdom" chart August 23, 1921 is extraordinarily correspondent to Iraq character and responsive to its development. I have worked intensely with it for five years. It is the archetype that may be ingrained in the national spirit of the country, more so than the release from British Mandate and the subsequent coups. It is similar to the choice of time for Israel (Ben Gurion's conviction and diary record), for England (the 1066 chart apparently still prevailing), and many others. See the extraordinary example of the history of Spain astrologically, page 193. *The latest chart important to the nation is not necessarily the most efficacious one for the country.* Historian-Astrologer Campion presents data thoroughly; he is not proving the data. That's our job, and the next step, checking against events, is essential. Time (events) eventually sorts out choice (determines angles).

282 The Iraq-Iran war erupted on September 22, 1980, with Iraq having SA Pluto opposed Uranus in the 7th, SA Mars square Pluto, SP Moon square the Jupiter-Saturn conjunction, with tr Jupiter conjunct and Neptune square the Conjunction.

283 *TIME* magazine, August 28, 1995, 46, and personal interviews with recent visitors to Iraq.

Saddam Hussein's aggression in the Gulf War was a thrust of ego-aggrandizement perfectly consonant with the Iraq Astro-profile. His defeat set him apart from all other Arab states. Iraq is completely self-absorbed and without ally.[284*]

■ Prediction ...

Saddam's Rule Now Ends—A major astrological vector affects the horoscope for Iraq incontrovertibly. It is a signal of government overthrow; the party (person) in power is toppled, brought down.

The time periods when this vector is at its highest are between May–June 1996 and November 1996.[285*]

There have been other indications of the building of energies for overthrow, but Saddam and accident have been able to control the situation. For example, the Republican guard tried to mutiny; in May 1995 the large Dulaymi tribe rose in a quickly suppressed revolt; there was an Israeli plan to assassinate Saddam in 1992, literally blowing up in a practice run on November 5,[286] and Saddam's cousin and son-in-law, Hussein Kamel al-Majid (who oversaw Iraq's program to develop weapons of mass destruction and was head of the Republican Guard), defected to Jordan in August 7–8, 1995, along with his brother Saddam Kamel, the head of Saddam Hussein's personal guard.

In his first interviews with the American media, Hussein Kamel said, "The Iraqi opposition is now in place to overthrow the regime. I am talking now about the opposition inside the country. I know everything about it, all the details—Iraqi army officers, government officials, university professors, and all the graduates, and also the Iraqi citizenry [It will require leadership by the army], this is true. The catalyst will be for the people to join the army in taking the initiative. All the Iraqi people are

284 Tyl, *Prediction in Astrology*, is primarily focused on the Gulf War, written before the War, predicting the war and concomitant details most specifically. It is a full presentation of Solar Arc theory in astrology.

285 Tr Pluto conjunct the fourth cusp, opposing the Midheaven, with SA Pluto conjunct Jupiter; with SA Mercury square Mars, SA *Saturn square Uranus* (May–June 1996); with SA Pluto=Jupiter/Saturn (major change of situation, in November 1996).

286 See *The Jerusalem Report* magazine, August 10, 1995, 18–19; also issue December 1992. Special weaponry had been developed. Safety procedures broke down in rehearsal, there was an explosion, and five men died.

armed. Everybody is now ready. But there are things that must be done before the first spark is ignited."[287]

What these "things" are is a mystery to the west. Perhaps the plan is to play into the reputedly wild, blood-thirsty ego of Saddam's son, Uday, "easing" his father aside, and then mount the revolt against the impulsive, unsettled son, who apparently has no support except from his father.

It appears impossible for the Saddam Hussein regime to continue. If he does escape overthrow in 1996 (for instance, because of the absence of a figurehead around whom the revolt could focus), there is another critical time in February–September 1997, a protracted period that also shows an uprising of the people. The key time within this period is July 1997. The probability of Saddam Hussein passing this outside time of revolt is extremely low. If Saddam is overthrown in 1996 and a second dictator follows, he too will be ousted in the late Summer of 1997.[288*]

■ Prediction ...

Iraq Begins Recovery—Beginning in January–February 1998, Iraq will begin its era of freedom and new alliances with the world.

The United States will be involved with the new Iraq, at the latest, between February and August 2000 (see page 238). This will be a vital injection of reconstruction energy for Iraq, and the United States will be extending its continental staging area platform from Israel eastward, *vis a vis* the Far East.[289*]

---

287 *TIME* magazine, September 18, 1995, 81–82.

288 All 1997, *tr Pluto square the Ascendant; tr Saturn square Pluto* and tr Saturn conjunct the Moon in May-July, with *SA Pluto=Sun/Moon, SA MC=Saturn/Pluto*. Additionally, *SA Pluto conjoins Saturn* throughout the Summer and partile in September.

289 For Iraq: SP Moon conjunct Uranus in the 7th, tr Mars-Saturn (partile: 4/15/00 at 8:28 P.M. GMT at 17 Taurus 16) square Sun-Mercury in July, tr Uranus Sun-Mercury; Iraq Mars-Neptune natally opposing the United States Midheaven and Moon in Aquarius which are activated by tr Mars-Saturn square.

5

RELIGIOUS FUNDAMENTALISM AND NATIONALISM

Considerations of Islam

Benjamin R. Barber, Political Science professor at Rutgers University, in his study *Jihad vs. McWorld*, positions the thrust of nationalism this way: "Nationalism established government on a scale greater than the tribe yet less cosmopolitan than the universal church and in time gave birth to those intermediate, gradually more democratic institutions that would come to constitute the nation-state." He sees world pains today in the clash between "choices that are secular universalism," what the national image demands, and "the everyday particularism of the fractious tribe," the vestigial needs for expression that are usually ethnic/religious in origin and preservation; the new ways and the traditional ways. Again: liberalism and conservatism.[290]

The complex four-year clash in the former Yugoslavia, for example, showed "tribal" needs destroying or reorganizing one larger nation to form other smaller ones; the break-up of the Soviet Union for the autonomy of the satellite states, the sectional warfare in Rwanda, the Zulus and other tribes of South Africa, still fractious in its newness, the Palestinians in Israel, the Kurds in Iraq, the Basques and the Catalans in Spain, Ireland in Great Britain, and Quebec in Canada, defining itself with the threat of secession. Other examples include the Welsh Independence movement, based as much on language as is the Quebec movement, and the Scottish National Party seeking to

---

290 Barber, 7

establish an independent Scotland within the European Union. We can add the Black Muslim movement in the United States, seeking its own nation. There are many more examples.

With Quebec, a second vote will bring autonomy. The precedent for separatist nationalism will be established even more strongly. European nationalist movements will soon reshape the business balance and political leverage of the entire market; nationalism becomes the catalyst for a busier and more variegated world, yet a smaller, closer one at the same time. This is the profile of the next century.

The Middle East is fraught with the clash between the two religio-economic worlds: the "Jihad" (literally, "striving," i.e., striving to advance Islam; popularized now as "holy war" with the sense of vendetta) world of religious tradition and conviction—the memory of Islam's dominance in the world throughout the first Millennium; and the "McWorld" of westernization, that is essential (synonymous) for modernization, that is the evil of Islam. Within the battle, the sense of nationalism becomes a fury and the separation of state and religion an evasive antidote.

In his study of nationalism, *The Wrath of Nations*, William Pfaff portrays Islamic fundamentalism as a form of "national" resistance, an assertion of political autonomy and independence, and "an attempt to reclaim a jeopardized cultural independence and wholeness, in which statehood or nationhood is merely means to an end." Islamic fundamentalism is a product of the failure of secular nationalism. Without a say in government, voices shout together through religion.[291]

The Islamic regimes that have survived the World Wars and now reach toward the Millennium are the conservative monarchies in Saudi Arabia and Jordan where the monarch's legitimacy has been linked to a religious role as descendant of the Prophet or protector of the Holy Places. Pfaff asks, what will happen in these countries when these monarchs are gone? (See page 144.)

Pfaff projects continuing crises in the Middle East since the fundamentalist movement is virtually the *only consolation* the doctrine and its adherents have. Fundamentalism is disruptive and isolationist, and certainly goes against, clashes with, the trend of the world to unite.

---

291 Pfaff, 128–129.

Barber studies oil production and oil reserves in the world, with these findings: "better than three-fifths of the world's current oil production (and almost 93% of its potential production reserves) are controlled by the nations least likely to be at home in McWorld [the Western way] and most likely to be afflicted with political, social, and thus economic instability." These "high risk" countries are Algeria, Iran, Iraq, Libya, Nigeria, and the former Yugoslavia.[292]

Almost all industrial nations are import-dependent (under fifty percent for the United States and more than ninety percent for Japan with Germany somewhere in between, for example). In objective terms, *the major fuel supply sector of the world is weighed down with "pathologies,"* supplier nations that are ripe for episodes of internal turmoil, political instability, civil war, or tribal fragmentation.

Barber observes that the concept of Jihad splinters nations but then also increases their dependency on McWorld—look at the exploding need now in the Palestinian settlements for technology to support urbanization, industry, i.e., paving streets, regulating construction, managing telephone communications, outfitting hospitals, fulfilling creature comforts, etc., and for ways to attract major foreign investment. Barber observes that the concept of McWorld gives nations stature but also then increases *their dependency upon imports*, thereby reducing their power.

The United States is dependent upon the Pacific and Middle East staging areas to protect its Super Power position and is vulnerable to losing it through that dependency. Japan is life-dependent on the Pacific Market especially to fulfill its needs for natural resources and is vulnerable to interruption of its supply lines ... and both—indeed, all industrialized leaders—depend on the oil-producing countries for fuel to energize the effort.

Pfaff adds to this that "When observant Moslems try to rule without westernized systems and ideas, they are left with unsolved problems: how to define an 'Islamic economics,' an 'Islamic finance,' an Islamic way to run industry." The main function of Muslim government is to enable the *individual* Muslim to lead a good Muslim life; that is the purpose of the state.

---

292 Barber, 44–48. Barber excludes from the profile the OPEC nations like Qatar and Bahrain which have minuscule populations and gargantuan production surpluses.

No Muslim teaching is prepared for the administration of a twentieth century nation.[293]

In the political arena of religion, one man's holy thrust/war (*Jihad*) can be another man's terrorism. Many analysts see the hijackings, the bombings, the assassinations and kidnappings as frustrations within the Islamic world (and, indeed, elsewhere: the Oklahoma City bombing, the Japanese subway gassing, etc.), as manifestation of Islam's impotence with being successful in terms of progressive government and, in western terms, material acquisition. The Islamic turmoil projects its upset upon the work of "Satan" manifesting in the United States, leader of the West, and the abomination and sacrilege of Israel, reminder of the past.

Fernandez-Armesto observes that Islam is too big for coherent political action, too diverse to turn into a single amalgam. "When the wave rolls, leaders sometimes ride its surf but rarely succeed in controlling its power." He quotes President Hosni Mubarak of Egypt that Arab unity "changes with the weather." All the United Arab Republics of the second half of the century, which have included, in different combinations, Egypt, Syria, Libya, and Sudan, have quickly fallen apart.[294]

J. M. Roberts, in his observance of violent politics in Arab states between repressive authoritarianism and impassioned fundamentalism, notes that the average age of most Islamic societies today is very young, between fifteen and eighteen (as of 1993). This is history *in development*, in explosive adolescence. "There is just too much youthful energy and frustration about for the outlook to be promising for peace."[295]

Islamic history is packed with revivalist movements, yet no Islamic resurgence has lasted for long without getting deflected somehow or losing outright. A clear case in point is Iran: the Ayatollah Khomeini who transformed Iran to an Islamic regime upon his return from exile on February 1, 1979, was burned in effigy in the streets of Teheran during riots just eleven years later in 1990 and 1992; Mullah representation in the legislature dropped from one-half to less than a fifth. Nationalism and religion, specifically Islam, are falling apart, separating still.[296]

---

293 Pfaff, 125.
294 Fernandez-Armesto, 587.
295 Roberts, 893.
296 Ibid, 590.

While airport signs and hotel-room cards in Teheran proclaim "Death to America," religious leaders and university groups are examining and debating the validity of Khomeini's claim to absolute clerical power. An underlying current of dissent lives. Nothing inspirational is holding Iran's system together. A former professor at Teheran University can not see the Islamic state lasting another decade; a philosopher says—capturing thoughts of many student groups and intellectuals—"Religion is for the next life, not this one. The danger to Islam is that the revolution will give it a perpetual bad name."[297]

Fernandez-Armesto portrays Iraq as "a conglomeration of minorities crushed into a national mould." Saddam Hussein used Iraqi nationalism "in defiance of Arab nationalism," that which was espoused by his own party, and, as well, against the Islamic revivalism of his opponents. Here are the different winds, changes of climate, if you will, within Islamic government. Saddam went beyond Islamic and Arabic identities to the glories of ancient Mesopotamia, the new Nebuchadnezzar, as we have seen, in decided ego indulgence.[298*]

Islam is a religion, not a government. It is a theology to guide the way of life for the individual and has no reference to modern national development. Muslim fundamentalism, according to Fernandez-Armesto, Barber, Pfaff, and many others, is incompatible with technical and scientific progress. It insists on *the sufficiency of ancient knowledge and the perfection of Koranic society.*[299]

Strangely, modernism and success have been tolerated by Islam in Turkey. While the country has become a secular Republic with the deep reforms achieved by Kemal Ataturk, instituted as the Ottoman Empire fell apart in the early 1920s. Turkey is the singular shining star of Islam's achievement in this century, an extension of ancient Turkey when it became the center of Islam in its great empire of the previous Millennium. Turkey is the sole Muslim

---

297 *Foreign Affairs* magazine, November/December 1995, Milton Viorst, Middle East Analyst, "The Limits of the Revolution."64–76. Yet, the militant group *Hesbollahi* is part of Iran's Israel policy, and the country vies for leadership of radical Muslims worldwide (page 76).

298 This is dramatic manifestation of the portents of the Jupiter-Saturn Great Mutation Conjunction chart, December 31, 1980, at 9:23 P.M. GMT, drawn for Mecca (10 Libra 15 Ascendant), pitting Arab against Arab in the name of religious philosophy and government enforcement (Jupiter-Saturn).

299 Fernandez-Armesto, 591. It is irony indeed, that scientific erudition and skill were emblematic of the height of Islam a thousand years ago.

country in NATO, and a woman, Tansu Ciller, was named Prime Minister (women have had voting rights since 1935). Yet, the leading political parties in Turkey now fear the growing strength (electoral gains) of the Islamic *fundamentalist* party. "Turkey is now poised between East and West as never before in its seventy-three years as an avowedly secular state."[300]

Conversely, and more the norm, in Egypt—a country of incomparable grandeur past—the song is of sorrow. Arab radicalism has brought about ruin and bankruptcy.[301] Anwar Sadat had begun revival by negotiating peace (and trade) with Israel. The Palestinians and other Arabs shouted treason; and Sadat's acts of vision ultimately led to his assassination by Islamic fundamentalists in his own army, a nd the breakdown continued into the realm of international terrorism and relative isolation.[302*]

The Islamic fundamentalist movement is targeted against the West; in Egypt during Sadat's time, criticism was launched at his capitalism. Although both profit and private enterprise are sanctioned and regulated by the Holy Law, the issue is with the "crass materialism and corruption" which are part and parcel of the western way.

The fundamentalist movement is anti-peace and anti-Israel: "In God's good time, the stranger will be evicted and the land restored to the realm of Islam." The major problem faced by Islam is the domination of the Muslim lands, in Egypt and elsewhere, by *secularists* who are destroying Islam from within, losing the primacy of religious perspective.[303]

---

300 *The European*, December 28, 1995–January 3, 1996, 1.

301 *Foreign Affairs* magazine, September/October 1995, Fouad Ajami (Majid Khadduri Professor of Middle Eastern Studies, Johns Hopkins University), "The Sorrows of Egypt," pages 72–88.

Fouad Ajami cites Egypt's "endless alternation between false glory and self-pity," a country of sixty million people producing a mere 375 books a year (in contrast with Israel's five million people and 4,000 titles), and "the people in a state of utter backwardness."

302 It appears that the horoscope for the Egypt Republic (Campion, *World Horoscopes*), June 19, 1953 at 1:30 A.M., EET in Cairo is reliable. It tracks the assassination (October 6, 1981) of Anwar Sadat accurately: SA Mars square the Ascendant (within 54 minutes) and tr Neptune square Moon in the 6th (Armed Forces), ruling the 4th (other political power). Sadat was born on December 25, 1918 at 2:00 A.M., EET in Cairo; time speculative, "shortly after midnight," international compendia. Taeger Archives 00:20 A.M.

Egypt shows complete depression of planets under the horizon, with the retrograde conjunction of Saturn-Neptune square the Midheaven, Uranus-Mercury axis.

303 Lewis, 378–379.

In the fundamentalist view, Sadat's crime—as our example focal point, similar to that of the Shah of Iran, Saddam Hussein in Iraq, Assad in Syria threatening peace with Israel, and Ataturk in Turkey—was/is the nullification of the Holy Law of Islam and the paganizing of Islamic society. Laws from the outside world can not be introduced and imposed in Muslim life.

■ Prediction ...

Egypt Begins Recovery—Over the past few years, in Egypt particularly, militant Islamic violence has escalated.[304*] Present Egyptian president Mubarak has directed his security forces to crack down on the Gama al-Islamiyya (ardent Islamic nationalists), the Islamic Jihad, the non-violent Muslim Brotherhood, opposition political parties, opposition newspapers, and even Human Rights agencies fronting for Islamic reformists. Supporters see the crackdown as a show of the strong leadership that taps the people's nostalgic allegiance to the pharaonic era. Detractors see it as further evidence of Mubarak's western-influenced despotism and ego aggrandizement.[305]

While there was a failed assassination attempt on Mubarak's life in late June 1995, claimed by the Islamic Gama group, the crackdown seems to be working, and, after a difficult time (terrorism outbreak) in the early Spring of 1996, success with the program will be emphatically seen in August.[306*]

Mubarak will take a major trip in January 1997 to tie down a major investment project to be made in Egypt. The plans will be concluded in May 1997, and Mubarak will present a new picture for Egypt, solidly backed up with the investment success and secured by the crackdown on violence. He will be presented yet once again by the Peoples' Assembly as presidential candidate and will be reelected to his third six-year term in November 1997.[307*]

---

304 The Egypt horoscope tracks the new rise of fundamentalism with tr Neptune conjunct the Midheaven throughout 1993 and extremist attacks with tr Uranus square the Ascendant in 1995.

305 *The Jerusalem Report* magazine, October 5, 1995, 38–39.

306 Tr Sat square Sun in March 1996; tr Jupiter opposed Uranus, tr Uranus conjunct Node, tr Pluto entering 8th House (investments in Egypt) in April–August 1996, with SA Jupiter square Saturn (law and order, proving a point).

307 SA Jupiter conjunct Mercury, rulers of 9th and 2nd Houses, respectively. SA Jupiter square Neptune (idealism); SA Pluto square Mars, the strong "sell."

Egypt should be conspicuously revamped culturally and educationally by August 2000, with much cause for and show of celebration.[308*]

Islam vs Israel

Bernard Lewis, Professor of Near Eastern Studies Emeritus at Princeton University, in his *Islam in History*, presents "An Ode Against the Jews" written almost a thousand years ago by Abu Ishaq, a prominent jurist in Spain. The old ode is one of outrage, and the essence of that outrage lives today.

Life and livelihood and the practice of their religion is not denied to the Jews; those rights are guaranteed and protected by dhimma, the contract between the Muslim state and the tolerated non-Muslim communities. Rather, it is argued that the Jews have violated that contract and it has ceased to be operative.[309]

Presented by Lewis through the old ode, the Jews have failed to keep their proper place, i.e., to remain in the station that is assigned to them. The primacy of Islam "in this world and the next" has not been accepted, and, as a consequence, certain fiscal disabilities and social limitations follow. "Second-class" citizenship should be understandable and acceptable.

Considerations of Judaism

The assassination of Prime Minister Yitzhak Rabin (see page 113) has brought to light yet once again the imbroglio of religious fundamentalism within Jewish life.

Zionism

Zionism (see page 112) was the socio-political movement that spurred the birth of the modern state of Israel. This fervent movement emerged from the Jewish dream, in exile and under persecution so many times in history, to establish a national home, its promised nation.

Zionism was influenced by national currents in late nineteenth-century Europe. A Jewish nation was thought to be the answer to the Diaspora and anti-Semitism. An early explanation of why the

---

308 SA Sun square Venus, December 1999; accumulated semisquare Solar Arc in August 2000, with tr Neptune conjunct Node, tr Pluto opposed *Jupiter*.
309 Lewis, 167–185.

Jews were hated so was that they were landless, and thus a threat (perhaps much as the Palestinians came to be after 1948).[310]

The first World Zionist Congress was organized in 1897 by Theodor Herzl, an Austrian Jewish journalist. Two hundred delegates attended the Congress in Basel, Switzerland, on August 29, and soon thereafter Zionist groups were established all over the world.[311]*

Some six years later, the Zionist movement rejected the British offer of land for a homeland in Uganda. Palestine was deemed essential for the Jewish identity.

Upon Herzl's death, Haim Weizman took leadership of the movement. In 1917, while still at war with Turkey and hoping for international Jewish support, Britain presented the Balfour Declaration which was designed to help the Jews establish a national home in Palestine. Great Britain was given mandate of Palestine by the League of Nations in 1920 in part to implement the Balfour Declaration.[312]

After World War II, the Zionist movement was split by Britain's adjustment of the Declaration: Zionist "revisionists" wanted *all* of Palestine; the "general Zionists" reluctantly accepted the United Nations plan to partition Israel.

Today, in Israel there are the religious Zionists (blending state and religion) and those Religious Zionists with an extremist messianic bent (see "Zionists," page 112). Another group, the ultra-orthodox non-Zionist Jews, has nothing to do with Israel as a political entity.

Analysts see a complex relationship in some sectors of the movement between modern Zionism and the medieval Crusades. The Zionists needed to disprove the make-do existence of their faith and togetherness in exile, the Diaspora, asserting the necessity of the land, regaining their Promised Land. The Christians were

---

310 Maccoby, 18.

311 The horoscope drawn for that day, August 29, 1897, is indeed revealing and significant: the Sun and Moon were both in Virgo, with the Sun peregrine (the emphasis on intellect, principle, and dignity); the Moon-Jupiter conjunction is squared by Neptune (idealization); Mars-Mercury in Libra (social promotion), Saturn-Uranus conjoined in Scorpio (bringing tradition forward differently), and the Nodal axis at 4 Aquarius-Leo 25 (associations, networking) is *exactly conjunct the Moon position of the future Israel at 4 Leo 21.* Additionally, Pluto=Sun/Moon (new perspective, driving force).

312 At this time, some 600,000 Arabs had been living in Palestine beside 80,000 Jews. See Roberts, 791.

shut out of Jerusalem by the Moslems and fought for two centuries to regain *their* Holy Land; while *they* failed, the Zionists would *not*.

Many Arabs perceive the Jews as a "reincarnation of the Crusaders. The failure of the Crusades is history's promise that Zionism will fail someday too." [313]

Yigal Amir, the assassin of Yitzhak Rabin, was part of a rightwing group of extremist fundamentalists called Eyal, an offshoot of the anti-Arab Kach movement, formed by Rabbi Meir Kahane. The Kach movement is outlawed in Israel; just twenty-two days before Rabin's assassination, a Kach member was arrested for vandalizing Rabin's car.

Over the two years before the assassination, the fundamentalist hate was extreme: Rabin was accused of "bringing on a new Holocaust"; Rabin and Peres were "Wanted for treason"; the government was denounced as illegal by a former Knesset member; protestors blocked and attacked Rabin's motorcade; accusers chanted "Kill Rabin, the murderer of Jews"; a Likud member of the Knesset preached, "Rabin hates you. It's simply hate that knows no boundaries and has no measure"; the Rabin "junta was raping the Jewish people"; and thousands of demonstrators railed in Jerusalem against Oslo II, with effigies of Rabin in a Nazi SS uniform, the crowd chanting "Rabin is a traitor, etc." [314]

Christian Crusades

Extremism abounds in Islam, in Judaism—*and* in Christianity. Witness the Crusades, 1095–1291, that changed the relations between East and West forever. The First Crusade was proclaimed by Pope Urban II at a church council meeting in Clermont, France, in the late afternoon on November 27, 1095. At the end of the Council, he spoke before a horde of people, outdoors in a field, calling upon French knights to vow to march to the East, to Jerusalem, to free Christians from the enslavement of Islamic rule and to liberate the tomb of Christ from Muslim control.[315*]

---

313 *The Jerusalem Report* magazine, November 30, 1995, 47–48, quoting Benjamin Kedar of Hebrew University. Some Arabs called the Gulf War the 12th Crusade.

314 Ibid, 6.

315 Riley-Smith, 1. The horoscope for this momentous event (set for 3:00 P.M., LMT) is extraordinary: Sun in Sagittarius-Moon in Scorpio, both in the 7th ("inspiration solidified; well-armed mission; demanding opportunity for fulfillment; emphatic clear expression of opinion and philosophy"); Sun exactly squared by *Saturn in Virgo*, ruler of the 10th (the papal authority, didactic opinionation) and 9th (philosophy, foreign land);

Men "took the cross," which involved taking a particular vow at highly emotional gatherings and adopting a dramatic white tunic attire over their armor, emblazoned with a Red Cross; some knights became hysterical with dedication and branded crosses on their bodies.

The First Crusade (1095–1099) was fought initially by French and German peasants, who started out prematurely, impetuously, without organization or proper leadership, slaughtering Jewish communities throughout the Rhineland, the beginning route to the Holy Land. This horde was in turn massacred by the Turks in Asia Minor. A follow-up force of four large European armies then routed the Turks and, led by the heralded Godfrey of Bouilon, captured Jerusalem in 1099, slaughtering thousands of Muslims and Jews, committing violence so terrible that history even recorded cannibalism among the horrors. The conquerors set up the Latin kingdom of Jerusalem, with outposts established at Tripoli, Antioch, and Edessa (in Greece between the boot of Italy and northwestern Turkey). Forays were extended as well south into Egypt and east to Constantinople.

The Turks recaptured Edessa in 1144, and this motivated the Second Crusade (1147–1148), led by Louis VII of France and Conrad III of Germany. Their attack on Damascus failed because of the leaders' mutual jealousy and lack of cooperation. Then, under the great Saladin, sultan of Egypt, Syria, Yemen, and Palestine, on July 4, 1187, the Latin-Christian army was completely routed at all installations by the Muslims. Jerusalem was regained by Islam after eighty-eight years of Christian occupation.[316*]

Neptune is in the 4th (the infidel Muslims in the Holy Land) opposed the Midheaven and quindecile (upheaval) Venus in the 9th, ruling the Ascendant; Jupiter conjoins the Midheaven and is tightly squared by Uranus; Mars in Leo ("getting away with murder") squares the Ascendant. Mercury, ruler of the Virgo 6th (along with Venus), military forces, is in 00 Capricorn, the public thrust of the Aries Point.

Key midpoint pictures are startling: Pluto=Sun/Neptune ("use of the spiritual, psychic, or illusory as a force for persuasion; fateful deception"); Uranus=Sun/Node ("attraction to unusual individuals; upsets through intensity"); Neptune=Pluto/Ascendant ("something paranormal influences situations; vision to fulfill"); Moon=Sun/Uranus ("emotional excitability"). All quoted phrases: Tyl, *Synthesis & Counseling* or *Prediction*, Appendix.

316 It is fascinating to note that Saladin's "victory chart" contains a tight Jupiter-Saturn conjunction in Air (the Great Conjunction had occurred on November 8, 1186 at 8:11, UT, at 12 Libra 04 squared by Pluto, almost exactly conjunct the 9 Libra 30 Great Mutation Conjunction of Jupiter-Saturn (December 31, 1980 at 9:23 P.M. GMT) that signalled the development of the current 20-year era of the Middle East Crisis, again centered on Jerusalem. Charts for this 1186 conjunction from Rome's (9:11 A.M. LMT) and Jerusalem's perspective (10:11 A.M.) are extremely instructive.

Saladin declined to persecute the defeated Christians as the crusaders had persecuted the conquered Muslims years before. He innovated enormous cultural developments and a growth in learning throughout the Islamic empire. Motivated by the true notion of expanding the faith, *jihad,* Saladin made Islam a haven for religious scholars and teachers.[317]

A third Crusade was inspired, to be led by Richard the Lionhearted of England, and the kings of France and Germany. It was a dismal failure.

From 1101 then, onward, i.e., after the First Crusade (1095–99), the Crusades to retrieve the Holy Land from the infidel Moslems—one holy summons for each generation throughout the twelfth and thirteenth centuries—were all failures. This brought enormous criticism upon the crusaders and drove hordes of them to even greater hysteria and brutality. The reasoning represented extremism to a fault: the failure in God's own war, which was being fought at his own bidding, could not possibly be attributed to God, but only to the instruments at God's disposal, the crusaders themselves.[318]

The intensity and rationales of extremism bring people together to form sub-groups (minorities). Whatever trait or philosophy is isolated as fundamental and indispensable attracts others who share it; they gather with like others for company, community, importance, for nation, for power and pride. For example, if ethnic identity becomes the basis of nationhood, all unlike others become rivals, threats to purity and solidarity. This leads all too familiarly to the concept of ethnic cleansing, exploited by the Germans during World War II and in the Serbo-Croatian conflict to keep the core pure.

William Pfaff says that nationalism is intrinsically absurd. "Why should the accident—fortune or misfortune—of birth as an American, Albanian, Scot, or Fiji Islander impose loyalties that dominate an individual life and structure a society so as to place it in formal conflict with others?" [319]

---

317 Axelrod & Phillips, 266. President Assad of Syria has a tapestry of Saladin defeating the Crusaders hanging in his office; Saddam Hussein has emphasized the fact that he shares a birthplace with Saladin, Takrit in southern Iraq. (*The Jerusalem Report* magazine, November 30, 1995, 46–47.)

318 Riley-Smith, 66–71.

319 Pfaff, 17.

To be a European in the Middle Ages was for the vast majority to be a Christian. Upon this trait, a homogeneity was achieved among Spanish, French, Germans, and Italians, and that made the Crusades not only possible, but blindingly focused as well.[320]

In the United States today, the Christian Movement (including the Christian Coalition) is growing in influence constantly, held together nationally through cable television and telecommunication networks, newsletters, etc. The Christian Coalition has become one of the most powerful grass-roots organizations in American politics. In two years (1993–1995), active supporters have grown in number from 500,000 to 1.6 million, and the budget from $14.8 million to $25 million.[321]

Religious belief brings conviction—the sense of infallibility—to political expression. In our day now, the Pope is infallible in his pronouncement on Church matters, which have become exceedingly personal in modern times (see "Vatican," page 26). To be Islamic is to be right, "in this life and the next." To be Jewish is to deserve what God has promised.

With intermarriage, with mingling across borders, the purity of these views is threatened. The sense of nation dilutes itself, and the core of the national concept remains fired in the mind in compensation. Just as Poland existed during the years of the two great wars *without actual territory*, by living in the minds of its people, just as the sense of Return has driven Jews to a land promised over 3,000 years by invigorating their faith and determination, just as the grandeur of Islam, which ruled the western world for half a thousand years after Muhammad's vision, has burned in the convicted memories of Koran-bound Arabs today, so the world must now see the bond of humanity as transcendentally important. In practical terms of survival and development, material trade—the exchange of resources—must expedite the sharing of spirit.

---

320 Mass crusading armies moving together thousands of miles to reach the Holy Land, while sharing faith, did not share language, for one exceptional trait. Confusion was extreme, chaotic.

321 *TIME* magazine, May 15, 1995: Cover story, 28–35. The Coalition is credited with providing the winning margin for perhaps half the Republican fifty-two-seat gain in the House and a sizeable portion of their nine-seat pickup in the Senate in 1995.

Jordanian Leadership

In late October 1995, a Middle East and North Africa Economic Summit meeting (MENA) was held in Amman, Jordan. This auspicious event, Jordan taking the initiative in bringing the entire Middle East region into the world marketplace, follows on the Jordanian peace achievement with Israel, signed October 26, 1994,[322*] to define a period of triumph in King Hussein's rule. The summit was co-sponsored by the United States and Russia with strong European Union and Japanese backing.[323*]

Crown Prince Hassan, King Hussein's younger brother and heir apparent, projects Jordan's own national agenda as focusing on bringing Jordan into the global market, toward global financing. Jordan is defining the Middle East region and its extension into North Africa as the "Asian rim of Europe and the European rim of Asia." [324]

Even though Iraq was excluded and Syria (and Lebanon) boycotted the meeting, progress was begun. The market of the Middle East—Jordan, Israel, Syria, Lebanon, Iraq, and Egypt—was opening the way to togetherness regionally and globally, gaining a stature not achieved since pre-World War I.

---

322 October 26, 1994, at 2:17:20 P.M. at Wadi Arava, Jordan (35E00, 29N30): a tragically disappointing chart, which I can not as yet project: Moon opposed Uranus-Neptune (Neptune ruling the 7 Pisces 12 Ascendant); Saturn retrograde rising at 5 Pisces; Venus (ruler of 3) squared by Mars; the Mars/Saturn midpoint was 23 Taurus 46, the Sun of Israel, the Moon of Arafat. The redemption of the chart could be the Jupiter-Pluto conjunction in the 9th, Pluto ruling the 9th, and Jupiter the 10th: resourcefulness, trade, etc.

323 King Hussein was born November 14, 1935 at 10:35 A.M., according to his birth certificate (via Taeger Archives), in Amman, Jordan. In December 1994, his SA Sun was exactly conjunct his Ascendant; SA Jupiter was applying to square his Uranus (the big break, success; exact July 1996), with tr Pluto upon his Jupiter in Sagittarius (which opposes the national Sun, see below).

Jordan's horoscope: probably May 25, 1946, at noon (or before) in Amman; Campion, *World Horoscopes*. In October 1995, SA Sun conjunct Saturn, tr Jupiter conjunct Uranus at the Midheaven, *tr Pluto applying to opposition with the national Sun in the 9th*.

The Pluto transit opposed the Sun, classically refers to the monarch in jeopardy, to the ruling power ousted [recall the Pluto transit opposed the Israel Sun at election time in June 1992; see page 115]. At this time—as perhaps all the time—King Hussein was undoubtedly guarding vigilantly against assassination; at the time of the peace-signing with Israel, having turned on Saddam Hussein in Iraq, the king was being burned in effigy by the Palestinians in Gaza [the Palestinians make up about 65% of Jordan's population!].

324 *The Jerusalem Report* magazine, November 2, 1995, 36–37.

■ Prediction ...

King Hussein's Road Ahead: Transfer of Power—When King Hussein was just four months before his 16th birthday, July 20, 1951, his grandfather, Abdullah ibn-Husein, king of Jordan from 1946, was assassinated by a Palestinian in a Jerusalem mosque. Young Hussein was witness.

Abdullah had annexed the West Bank of the Jordan river, a part of Palestine that the United Nations had designated as Arab territory. The Palestinians had anticipated the creation of a new country.

Abdullah's son (Talal) succeeded him on September 26, but the son was deposed by the Jordanian Parliament just four months later on February 11, 1952, unfit to rule because of mental illness.

On February 11, 1952, young Hussein became king, three months after his sixteenth birthday.[325*]

King Hussein faces two major periods of challenge and development through the Millennium. The first period, July-October 1997, after a year of intense, successful trade and investment development, the king will achieve world recognition. Then, there is a high probability that the king will be seriously ill, perhaps with his lungs in the Fall of 1997. He will not be out of danger until early February 1998.[326*]

The second period is in April–May 1999. It is probable that King Hussein will seriously consider stepping aside in favor of his younger brother Crown Prince Hassan.[327*]

---

325 The astrology is remarkable: Hussein's SA Uranus opposed his Sun in the 10th; SA Moon conjoined his Pluto in the 7th; SA Jupiter squared his Midheaven; *Tr Pluto was exactly square his Sun in the 10th;* tr Uranus conjoined Mars and Jupiter squared Mars in the 12th. The TP Moon and Midheaven squared Neptune in the 8th, TP Ascendant was conjunct Neptune in the 8th, and Neptune in the 8th is the natal midpoint of Hussein's Sun/Moon!

326 SA Mars=Sun/Moon, SA Mercury (ruler of 6th) opposed Moon, SA MC conjunct Mars in the 12th with *SA Saturn opposed Mercury.* Tr Uranus applying to square the Midheaven and tr Saturn applying to square the Ascendant. TP chart for February 1, 1998: Sun=Saturn, Saturn=Venus, Jupiter=Sun, Moon=Neptune (natal Sun/Moon), all exact.

327 SA Neptune conjunct the king's Sun, tr Saturn conjunct the 4th cusp opposed the Midheaven. Jordan's SA Saturn conjunct the Ascendant (August 1998), *tr Pluto conjunct the fourth* and tr Saturn conjunct Mercury, ruler of the Ascendant and Midheaven, in July 1999.

Transition of power should be very positive, completed grandly, perhaps in May (the Summer) of 2000. Provisions to shift from monarchy to democracy thereafter will be made.[328*]

As the world becomes smaller through trade, communications, and travel, we can ask if it becomes more intelligent as well, more aware of neighbors' histories, spirit, and natural land assets. Will the collisions settle into cohesion? In the large view, astrology can suggest broadly but strongly that, yes, the world is coming together, geographically, commercially, *and* philosophically as well.[329*]

Real-time communications inform and bind people with each other's struggles and achievements. Populations have more to say about their destiny. Trade and investment dramatize interdependence. And the restless spirit of various beliefs in God—perhaps following the Vatican's unifying example within Christendom (see page 38) early in the next Millennium, more than ever before, will find understanding with grace and coexistence with honor.

Fracture and Failure in Africa

The continent of Africa is an enormous bulbous geographic barrier between West and East, between the Atlantic world and India. Portuguese and Spanish explorers in the fifteenth century traced discoveries along all the coasts of Africa, making inroads into western and eastern Africa to mine gold, gather ivory, and capture slaves, en route to the mysteries and riches of India and beyond. The Arabs of northern Africa and the native Swahili had competition.

The long, treacherous southern route around the Cape of Africa become established, and the British joined the expansion and stationed themselves strategically to protect their gains. The French followed also, pursuing riches down through the fertile Levant area of the eastern Mediterranean (the Middle East) and into northern Africa, á la Napoleon's expedition to Egypt in 1798.

---

328 The king: SA Saturn opposed Midheaven (11/00); SP Moon conjunct the Midheaven (06/00), tr Uranus square Sun, tr Saturn opposed Sun, tr Mars opposed Sun, tr Jupiter opposed Midheaven 03-06/00). TP Jupiter square Sun, TP Moon conjunct Ascendant, TP Mars conjunct the fourth, TP Ascendant conjunct the Moon, TP Sun opposed Venus—all exact—May 12, 2000. For Jordan: SA Jupiter exactly opposed the Midheaven and SP Moon exactly conjunct the Descendant in May 2000.

329 Pluto in Sagittarius supported by Uranus and Neptune in Aquarius 1999–2003.

The whole of North Africa was opened to imperial expansion by "European predators" because of the decay of the formal over-lordship of the Ottoman sultan (the Turkish rule of that area of the world).[330]

The Suez Canal

The passageway between the Mediterranean and the Red Sea, out through the Arabian Sea and on to India, called the Suez Canal, is not a modern achievement; the short-cut was explored in antiquity (in the twentieth century B.C.E., several hundreds of years before Israel's King David), was later developed by Persian conquerors and then the Romans, but was abandoned in the eighth century C.E. Modern construction by the French took place in 1859–69.

Free passage and political neutrality were chartered for the Canal in times of peace and war, and Britain was the guard of that neutrality. But after World War II, Egypt pressed for British with-drawal. Egypt's Gamal Abdal Nassar then nationalized the Canal in 1956. Israel was denied access.

Supported by the French and the British, Israel invaded Egypt October 29, 1956, and the United Nations took over the Canal. Yet, Egypt still prevented Israel from using the waterway. During the Arab-Israeli War of 1967 (the "Six-Day War," page 113), the Canal became the border between Egypt and the Israeli-occupied Sinai Peninsula, and was closed.

After the war of 1973, Egypt and Israel withdrew from the Sinai. Both banks of the Canal reverted to Egyptian control, and the waterway was reopened in 1975.

Technology and Change

With improved medicines to fight African diseases (especially qui-nine against malaria) and steam propelling ships faster and more safely, European intrusion and rule bloomed under the guise of pro-tecting trade and investment. The technology of the Europeans was miraculous to the Africans. Upon this impression, missionaries and investors followed to enlighten the "Dark Continent" with the "blessings of civilization." The colossal extension of European power transformed African history.

---

330 Roberts, 652–658.

The suppression of inter-tribal warfare, the improvement of medical care, and the introduction of new foods encouraged enormous population growth among the Africans. The *need* for European skills, services, and structures grew similarly. Colonization by the British and the French was rampant. When one power got a new concession or a colony, it almost always spurred on other powers to go one better. The process was surprisingly peaceful, so dominant were the Europeans.[331]

In the 1950s and 1960s, Africa underwent a dramatic *de*colonization. With the pull-out of imperial powers, fragile infrastructures wobbled. A thrust to nationhood, in emulation of the former colonizers, followed the boundary lines of the colonies, and often enclosed peoples of many different tribal languages, gene stocks, and customs. Disruption threatened and erupted.

The doctrine of nationalism appealed to the elite African leaders who were European educated and mercenary despots who were kingly-riches motivated. But, in the isolationism that always accompanies national birth, the new states/nations of Africa still desperately required economic resources, capital, and marketing facilities, which could only come in the near future from the world outside (and white South Africa was for a long time regarded as "outside" by many black politicians).

On March 6, 1957, British Togoland and its Gold Coast colony united and were granted independence within the Commonwealth of Nations as the state of Ghana, the first ex-colonial new nation to emerge in sub-Saharan Africa. In the next twenty-seven years, twelve wars were fought in Africa and thirteen heads of state were assassinated.[332]

The "Belgian" Congo was particularly severe in its eruption, with the Soviet Union and the United States taking sides in the civil strife. Then, on May 30, 1967, the eastern region of Nigeria, stronghold of the Ibo tribe, was declared the independent Republic of Biafra. Nigerian national forces invaded Biafra on July 6 and a civil war continued.

And so it goes. The fractured state of African self-rule had unstable roots: the long history and human drama of being chattel in the European (and American) slave trade, the sense of political (educational) inferiority, and, as a country of self-isolating nations, there

331 Ibid, 656.
332 Ibid, 856.

was little hope of being taken seriously and respected by the powers of the world. The sense of black inferiority and white supremacy led to the harsh demarcation of *apartheid*, the policy of strict racial segregation practiced in South Africa after 1948 by the National Party government to maintain the domination of the white minority. The platform attracted the enmity of all the black world.

There was indeed an attempt in 1958 to found a United States of Africa, but the thrust of collective dignity and safety took until May 22–26, 1963 to form as the Organization for African Unity (OAU), under the leadership of Ethiopian Emperor Haile Selassie. The OAU was structured to eradicate all traces of colonialism, to defend each member nation, and to promote economic, social, and welfare measures, and then the OAU was split up by civil war in Angola.[333*]

In spite of all these efforts to national integrity, the attachments of Africans remain those of family, community, tribe, ethnic group, and religion, *not* nation. This is William Pfaff's studied analysis. "Even South Africa's African National Congress, the closest there is to a modern national movement in Africa, has its basis in a tribe, the Xhosa," rivalled in extremism by the Zulu tribe.[334]

The KwaZulu in the state of Natal, the headquarters of Mangosuthu Buthelezi, President Nelson Mandela's chief rival, fight on. The new obstacle is South Africa's new constitution due to be completed by July 1996: Buthelezi is demanding virtual autonomy for his province, including letting the eight million KwaZulus (the majority living in Natal) have their own army. But these subnational, extended tribal considerations do not fit in with Mandela's ANC Party's desire for a unified country with authority in the hands of elected officials. Buthelezi has exhorted more than 40,000 tribal elders and their followers to "rise and resist." On December 25, 1995, some 800 attackers arrived at Izingolweni south of Durban and attacked the village, raging, maiming, and killing from house to house. The men had AK-47s; the women set the huts on fire. The local ANC leader was found near his hut, castrated and disemboweled.[335*]

---

333 The chart for the OAU Conference, May 26, 1963, in Addis Ababa, Ethiopia (say, for noon) shows a terribly fractious profile and outlook: Mars-Uranus conjunction square Mercury and Sun, and opposed Saturn, also square Mercury.

334 Pfaff, 134–135.

335 *New York Times*, January 7, 1996, 1. Nelson Mandela, July 18, 1918, at 2:54 P.M. EET, Umtata South Africa (28E47; 31S35); source: Noel Tyl rectification proofed by Rod Suskin of Cape Town, South Africa. Then, after this process, Mandela himself reports "2:45."

Pfaff states that democracy will fail in Africa, "in most places at least, because the civil society, civil culture, and enlightened middle class essential to democracy are not there." [336]*

The frequent upheavals and changes baffle astrology in its need to establish a reliable time for the birth of any nation. In astrological and political perspective, Africa is undeniably unpredictable.

So, as the world grows smaller, as grand markets homogenize and demarcate themselves to gird the globe, the African barrier still exists at the political level. The continent is called the "Third World," a racial, geographic, and culturally isolating label for a world trying to understand itself, establish the reliability of its roots, leave a stormy winter and take its position in the supposedly enlightened world upon which it depends.

---

336 Pfaff, 157.

6

THE
UNION OF
EUROPE

The Balkans —
Europe's Future Bridge to the East

The Balkan region begins directly across the Adriatic Sea from Italy. The region forms the massive headland above Greece, with the former Yugoslavia in the West abutting Romania and Bulgaria to the East, which are in turn bordered by the Black Sea and the great peninsular city of Istanbul (Constantinople). The region is at the crossroads of European and Asian civilizations. Ancient Greece, the Byzantine Empire, and the Ottoman Empire flourished there throughout the ages.[337]

The former Yugoslavia was comprised of six states and several subsidiary territories. The larger and most influential are (West to East) Croatia, Bosnia, and Serbia [*think* "C-B-S"]. Since 1991, the Serbs have clashed with the Croats with the fighting centered in Bosnia, between Croatia and Serbia.

Pfaff attributes the Balkan War of the 1990s to the Serbian protest in 1902 about the existence of the distinct Croat nation.

---

337 *Ottoman* is the designation for Turkey's former vast empire. The term was derived through English mispronunciation of the name of the great Sultan Osman I who entered Asia Minor in the late thirteenth century. The Turks then entered the Balkans in 1345, securing Constantinople in 1453. At its Zenith under Sultan Suleiman I in the mid-sixteenth century—having annexed lands extending to the Persian Gulf, embracing the entire southern coastline of the Mediterranean as well, including Alexandria—Suleiman began to advance into Austria. He failed to capture Vienna, and the grand Ottoman Empire began its decline. The Turkish fleet was annihilated in the Eastern Mediterranean in 1571. The vestiges of the Empire were completely reorganized finally during the First World War.

When, in 1918, there was the enforced mingling of the two ethnic peoples in the Yugoslav monarchy, which the Serbs dominated, the Croats became frustrated as well.

The religious dimension complicates the issue: the Ottoman invasion of Serbia late in the fourteenth century introduced Islam to Serbia. Gradually, over 250 years, the Muslims became an absolute majority in the territory of modern Bosnia as well. Through this religious outreach, the Muslims of Bosnia (the main central region are Islamicized Serbs, and the Croats (those people with roots in Croatia farther West) are chiefly Catholic Serbs. *Serbs*—Muslim or Catholic—could not tolerate the central importance of Bosnia.[338]

The borders of these states, with the people behind them all sharing the same language, are exceedingly porous: trade, intermarriage, travel, and give-and-take skirmishes have mixed up the populations. This demands terminology elastic enough to describe the many ethnic and political factions fighting with each other within the larger picture of Serbian insistence of regional dominance: there are the Serbian Croats, the Bosnian Serbs, the Croatian Serbs, the Bosnian Muslims, etc. In the main, the fight pits Muslim and Catholic Serbs anywhere against the Muslims of Croatia and Bosnia.

The Mujahideen are the Islamic foreigners (mercenaries) imported to help the Bosnian Muslims in their fight against the Serbs. They are dedicated to defending Bosnia to the death: "Bosnia is a sacred Islamic land. It is our duty to defend it from occupation." Sarajevo, the capital of Bosnia, has become the "Jerusalem" of the Balkans.[339]

Croatia's Assembly president, elected in 1991, Zarko Domljan, has observed, "Yugoslavia is not a nation—it is a mixture of ancient tribes," and news stories about those tribes refer regularly to the "whirlwind of hatreds" there.[340] While the combat of the ethnic tribes involved in the complicated conflict is centuries old, the escalation of it to a war among nation states goes back only to post-World War I American policy and the setting of arbitrary boundaries.

---

338 Malcom 54, 226–227.

339 *The European*, January 4–10, 1996, 2. And Sarajevo, of course, was the scene at which the First World War was ignited. See page xxx.

340 Barber, 195–196.

American president Woodrow Wilson believed that he (the United States) could make over international life by arbitrarily setting the new boundaries of countries within defeated Europe in terms of ethnic nationhood. The plan was to create frontiers and boundaries by drawing map lines where concentrations of ethnic groups and natural landfalls dictated, so that ethnic entities could be granted self-determination without triggering new European rivalries.

The results of those new boundaries, with the pressure cooking over seventy years in Yugoslavia, for example, erupted in the four-year Balkan war, with realities of ethnic cleansing horrors on both sides, and a bitterly negotiated peace under NATO and United States military surveillance and control achieved in December 1995.

The Balkan war has not been a war of good versus evil, according to Charles G. Boyd, former Deputy commander in Chief, U.S. European Command: "All factions in the former Yugoslavia have pursued the same objective—avoiding minority status in Yugoslavia or any successor state."

■ Prediction …

Peace in the Balkans Can Not Hold—The utopian view for larger states of the greater Bosnia area (Croatia and Serbia, Macedonia, and Montenegro especially) into a series of mini-states, proud and self-sufficient, will eventually have its fulfillment. The instrument to this eventuality will be renewed warring among the factions.[342]

Serbia will break the peace or jeopardize it in March–October 1997 at the familiar city centers in Bosnia and Croatia.

---

341 *Foreign Affairs* magazine, September/October 1995, "Making Peace with the Guilty," by Charles G. Boyd, page 24.

342 It is important to note that Greece is railing strongly with Macedonia, which seceded from Yugoslavia in 1991, about the state's use of the name "Macedonia." To avoid the spread of Balkan conflict into Greece, Bulgaria, Albania, and Turkey, President Slobodan Milosevic of Serbia has *not recognized* Macedonia, considering it part of southern Serbia, and has had a trade embargo imposed since February 1994 (which costs Macedonia about $50 million per month). The United Nations has a peace-keeping force in Macedonia (birthplace of Alexander the Great). *New York Times*, May 14, 1995. *The European*, September 14–20, 1995.

We can expect much more about this situation in June–November 1996 (Macedonia sovereignty: January 25, 1991, at noon, CET in Skopje, Yugoslavia [Campion, *World Horoscopes*]: tr Uranus conjunct Sun, tr Pluto conjunct 7th).

The United States will be militarily involved (especially in the 1997 period), with enormous national outcry *against* the involvement in the United States.[343*]

In the 1480s, Leonardo da Vinci conceived of a bridge from Istanbul to Pera, a link between Europe and Asia. Leonardo's design was amazingly modern, with a colossal span of 240 meters. He presented his plans to the Turks and there was no response; they didn't believe it could be done.

Now in the Balkans—with Rumania already fallen, with Albania suffering terribly, with Greece anxious about its loss in tourism from the devastation to its north—and the Serbs poised to erupt from a cold peace settlement, the open bridge from Europe to Asia still must be built. One day, Europe *will* extend through the Balkans to the Ural Mountains, with the ministates federated somehow within the European Union, but that must wait for negotiation in Summer 2000, when Serbia is finally appeased, and the togetherness of world markets is that much closer.

Germany: Fall and Winter

Not only is Germany the center of Europe geographically, Germany was also all-pervasive in early European military and cultural history. German tribes began to expand their outreach in the second century B.C.E. They were contained by the Romans for some 300 years, but then finally overran the Roman Empire with enormous migrations. Intermarriages constructed complex networks of influence and territorial possession throughout the continent and into the Eastern world.

---

343 Serbian Minority Republic-in-Bosnia chart, March 27, 1992, at 12:00 P.M. in Sarajevo: peace with SA Mercury conjunct Midheaven but *tr Neptune conjunct the 7th*. In late Spring 1996: tr Neptune conjunct the 7th; in 1997, tr Saturn conjunct the Sun with tr Neptune on the 7th; March 1999, SA Neptune opposed Ascendant, SA Pluto square Mars, ruler of the Midheaven.

Serbia chart: July 13, 1878, at 2:58 P.M., LMT in Belgrade. Peace with *SA Neptune conjunct Midheaven*. Tr Saturn conjunct Saturn, April 1996, January 1997. SA Sun conjunct Ascendant March 2000.

Croatia chart: June 25, 1991, at 6:10 P.M. CED in Zagreb. Note Croatia's peregrine Sun in Cancer and Serbia's peregrine Sun in Cancer! Peace with tr Pluto conjunct Ascendant. Tr Uranus conjunct Saturn in Spring 1996; February and September–November 1997, tr Saturn square Sun and tr Uranus conjunct Saturn again. In September–October 2000, tr Saturn conjunct the 7th and tr Neptune conjunct Saturn.

All chart data, Campion, *World Horoscopes*.

As the Middle Ages began in the tenth century, political and financial localization gave birth to feudalism, numerous fiefs and duchies ruled by elite families and supported by serfs. For trade and protection, one leader would pledge fealty to another leader of higher rank and greater resources. The pledge would be profound and have lifelong significance—and life and death import as well—from serf to vassal to duke to prince to king. Eventually, with the crowning of the mightiest military monarch Otto I, King of Saxony (the most powerful territory), King of the Lombards in Italy, subduer of the Poles and Bohemians and Hungarians, invader of France, ally of the pope (John XII), as Emperor of all others, the Holy Roman Empire came into being in 962, centered in Germany.[344*]

Otto then deposed the pope, named the successor Leo VIII, suppressed a Roman revolt and installed a new pope, Benedict V, and yet another, John XIII, who also was driven out by yet another revolt. Otto then invaded Italy for a second time and then arranged a strategic marriage between his son and successor, Otto II, and a Byzantine princess.

In addition to all his warring and positioning for control, Otto brought to Germany its first unification, unification that had never been known in the sprawling domain. Intellectually and artistically, he also brought about a grand national flowering and productivity that became known as the Ottonian Renaissance, Germany's first Summer.

Upon Otto's death in 973, everything collapsed, and for five years there were violent civil wars as powerful city states challenged Otto II. The feuding and territorialization of Germany promoted a fall into enormous fragmentation, extending into the fourteenth century: there were "bewildering congeries of independent units, governed under separate rulers and recognizing only the vaguest connection with the Imperial authority ... The German crown was a nullity and German unity a mere facade."[345]

---

344 Otto I was born October 23, 0912 (Sun in Scorpio, probably Moon conjunct Uranus in Aquarius, Jupiter square Saturn-Pluto) and was crowned Holy Roman Emperor by Pope John XII in Rome on February 2, 0962, probably near noon (the event chart is revealing). Axelrod & Phillips, 227–228.

345 Craig, 17.

The Holy Roman Empire

The Holy Roman Empire—in fluctuating degrees of solidarity and upset—included all the German lands, Austria, and modern West Czechoslovakia, Switzerland, Eastern France, and Northern and Central Italy. The emperor was usually the dominant German sovereign. The Empire was the temporal equivalent and ally of the papacy itself, *but it clashed repeatedly with the Church for the ultimate position of European supremacy.*

The Empire's stature and influence diminished with the Protestant Reformation, with theological and political schisms established between the Catholic emperor and Protestant princes. Finally Napoleon, as Emperor of the French, simply ceased to recognize the Holy Roman Empire in 1806 and reorganized the many territories and factions of Germany into the Confederation of the Rhine under French protection. Emperor Francis II of Austria then abdicated the imperial title to end the Empire.

The First Reich

Otto I, the Holy Roman Empire, became the First *Reich* (the German word for kingdom, empire: *rrighchh*) in the view of historians of the nineteenth century. Its collapse was precipitated by the Reformation and rampant territorialization, as we have seen, and by the Thirty Years War (1618–1648). This was a grievous Catholic-Protestant religious conflict that devastated Germany in particular (by then, viewed as a lesser power, torn apart and disunited). Politically, the European powers warred against the Hapsburgs, who at that time were ruling the Holy Roman Empire. All powers wanted more power; each religion wanted to better the other; all powers were afraid of each other, with the common enemy being the Hapsburgs from Austria.[346]

In the extended fighting over a generation, Germany suffered a population loss of about 35%, declining from twenty-one million people to about twelve and one-half million! The settlement of the War in 1648 actually compounded the problems of destruction and impoverishment: Germany was deprived of access to the sea, and, to

---

346 The Hapsburg dynasty infiltrated and seeded the monarchies of many countries of Europe through conquest and marriage: Germany, Austria, Hungary, Bohemia, and Spain. The last ruler, Charles I, emperor of Austria and king of Hungary, abdicated in 1918.

preserve its low-threat fragmentation within the European overview, over 300 German states were recognized as sovereign entities. German disunity and powerlessness became part of the natural European order. A Germany *unified* would undermine the European balance of power.[347]

Gordon A. Craig, Professor of Humanities at Stanford University, in his award-winning study *The Germans*, shows that the power of the German princes was actually *enhanced* by the long, horrible war. While the land holder who survived the war with assets rose in status and significance (the landed aristocracy), the devastated, provincial citizenry were engulfed with suffering. The separation between social strata was dramatically defined. The people's only reliable tie—security—with the elite was through obedience. The daily presence of death had made the German people willing to submit to any authority that appeared able to avert a recurrence of the terror. This socio-political obedience became linked with religious ethic. By the end of the eighteenth century, the nation-states of Germany had developed one cultural trait in common: obedience to the protectors. It endured through World War II, and undoubtedly to today.[348]

The Second Reich

The Second Reich belonged to the era of Otto von Bismarck (1815–1898), Chancellor of the Empire under Kaiser Wilhelm I (William I, 1797–1888).[349]* Prussia had become the most powerful state among all the German sections. William became king of Prussia after his older brother was declared insane. William appointed von Bismarck his prime minister in 1862. From then on, until William's death, Bismarck, the "Iron Chancellor," guided the militaristic policies (defeating Austria in the Austro-Prussian War and Napoleon III in the Franco-Prussian War; see page 179) and shaped the ascendant destiny of Prussia and, later, of the whole of Germany, when Wilhelm became Emperor (Kaiser) of all Germany.

---

347 Craig, 17, 20–21.

348 Ibid, 22–23.

349 Bismarck: April 1, 1815 at 1:30 P.M. LMT (between 1 and 2 P.M.) in Schoenhausen, Germany; Kaiser Wilhelm, March 22, 1797, at 2:00 P.M., LMT in Berlin. Coronation: January 18, 1871, at 11:50 A.M. in Versailles (Swiss astrologer Claude Weiss says 1:00 P.M.). Taeger Archives, 1* classifications.

These two leaders *re-created Germany unity*. Radical factions fought against their military ways and against Bismarck's struggle with the Catholic Church. There were assassination attempts upon William's life, but Bismarck pressed forward strongly with the late-coming, roaring industrial revolution and levied severe legislation against socialist movements to control the middle class.

In spite of all, Germany was united and once again powerful. It was again Summer. The State was decidedly authoritarian; it did not recognize the practice of popular sovereignty and the concept of self-government that were the current thought in the rest of Europe, having issued from the Enlightenment movement of the late eighteenth century in France (see "Enlightenment," page 176). Germany had been isolated from the humanist movement during the protracted duress of the Thirty Years War.

Craig observes that unity of society, the concept of a common law, a Natural Law among people, answering the fundamental demand for personal liberty and the right of the people to control the leaders they themselves had chosen, was "uncongenial to the German mind." Instead, the Germans developed an *inner* state of specialness, the concept that the German nation was a unique expression of culture.[350]

This was a self-absorption that separated Germany from the enlightened drive in Europe that was working to enrich mankind through reason and unity. It was self-aggrandizement that was extreme and it defined the nation's profile entering the twentieth century.

On June 28, 1914, in Sarajevo, the Austrian-Hungarian province of Bosnia, Franz Ferdinand, the heir to the Austro-Hungarian throne, and his wife were assassinated by a Serbian nationalist. One month later, on July 28, Austria-Hungary declared war on Serbia. Russia began to mobilize its forces to aid compatriot Slavs. Germany wanted the Russians out of the flare-up and sought to defend its new ally Austria. Germany declared war on Russia on August 1. (Austria followed suit on August 6.)

---

350 Craig, 33. This sense of German spirit is captured eloquently by Richard Wagner in the final staement of poet Hans Sachs in the opera *Die Meistersinger von Nuernberg*: "and if we Germans ever should fall to any foreign land, no Prince will understand us, but the art that is German and true will live on. Honor your German Masters and give them their due: though the Holy Roman Empire is gone, the holy German art remains." ["Sachs: *"Uns draueuen ueble Streich .... die heil'ge deutsche Kunst!"*]

Essentially, this very first conflict that was extended to involve the whole world of nations began as an essentially European war between the triple alliance of Russia, France, and Britain on one side and the powers of Germany and Austria-Hungary on the other. Serbia and Belgium were drawn in; Turkey and Bulgaria joined Germany and Austria; Italy was brought in by Germany; Greece, Romania, and Portugal were involved; Japan rushed to take over German positions in the Far East and the Western Pacific.

On February 3, 1917, the Germans announced their plan for unrestricted submarine warfare, President Wilson severed diplomatic relations with Germany, and the Germans sank the United States liner, the *Housatonic*. Brazil, Bolivia, and Peru immediately broke diplomatic relations with Germany, and then, two months later, the United States declared war on Germany.[351]

The most devastating war of world history—a terrible Winter—ended with the Treaty of Versailles, June 28, 1919. The dead numbered 8.4 million. The German Reich crumpled. The old rulers of the German states were swept off their thrones by the Liberal movement, and a new constitution was framed with a centralized federal government. It was ratified at the industrial and cultural center of Weimar *[veye'-mahr]* in middle eastern Germany. Germany became known as the Weimar Republic and was headed first by Freidrich Ebert. The postwar years were marked by economic crises, mass unemployment, rampant currency inflation, and the strengthening of the extreme right wing.

When Ebert died, Paul von Hindenburg was elected president. The world economic depression of 1929 further hurt Germany's recovery. Political and social tensions mounted. For a more energetic approach to solve the problems, the tired, aged middle-of-the-road Hindenburg appointed Adolf Hitler chancellor in January 1933.

---

351 Hobsbawn, 24. This *Housatonic* was the namesake of the Union ship, the *Housatonic*, sunk by the Confederate submarine *H. L. Hunley* on February 17, 1864 in Charleston Harbor. Another celebrated ship, a luxury transatlantic passenger liner, named the *Lusitania*, was also sunk by German submariners, thinking the ship loaded with explosives for the war, on May 7, 1915.

The Third Reich

The Third Reich—the new kingdom—belongs to Adolf Hitler.[352*] Germany was united under his spell. It was again a new Summer.

Joachim C. Fest, author of *Hitler: A Biography*, offers three key reasons for Hitler's success with the German people at the outset of the passionate movement. First, there is *die grosse Angst* (the Great Fear), a panic about the growth of the Communist Revolution and the relentless advance of modernization, that these dimensions would erode Germany's cultural and moral values. The Jews were seen as the people who would benefit from such urbanization and industrialization. They were foreigners, not genuinely German. All of this led to a tremendous longing in Germany for its romantic past.

Second, there was Hitler's extraordinary oratorical skill, a personalization of communication that addressed the private fears about Germany's dilution, weakening and disappearance—all of which had occurred before and were alive in memory still. And third, Hitler offered a dream, a salvation through the means of art and myth.[353]

Hitler had accomplished an enormous amount by peaceful means to raise the living standard for Germans. The people could not deny progress. Anything unpleasant was disregarded. Hitler's evil deeds—even his personal gruffness—were mere blemishes compared with his accomplishments for the Fatherland.[354*]

---

352 There are occult references to the labeling of Germany's historical kingdoms (Reiche in the plural): that Atlantis was the First; the flowering of Europe in the Renaissance, the Second; and the Hitler projection as the Third. One can not take this seriously in its extremism, but it does indicate a powerful sensitivity to the sense of destiny within the Hitler movement. And, as corroborated by the German Historical Society of Washington, D.C., there was a projected Fourth Reich referring to post-Apocolypse projections of the world purged by war for the return of the Messiah and 1,000 years of peace. [Hitler blended the two, claiming his third Reich would last a thousand years. This infers his own Messianic nature.]

   Hitler: April 20, 1889 at 6:30 P.M., LMT, Braunau am Inn, Austria. Taeger Archives 1*, widespread usage.

353 Craig, extensive discussion, Chapter 3.

354 The Third Reich began with Hitler's appointment as Chancellor: January 30, 1933 at 11:15 A.M. in Berlin. *Neptune is peregrine*, ruling the 12th, with the Moon in the 12th in 5 Aries. And there is an Earth Grand Trine forming among Venus, Mars-Jupiter, and the Taurus Ascendant. Campion, World Horoscopes, #126.

   The beginning of World War II (the Germans opening fire on Polish-occupied points in Danzig) was September 1, 1939 at 4:17 A.M., CET at Danzig, Poland. There is an Earth Grand Trine and the Moon-Jupiter conjunction in 2 and 7 Aries conjoins the 12th House *Reich* Moon. The Uranus at 21 Taurus conjoins the Reich Venus at 20 Capricorn and the Midheaven at 24, opposed by Pluto at 21 Cancer. The Sun was conjunct the Reich Neptune. Campion, *World Horoscopes*, #427.

Hitler began World War II on September 1, 1939, without a declaration of war, with his invasion of Poland. In Spring 1940, Hitler invaded Denmark and Norway, Luxembourg, the Netherlands, and Belgium, and advanced into France.

Italy declared war on France and Great Britain in June 1940 and invaded Greece from conquered Albania late in the year. Great Britain and France declared war on Germany on September 3. (See "The Vichy Republic," page 181.)

From July to December 1940, the Battle of Britain was fought in the skies over England as the German Luftwaffe sought to destroy the Royal Air Force.

At the same time, Japan began an invasion of northern Indochina and signed a pact with Germany and Italy that bound each of the nations to declare war on any nation that warred against any one of them.

Germany then overran both Greece and Yugoslavia in April 1941 and began its invasion of Russia.

Japan had occupied all of French Indochina and then reached across the Pacific to strike Pearl Harbor on December 7, 1941. The United States declared war against Japan on December 8, 1941, and Germany declared war on the United States on December 11.[355]

The Second World War ended with Hitler's suicide on April 30, 1945, shortly after 3:00 P.M.[356] The formal ceremonies of surrender ended at 11:01 P.M. CET on May 8, 1945 in Berlin.[357*]

Germany Divided

Out of this War emerged the strains and fears of still another world tension, the Cold War. The Soviet Union, which the United States had recognized officially in 1933 (on November 16, after a year of Nazi build-up), had common cause with the United States against

---

355 With Japan so completely in control of Indochina (the strategic western area of the Pacific Market as studied in this volume), the United States was outraged and threatened. The U.S. put severe economic pressure on Japan, whose trade and supply lines (then as now) depended entirely on maritime communications. It was this conflict that led to the attack of Japan and the Pacific war.

It was irrational for Hitler, fully extended into Russia, having conquered most of Europe, to have declared war on the United States and given the U.S. the opening to enter the European war on the British side. Hobsbawm, 41.

356 Craig, 61. Taeger Archives says 3:30 P.M. Hitler's mistress, Eva Braun, committed suicide with Hitler.

357 Campion, *World Horoscopes*, #428.

Hitler, who represented "a greater danger than each of the two saw in the other."[358]

Stalin feared any reunification of Germany, except under government leadership he could control. The memories of German attack from the West were too strong for him to trust a united Germany (the old fear from the end of the Thirty Years War). That a united Germany might be capitalist made it worse.

Stalin ingratiated the Soviet Union further with the United States by entering the continuing war against Japan in the Pacific within three months of Germany's surrender in Europe. At the Yalta Conference, on the Black Sea in southwest Russia, February 4–11, 1945, Winston Churchill, Franklin Roosevelt, and Joseph Stalin divided Germany into four zones of occupation, the fourth one to go to the French. Additionally, a four-power commission would control the city of Berlin. Russia was given extra considerations in the Pacific and *Korea* (see page 69). These plans were confirmed and made more specific at the follow-up Potsdam Conference in East Germany among the leaders July 17–August 2, 1945 [Truman in place of the deceased Roosevelt]—Germany was divided.[359*]

The Astro-profile of Western Germany, the Federal Republic of Germany (Bundesrepublik Deutschland) is determined by two horoscopes.[360*] The astro-profiles are echoes of one another: each promises prosperity from hard work, a tremendous sense of

---

358 Hobsbawm, 143.

359 The Communist German Democratic Republic, installed October 7, 1949, achieved complete independence from the Soviet military authorities with the announcement to that effect made on March 25, 1954, at 11:30 P.M. CET in Berlin. [Campion, *World Horoscopes*, #128]. This chart stands up strongly to test: note the importance of Mars in Sagittarius conjunct the Moon, opposed Jupiter: Mars rules the 5th, Mars-Jupiter, all classic references to athletics, i.e., East Germany's Olympics record.

Note as well, the Scorpio 12th House and its ruler, Pluto retrograde square to the Ascendant: a tremendous suppression of the people. The dreaded Stasi Secret Police and informer network among the people employed about one of every 25 adults; it was the "sword and shield of the party." See Jarausch, 35.

Neptune=Neptune, SA Saturn=Moon. The demise of the GDR was coming on for almost four years (SA Pluto=MC).

360 Signing of the Constitution: May 23, 1949, at 4:00 P.M. CED, Bonn, Germany. At the fall of the wall: SA MC conjunct MC, SA Saturn conjunct Ascendant, SP Moon conjunct Ascendant, tr Saturn conjunct the fourth cusp, tr Pluto square Pluto, tr Neptune square Neptune.

Full independence from the Allied powers: May 5, 1955, at Bonn (noon mark). At the fall of the wall: SA Venus conjunct Sun, SA Sun conjunct Mars, SA Jupiter-Uranus square Mercury; SP Moon opposed Jupiter-Uranus; tr Pluto opposed Sun.

Campion, *World Horoscopes*, #129, 131, respectively.

responsibility (guilt?), and keen involvement with internationalism. In its division, the Federal Republic is seeking unity with the
rest of Europe, the rest of the world.[361*]

And another dimension shows remarkably: the dream, the
vision—and the bewilderment, the possible deception—within the
German ethos. This dimension was present as well in the Astro-
profile of the horoscope for Hitler's Third Reich: extreme run-away
vision, and we can recall Hitler's "management of art and myth" the
colossal images of glory built by Albert Speer, Hitler's architect and
Armaments/Production Minister, for the gigantic rallies, the
imagery used by Hitler to ally the Germans with the pantheon of
the gods.[362*]

When the Berlin Wall toppled in November 1989, a national-
izing—"blinding"—euphoria gripped Germany. Chancellor Helmut Kohl, Germany's most influential politician leader of the
postwar generation in Germany, a Catholic, heading the Christian
Democratic Union, embraced the reunification of Germany with
fervor: his speeches conjured up *a vision of instant prosperity.* When
the necessary laws were passed, "thousands of entrepreneurs"
would come to invest "and quickly build, together with you, a
flourishing land." Kohl referred to the proven "safety net" of the
West as Germany's safeguard within the stupendous challenge of a
vastly expanded German responsibility.[363*]

While the reunited Germany was smaller and less threatening
than before the world wars, it was now increased by 41,817 square
miles, making it the third largest state on the continent, with about
137,931 square miles of territory. Berlin was restored as a metropo-
lis of some 3.5 million, and the national population increased by
16.34 million to 78.42 million—overnight.[364*]

The Astro-profile of the new Germany brings together in
remarkable, dramatic fashion the pervasiveness of hard work and
responsibility, the allure of the dream, and outreach of (and problems with) internationalism, and prosperity. The unification of

---

361 Each horoscope has Saturn strong with Sun and Neptune strong with Moon. Each
   horoscope's 2nd and 9th and 10th and 11th Houses are strongly emphasized.

362 The Neptune dimension. See earlier footnotes.

363 Jarausch, 125. Helmut Kohl: April 3, 1930, 6:30 A.M. CET at Ludwigshafen, Germany.
   Moon squared by Neptune; Sun squared by Saturn, a dramatic echo of German national charts. Taeger Archives, 1*.

364 Ibid, 197.

Germany is a unification within a national horoscope as well.[365*]

The Astro-profile echoes the rise and fall pattern seen through-out Germany's history. The Indian Summer of unification has quickly given way to the chill of new perspectives: the augmented responsibilities of internationalism that challenged the capacities of the people to continue the dream and develop success.

The Immigration Problem

Before unification, Germany had adopted a policy of grace and practicality to admit any immigrant who wished asylum from an oppressive homeland regime, to support the immigrant until the case would be thoroughly studied by the government. The policy of "Return" was an open invitation to restless or oppressed minorities in other countries to seek a new start in Germany. The policy was later absorbed into Chancellor Willy Brandt's *Ostpolitik* in the early 1970s, the political program designed to improve Germany's relations with Eastern Europe, which included treaties of non-aggression and cooperation with the Soviet Union and Poland.[366]

For Germany, the influx of immigrants was a supplementary work force during the post-war boom years in the 1950s and '60s. The immigrants are called *Gastarbeiter (gahst'ahr-bey-et-er)*, "guest workers." In Germany (and France), unskilled migrants from North Africa and Turkey make up 60% and 80% of total migrant flow, respectively.[367]

During 1993 alone, some 430,000 newcomers arrived in Germany while only 250,000 ethnic Germans resettled in Germany, and East Germans continued to move West. The housing shortage was severely aggravated. Serious concern was focused on the profile of being "German," upon what criteria can be used to determine citizenship: it can be easier for a child, for example, whose family

---

365 Date of political union: October 3, 1990, at Midnight to begin that day, for Berlin (the spiritual and future formal capital, the unification scene). Campion: *World Horoscopes*, #133. Saturn conjunct Neptune, both square Sun, ruling the Ascendant and 2nd; Moon in Pisces in the 9th; Mars rules the 10th, trine Sun. Mercury in Virgo conjunct Venus in Libra. And Note: Sun/Moon=Aries Point (public thrust, leadership); Sun=Mars/Saturn (enormous challenge, breakdown potential, weakness), MC=Mars/Jupiter=Neptune; Uranus-Saturn-Neptune square Sun-MC axis. This is the horoscope for today's Germany.

366 The policy allowed enormous numbers of discontented foreigners to enter Germany to find a better life. Germany had to change its Asylum Law in 1993 to allow German authorities to repel unqualified applicants at the point of entry. Asylum applications plummeted from 438,191 in 1992 to approximately 127,000 in 1995. *New York Times*, January 7, 1996, E6.

367 World Bank study, 6.

lived in Russia for 200 years (a descendant from the ethnic Germans brought over by Catherine the Great as workers) to return to Germany and become a German citizen than it is for an American or for the German-born child of a Turkish *Gastarbeiter*, even if the child speaks no Turkish and has been educated in German schools. Germany defines citizenship chiefly by bloodline.[368]

The people felt overwhelmed by unification, and, according to historian Konrad Jarausch, Professor of European Civilization at University of North Carolina, in his *The Rush to German Unity*, "young people, disoriented by the transition, blamed their problems on foreigners ... Bored teenagers turned into 'skin-heads,' adopting the forbidden symbols of a Nazi past for group identification ... Ugly public incidents erupted daily in 1992, totalling 2,200 with seventeen people dead. International observers experienced an alarming sense of *deja vu*."[369]

An example of the mounting problems—beyond the financial drain on Germany to build housing for immigrants seeking asylum, educating them to the German language, and providing schooling, shopping centers, etc.—is the two-million-strong immigrants from Turkey, more than 1.5% of Germany's total population, now working in Germany to establish a political party. Among them is the Turkish Kurdish population (approximately 500,000) now reaching for coercive strength in Germany, their host-country. The Kurdish Workers' Party (PKK) brings pressure on Germany to interact with Turkey, its NATO ally, on behalf of separatist nationalist Turkish Kurds. Kurdish activists rally sympathizers, and riots and burnings have taken place in the streets since 1992. Germany has outlawed the party.[370]

An allied problem is the rebellious youth, using the foreign immigrants as scapegoats for jobs lost to Germans, for assertion of Germanic spirit, and, to many observers, a revival and "rehabilitation" of Hitler and his vision.[371]

---

368 *New York Times*, January 7, 1996, E6: 6.9 million foreigners live in Germany, "barely a trickle" become citizens. Of two million Turks living in Germany, only 19,000 acquired German citizenship in 1994 (qualifying by having lived in Germany more than fifteen years). In 1992, 438,191 people from the Balkans, central Europe and elsewhere claimed political asylum in Germany.

369 Jarausch, 209.

370 *The European*, August 17–23, 1995; *International Herald Tribune*, November 14, 1995. Understandably, the near-success of Quebec in its secession from Canada and the explosive reorganization of Yugoslavia have encouraged all separatist movements.

371 Craig, 61.

A parallel example is dramatically obvious in Sweden—officially neutral throughout World War II and the Cold War, and declining for three decades to affiliate with the European Community or its successor, the European Union—which on November 13, 1995, did finally vote to join the European Union. New problems have migrated into Sweden's original separatist profile.

"Skinhead racism" has stunned Sweden. Over ten years, the neo-Nazi gangs have *quintupled* in number to beyond a thousand. Violence has increased as well. Swastikas abound in public display.[372]

■ Prediction ...

Social Unrest, Violence, and Political Change in Sweden— Life will change in many ways for Sweden, beginning in the Spring of 1997 and extending to April 1999. There will be demonstrations and violence by young radicals, with a complete overhaul of government coerced in the middle of 2000.[373]*

■ Prediction ...

Hitler Revival Escalates in Germany—A revival of Hitler—symbolized throughout the West by the "skinhead" movement—will continue. The revival has been in a visionary/conceptualization phase for some three years, since 1992. It should erupt and escalate sharply to another level of prominence late in the Summer of 1996 and early in 1997, in Germany first and then in Austria and elsewhere.[374]

An even more powerful third stage will occur in Spring of 1998. The vector of development is for the movement to take concrete and not insignificant political form. The unrest is extreme

---

372 *The European*, July 7–13, 1995.

373 Sweden: December 7, 1865, at 3:30 P.M. LMT in Stockholm. [Campion, *World Horoscopes*, #318] Joining EU: SA Moon just across the 7th cusp, SA Venus opposed Saturn, ruler of the 9th; SA MC opposed Sun; tr Saturn square Sun; tr Jupiter conjunct the Sun in Sagittarius.

Upheaval and change: tr Uranus conjunct the Midheaven in 1997, SA Pluto square Ascendant, tr Pluto conjunct Mars, tr Saturn square Midheaven in Summer 1998 and Spring 1999; tr Neptune conjunct Midheaven mid-2000.

374 Two neo-Nazis were apprehended in Vienna for sending a series of letter bombs which injured four people, including the mayor of Vienna. The purpose was to create a Nazi state. *The European*, September 14–20, 1995.

and, with the high unemployment—even on the decline—and high taxation, promises an incendiary state of social affairs.[375*]

In addition to the obvious "skinhead" extremists, there is an ultra-conservative, right wing movement in Germany—working in the same arena to the same goal—driven by articulate professors, aspiring politicians, and ambitious young people. They emphasize nationalism, anti-feminism, resentment of foreigners, and—quite tactically—they criticize extremism. The influence is pervasive, with 35,000 copies of the new right Journal, *Junge Freiheit* ("Young Freedom" or "Freedom for Youth"), circulated nationally (1995). The magazine is dedicated to "fighting ignorance about our nation, anti-authoritarian thought, pacifism, feminism, anti-militarism and obsession with the past."

The astrology of Germany shows all this eloquently, but it is unable to separate the liberal and conservative dimensions (as easily as the separation occurs in the astrology of the Vatican, for example; see "Vatican," page 26). The people of Germany are once again extremely bewildered and disillusioned, as they have been so many times in history, and it is time for a charismatic leader to rouse them for unity.[376*]

Germany and the European Union

The former East Germany is as well a *migrant to its stronger half.* The economic burden has been formidable and almost threatening to the stability of unified Germany.[377*] According to economics analyst Hamish McRae, the economic integration of East Germany eliminated West Germany's account surplus and cost more than $100 billion in public sector payments alone in 1992. Europe's recession in the early 1900s was in part a result of the

---

375 Progressing Hitler's horoscope into the future, extending its life influence: SA Sun=Saturn with tr Neptune square Ascendant all 1996; *tr Uranus conjunct the fourth mid-1996; SA Uranus conjunct the 4th with tr Saturn conjunct the seventh cusp and conjoining the Sun in mid-1998.* This technique is proved valid and significant in the extended lives of powerfully idolized personages in history, e.g., Eva Peron, May 7, 1919, at 5:00 A.M. Cordoba time, Los Toldos, Argentina (27 Aries 15 Ascendant). Taeger Archives, 2b; biography.

376 This is the Saturn-Uranus conjunction (conservative-liberal) in the national horoscope (October 3, 1990 at midnight, beginning that day for Berlin, see footnote, page 162), with Neptune at their midpoint (ruling the 9th, philosophy, foreigners, etc.), all square to the Sun, ruler of the Ascendant.

377 The Moon in Pisces in the 9th, Neptune conjoined with Saturn and Uranus, all square the Sun, ruler of the Ascendant, is the key concept here astrologically. Transiting Saturn through Pisces has represented the heavy burden for Germany in 9th House matters. The Moon rules the 12th.

costs of German unification, since all countries involved with the Deutsche Mark, investing in Germany (and facing raised interest rates), and trading with Germany—the world's biggest exporter— were affected in turn. In short, Germany's problems affect the rest of the world, most specifically the European Union. And the fiscal problems have slowed Germany's growth.[378] (See also, "Deutsche Mark," below.)

McRae anticipates that the potential of Germany's sluggish growth may pry the European Union apart. "Throughout its formative years, the EU never had to cope with a chronically weak German economy." The weaknesses introduced by the unification and persistent immigration flow have become pervasive and persistent. France and Italy, for example, may be forced to look elsewhere for markets.

McRae also sees the "economic logic" that is pressing toward an integrated European economic space to be so overwhelming that "it will take place." The question becomes the time scale. Perhaps with a down Germany, the European Union is reaching its practical limits at the present time.

The Deutsche Mark

Another dimension is important within this complicated issue of Germany's financial state: *the stability of its currency.* The Deutsche Mark is more than currency for Germany; it is a symbol of nationalism. Inhibited by war memories, the Germans eschew ostentatious patriotism; opinion polls show that Germans focus that patriotism on the Mark for their expression of faith and pride in Germany. Almost 80% of Germans identify their Germanness with the stability, strength, and international prestige of the Mark. It is a powerful symbol of Germany's recovery from the war and its phenomenal postwar prosperity.

On June 20, 1948, all people living in Germany were given forty new German Marks and told that the money would be legal tender the next day, i.e., beginning at 00 hours, June 21. The Mark was protected by the Bundesbank (State Bank) and integrated Germany into the economies of the new era.[379*]

---

378 MacRae, 63, 236.

379 The horoscope of the Deutsche Mark, set for Berlin (Bonn did not become the capital of Germany until 1949) is remarkable: Sun in tight conjunction with Uranus opposed by the tight conjunction of Moon and Jupiter in Sagittarius in the 10th, Jupiter ruling the

During crippling inflation following both world wars, the former (Weimar) Republic mark went from four to the dollar to more than four trillion to the dollar. Today, the Deutsche Mark has developed into Europe's dominant currency, and the Bundesbank is Europe's unofficial central bank. Within the European Union, the Deutsche Mark has been put forward for study to become the common currency standard among all the participating countries.[380]

■ Prediction ...

Germany's Indebtedness Stabilizes in Summer 1998—Germany's financial difficulties will have been at their worst in the Spring of 1996.

While Germany has the best workers in the world, it has the most taxed workers as well. Out of the average German worker's gross pay, 44% goes to taxes and social services, compared to about 30% available for personal spending.

As well, because of the memories of enormous family losses during the war years, the Germans are among the world's highest savers (along with Japan) and the most conservative investors. Only 5% of Germans own stock (as compared with more than 25% percent of Americans). This tightness with money scares away potential investors from overseas. Foreign investment in Germany averaged only $5.5 billion a year in the late 1980s and early 1990s, roughly one-tenth of the investment in the United States during the same period. Venture capital is rare in Germany.[381]

The federal debt in Germany is $1.3 trillion, because of the burden of reunification, nearly triple that of 1985, according to the German Association of Taxpayers (in spite of the "Solidarity Tax" on wages to cover part of the massive transfers to the former East Germany).

Late in 1996, negotiation for a major investment program in Germany (venture capital and aid) will begin for Germany,

---

10th! Saturn and Pluto are in conjunction, with Saturn exactly upon the Descendant (hard-working, stolid, "muscular"; a profile of greatness). Mars, ruler of the 2nd (value) is in Virgo, in the 7th and unaspected (aggressive with correctness, discriminating). Finally: The Sun and Venus/Jupiter conjoin the Aries Point of public projection and Uranus=Sun/Jupiter (success, great expectation).

380 *International Herald Tribune*, June 25, 1995.

381 *Washington Post*, February 22, 1994, A1, A14.

possibly in the world health-services field. This will signal a new program for reeducation and resources and deployment away from manufacturing and into professional services (see page 171). It will take several months for the agreement to be formed and announced, perhaps in April 1997.

Additionally, the government will move production of many of its products to other lower-wage countries to bring its world-highest labor costs down on selected items. Manufacturing research and development will make a shift to the electronics sector, in emulation of Japan and India. As the new eastern sector of Germany begins its recovery, the financial drain of reunification will be stabilized and begin to subside.

Due to these maneuvers and considerations—improving (auto) manufacturing processes with new technological concepts to streamline production and lower production costs, arousing the people for a recovery effort, having them work longer hours—unemployment, having soared to four million or 10.2% of the work force at end 1995, should start to drop. The national financial picture should stabilize and show improvement especially in the Spring–Summer of 1998, just before national elections. Germany will start on its gradual way to a second recovery, a reconstruction of its world leadership position in surplus savings.[382*]

■ Prediction ...

Deutsche Mark Becomes European Union Currency Standard—The Deutsche Mark (see "Deutsche Mark," page 166) will be confirmed as the planned currency standard for the European Union toward the end of 1996, perhaps in October. An intermediate step of introduction will be deployed late in 1997, and the common currency plan will be actualized in the year 2000, January–February.[383*]

---

382 Germany in 1997: tr Saturn=Sun/Moon giving way to tr Jupiter conjunct Saturn, tr Uranus conjunct the 7th; tr Saturn opposed the Sun, ruler of the 2nd; SA Venus conjunct Sun, July 1998. Kohl: tr Saturn conjunct Ascendant and more, Summer 1998.

383 *Mark chart:* SA Pluto square Sun (10/96), SA Sun conjunct Saturn, SA Jupiter-Moon opposed Pluto; tr Uranus square Ascendant, tr Saturn conjunct Nodal Axis, tr Jupiter trine the Moon.

World Trade

Germany is the mightiest manufacturer in the world, and the greatest exporter, as well. The countries of Europe specialize in the products they make and the natural resources their lands support. More than in any other market, the European countries specialize: Norway, Denmark, and Switzerland, for example, do not make automobiles; the French produce the preferred wines and perfumes; Germany tops all in Europe with personal computer manufacture (but lags far behind Japan and the United States).

As a result, the countries of Europe need each other, and, for everyone's best interests, the common market was born to make trade as easy over national borders as it is between states in the United States.

International diplomacy influences trade decisions, the sharing of "trade secrets," if you will; and trade maneuvers influence international diplomacy. For example, with the thawing of the Cold War and the collapse of the Soviet Union, the "common enemy" is gone, and the defense bonds, the preferences and allegiances connected to that are diluted or negated among the United States, Japan, and Germany, which has long bordered communist countries. This tends to push the United States *out of the German market and away from the Pacific Market.* At the very least, it undermines its bargaining position. When the United States announced (and called for others to observe) a trade embargo of Iran, *Europe and Japan ignored it.*

In the Middle East, considerations of common needs and specialization go hand in hand to affect diplomacy mightily: the historic decision for peace between Syria and Israel will be, in the main, dictated by Syria's need to ingratiate itself with the West to gain modernization through importing technology and investment. Germany's relations with Iran have had an impact on Germany's sensitive relations with Israel.

For example, Iran is now enemy of the United States, but Iran is Germany's biggest trading partner. France, Italy, Belgium, Sweden, Spain, Turkey, and to a lesser extent, Great Britain all do hundreds of millions of dollars worth of business annually with Iran. Japan has set aside $1.4 billion in development credits for Iran. All of these countries trading with Iran are allies of the United States.

384 *Foreign Affairs* magazine, November/December 1995, "Germany's New Ostpolitik," by Charles Lane, Senor Editor at *The New Republic*, 77–89.

Germany's *Ostpolitik* was designed to ingratiate itself with the Eastern countries. Engaging the East with issues of diplomacy and trade helped to "contain" the Eastern danger zones politically and militarily. Kohl's government, mired in sluggish economic growth (near zero at end 1995, with consumer sales down 2.5%, threatening recession) due to the cost of reunification, is eager to take lucrative Iranian contracts—for example, to build an atomic reactor for Iran; the German company Siemens—and penetrate the large market of 60 million people.[385]

The European Union, especially now with Germany reunified, is spreading its diplomatic wings. Opportunism is now the keynote of international trade. Less and less is the United States the catalyst for direct market activity.[386]

■ Prediction ...

Iran Becomes an Atomic Power—Iran has gone its way and shall return. The Astro-profile of Iran shows a country that is quick and aggressive, with a judicial attitude toward the rest of the world, a formidable superiority complex. The country withdraws to its own theatre, much as a big fish seeks to occupy a small pond for maximum safety. This is the manifestation of the religious suppression (confinement) of liberal internationalism.

The potential is for Iran to explode back onto the world scene in a leadership position, still didactic, moralistic, and severe, but with a more secular orientation—business is business, we need to be part of the world.[387*]

Iran will begin to use nuclear energy (become an atomic power) between January 2000 and June 2001. There will be investigations and international outcry as testing reveals activity

---

385 Ibid, 82. And yet, during the Iran-Iraq war 1980, Germany sold billions of dollars of industrial goods to Iraq.

386 This freedom should increase mightily for all nations. Pluto in Sagittarius.

387 Iran: February 1, 1979 (the airport arrival of Khomeini) at 9:50 A.M. IRT in Teheran. [Campion, *World Horoscopes*, the second option in the text; tested many times]. Sun in Aquarius-Moon in Aries, square the Midheaven, rising in the 12th. Sun-Mercury-Mars conjunction in Aquarius opposed by Jupiter, ruler of the 9th. Saturn in Virgo, retrograde, peregrine; Uranus in Scorpio, peregrine; Venus conjunct Neptune in Sagittarius in the 9th. The retrogradation pattern portrays the religious veil over the Aquarius-Leo internationalism bent. AP=Mars/Uranus, Saturn/Pluto; Uranus=Neptune/ Pluto, "disruption to gain recognition."

beyond peaceful deployment of nuclear energy, at the earlier end of the time span. August–September 2000 and/or June 2001 creates a major change in the world identity of Iran. The peaceful exploitation of atomic power will greatly dilute radical Islam's bureaucratic choke hold on Iran and introduce the invigoration of increased world trade and political interaction. The potential for atomic weapon development will increase circumspect Islam's international power position decidedly.[388*]

■ Prediction ...

Iran Exploits German Trade for Atomic Power—Iran and Germany are perfect partners in trade.[389*] An extraordinary trade accomplishment will be completed by Iran, most probably with Germany, in the Spring of 1997. Quite possibly, this trade period could be linked to the final stages of acquiring atomic power.[390*]

■ Prediction ...

Germany Begins Shift to Professional Services—Germany has the oldest population in Europe. In the world, only Japan is older (see "Social Resources," page 43). By 2020, 22% of Germany's population will be aged sixty-five or over, as opposed to 9% in 1950. This index is crucially connected with economic progress.[391]

An older country with a relatively lower birth rate (as Germany has) will inevitably be *a slower-growing country*. For progress to be maintained, the country must adapt its way of achieving Gross National Product to different considerations: how the people work and what the people do are critically more

---

388 Iran: SA Pluto=Sun/Mars in January 2000, SA Uranus=Saturn in September 2000 with tr Pluto conjunct Saturn and more; SA Pluto square Sun in June 2001.

389 Iran Moon in Aries opposes Germany Sun in Libra; Iran Sun trines Germany's Mars, ruler of its Midheaven; Iran's Jupiter, ruler of its 9th, is conjunct Germany's Ascendant; Iran's Neptune in the 9th in Sagittarius is squared by Germany's Moon in Pisces in the 9th.

390 Iran: tr Jupiter conjunct the Sun, tr Saturn conjunct the Ascendant with SA Uranus= Sun/MC, SA Jupiter=MC. Germany: tr Saturn conjunct Midheaven opposed Sun, SA Pluto=Sun/Uranus, Moon=Pluto/Ascendant, SA Mars=Moon.

391 McRae, 100.

important as opposed to *how much* they do. Services, for example (health care, promotion and marketing, information services, banking and investment, design, consultancies, construction, tourism, etc.) require different personnel "tooling" than manufacturing does. Services are low-cost, open-ended, and high-profit.

Services are top-line accomplishments in a country's economy because the demand for them is rarely exhausted: people always need health care, information and education, money, living quarters, adventure, etc. It is entirely possible that Germany will cut back manufacturing and build and sell its capacity for professional services throughout the world. It is the next step after manufacturing and export power to improve domestic living standards. Germany will begin to educate its people for jobs of the future, rather than for jobs of the past.[392*]

■ Prediction ...

Kohl Wins Again in 1998, Awakens Germany—Helmut Kohl became Chancellor of Germany on October 1, 1982. His tenure to date (1995) approaches that of *Der Alte* (the Old One), Konrad Adenauer, West Germany's first Chancellor after the war (May 21, 1949), who helped write its Constitution, founded the Christian Democratic party, headed its spectacular postwar economic and financial recovery, relating Germany to the rest of Western Europe, NATO, and the European Common Market. Adenauer served for over fourteen years, resigning in October 16, 1963 (Ludwig Erhard succeeded him).

The Astro-profile of Helmut Kohl shows a driven, robust, knock-over-the-table-to-get-across-the-room leader, with powerful communication skills. He is dedicated to hard work, is an austere administrator, and has a private part of his make-up that dreams, is hidden away in curious awareness of the unconscious, the hunch, the religious, the paranormal.[393*]

---

392 Germany: Sixth House accentuation; the dignity of Saturn in Capricorn, i.e., aging (square the Ascendant ruler); 6th House, professional services.

393 Helmut Kohl: birth data, see footnote to Kohl, page 161). Sun-Uranus-Mercury (ruler of the 3rd) conjunct in Aries, in the 12th, squaring the opposition axis of Saturn in Capricorn conjunct the Midheaven and Pluto in the 4th. Venus rises in the Aries Ascendant. Neptune, ruling the 12th, trines the Gemini Moon on the cusp of the 2nd.

Politically (like Pope John Paul II, see "Vatican," page 26), he is caught and pressed in the middle between Left and Right; the Liberal-Conservative battle is raging within him. Analysts write of public assessment of Kohl as a European version of Mao Tse-tung: omnipotent, unchallenged, the historic unifier. He has made it clear that he "fully intends to run for the chancellorship in 1998 and possibly beyond."[394]

Kohl is the man for Germany at this time. There are very significant and telling correspondences between his horoscope and that of the united Germany.[395*]

One drawback: Kohl has indications of potential debilitating ill-health, and this sector of symbolism in his horoscope is activated January–May, 1998, five months before elections, and coincident with a major business success Kohl will have arranged for Germany (see above). If his health prevails under the strain of his work, Kohl will run for an unprecedented extension of his terms and win once again.[396]

But Kohl will be threatened by and must manage adroitly and powerfully the severe socio-economic social unrest brewing in Germany: the drastic unemployment, the high taxation, the rebellious youth, the right-wing sophisticates blaming difficulties on political mismanagement, the aging and content population majority, the defensive isolationism brought about by the financial problems, and the instabilities of the European Union growing because of Germany's plight. With high unemployment there is an increase in welfare demands, which in turn raises taxes to pay for the unemployed, and then the increased taxes inhibit consumer spending and economic growth.

Trade, the European Union position, the revamping of export specialization, and the re-establishing of a vision for a future that recognizes the young's lust for freedom from eco-

---

394 *The European*, October 12–18, 1995, 4.

395 Kohl's Sun-Uranus conjunction in Aries conjoins Germany's Midheaven (even though it is a midnight mark, the Angles take on the identity of the nation); his Nodal Axis is conjunct Germany's Ascendant (very strong), and his Saturn is exactly conjunct Germany's Neptune, ruler of its 9th House and dispositor of the national Moon.

396 Kohl won his last election in 1994 by only 142,000 votes out of 50,000,000, i.e., by one quarter of one percent. A more vibrant candidate than the "sad sack" he defeated would have won. But this is less a critique of Kohl's achievement than it is an alarming indication of the people's plight, weighed down by debt, giving up in age, rebelling in youth, yearning for change.

nomic dross—this will representing the new way; identification with European institutions instead of exploiting the dangers of extreme nationalism.

Part of the German people's legacy throughout German history seems to be to carry a cross, to shoulder a burden, as they suffer the winters of their discontent and development. Nothing is moderate or "normal" in German life.[397]

The German people easily become resigned to fate. The dream goes to sleep easily. The unification of Germany was initially euphoric, quickly embarrassing, and thereafter tedious. Inspired leadership on a reconstruction track is essential.[398]

The people of Germany can be awakened by Helmut Kohl, who will run once again for Chancellor in the Fall of 1998, as predicted above. He will have to commandeer all of Germany to help the Eastern sector rebuild: some ten years are needed to restore production to an adequate level and twenty-five years to bring housing accommodations up to western standards, all costing billions of dollars. The haul is long; the dream must be vivid, and the younger generation must be the resource.

Konrad Jarausch provides a conclusion: "The Berlin republic is too big to fit harmoniously with its neighbors and too small to dominate them outright. The surprises of the unification process should caution against straightline predictions for the future. Unity opens a new chapter to come."[399]

---

397 Helmut Schmidt, Kohl's predecessor as Chancellor, has cautioned that "Germans are not yet a normal people." [Jarausch, 210]. And Goethe once said, "The Germans make everything difficult, both for themselves and for everyone else" [Craig, 15]. The Moon in Pisces.

398 Germany: AP=Mars/Saturn, Sun/Moon. Saturn conjoined by Neptune. Saturn=Moon-Pluto.

399 Jarausch, 210.

France — *La Politique, C'est Tout*

(For France, Politics is everything.) France is rebellion. Explosion. Protest. Its social movements against authority create historical seasons. International wars mask internal civil strife. It has been so for over 200 years; the people's revolution continuously transcends everything.

The Western world loves revolution. The American Revolution of 1775–1783 for independence from Great Britain was the model for the French Revolution 1787–1799, for ascendancy of the people over the privileged class and imperial rule. This Revolution in turn inspired the Latin Revolution(s) of 1809 by Spain's colonies in the New World, and then, in theory, the Communist Revolution in so many countries, and other revolutions. The United States, in its role of protector and nurse to the world at large (see United States, page 225), supports and abets revolution by any downtrodden people against oppressors, and then, for that support, extracts fealty for the future.

The French Revolutions

Although the French Revolution was accomplished during a protracted period of about ten years, with many, many mob eruptions and massacres and executions, Constitutions and Acts of Rights, it is the storming of the Bastille of Paris on July 14, 1789 that defines the nation's holiday of freedom from the *ancien régime* (the old monarchical way). The attack on the Bastille continues to inspire books, histories, art, operas, musicals, and films about the Romantic concept of explosive populist action for individual freedom, for liberty, equality, and brotherhood.

The Bastille, the fortress in Paris built in 1370 to house political prisoners, a long-hated symbol of monarchical absolutism, had been portrayed by anti-monarchy pamphleteers as an active threat during the restive times (1780s). These promoters disseminated a picture of the Bastille dungeons packed with wretched prisoners of the state and swollen with royal troops ready to emerge and defeat the populace. In reality, the Bastille was garrisoned by only 120 soldiers, whose leader promised the protestors that day in 1789 that there would be no gunfire unless the Bastille were attacked.

The angry crowd of some 800 agitators—protesting the economic crisis of France's finances, 50% unemployment, the coincident food shortage, the exorbitant cost of bread, and intense political agitation toward King Louis XVI, and fearing the foreign mercenaries gathering outside Paris— infiltrated the outer court-yard of the Bastille, looking for ammunition for other sieges. The soldiers panicked, opened first fire, and were then slaughtered by the crowd.

A rebellious detachment of the Gardes Françaises then marched to the Bastille and trained their five cannon on the main gate. After the explosions and collapse of the gate and inner walls, only seven prisoners emerged from the fortress, and the people set to the task of demolishing the citadel. King Louis had spent the day hunting. Upon his return to his palace, he wrote in his diary "14 July, nothing." In fact, the king had lost control of Paris and had no prospect of regaining it.[400]

The French Revolution—and the storming of the Bastille—becomes symbolic of the two most powerful forces affecting Western civilization in the last three hundred years: the influence of enlightened thought. (The Enlightenment) and the thrust of people demanding freedom and self-government. These forces ignite change and then politicize themselves into the modern concept of nation(alism). Rigid boundaries are erected to protect against any further change. Further development occurs only through open exchange of resources with other nations, internal upheaval, or external attack.

The Enlightenment

This evolution of thought in the eighteenth century, sometimes called the Age of Reason, was focused mainly in France. The great writers and thinkers of the era applied reason to religion, politics, morality, and social life. They did this with enormous energy and enthusiasm, on a solid philosophical base rebuilt from classical times.[401*]

The Enlightenment issued principally out of the somber and religious last years of Louis XIV, the "Sun King," who reigned for seventy-three years (1643–1715) and ruled for fifty-five upon the death of Cardinal Giulio Mazarin, chief Minister to the child-king

---

400 Cobban, Volume 1, 137, 139. 140, 145, 148–149. The 800 who stormed the Bastille represented perhaps 10% of the revolutionaries rampaging throughout Paris at the time.

401 The bloom of the Enlightenment corresponded to the previous transit of Pluto through Sagittarius, 1748–1762, giving way then to the practice of the philosophy within the revolutionary political movements with Pluto transiting Capricorn.

(and his mother-Regent). During his years on the throne, Louis regarded the arts as a celebration of his shining monarchy. Similarly, to honor the excellence of France, he waged many wars with Spain, the Netherlands and areas of western Germany, and persecuted the Protestant minority (the Huguenots). Louis XIV died on September 1, 1715, at the age of 79.[402]

The movement began with the reinspection and breakdown of older metaphysical and philosophical knowledge. Knowledge could not continue to exist as just a tradition, a system of pure thought to delight understanding or to prove premise—like Cartesianism—but *would be put into action;* reason would become a tool within a view of social betterment.

The sciences themselves—especially the earlier Newtonian discoveries (1642–1726) and the treatises of Francis Bacon and John Locke—were called *philosophe,* and they were re-studied and put to work to trace the evolution of man from the dawn of history into a future of liberation, equality, and human perfection. All this would be accomplished through better teaching, fairer laws, and magnanimous institutions. The thinkers of the day—so many contemporaneous geniuses—were looking for the Natural Law *that transcended any idea of social distinctions built upon privilege.* At the most significant level of application, Natural Law revealed that *divine-right monarchy belonged to the past.*[403]

The French ideas were developed by many, by Voltaire, Montesquieu, and Rousseau in the main; spread to the East into Germany through the Masons and Rosicrucians and Immanuel Kant (the supreme importance of the individual); into Italy by Giambattista Vico (the first modern historian, seeing history in human terms rather than God-ordained pronouncements); into England by

---

402 Louis XIV was born September 5, 1638 at 11:11 A.M. LMT (Penfield collection; international usage) at 02E05, 48N54. He was known by his extraordinary patronage of art, architecture (Versailles), literature, and women, his belief in absolute rule through his own person (*L'Etat, c'est moi*), and a consuming obsession with rigid etiquette and controlling administrative details. While French civilization bloomed conspicuously under his reign and he was known as the consummate symbol of majesty in behavior and spirit, he left the kingdom practically destitute because of his profligate spending and his international wars.

The astrology is striking: the *Virgo* Sun in the 10th is sextile Neptune rising in Scorpio; Moon-Venus conjunction opposed by Saturn in Aquarius, the axis squared by Jupiter in Scorpio, and much more. *Venus in Virgo rules the Midheaven and is squared by Mars in Sagittarius in the 2nd.*

403 Cobban, Volume 1, 164.

Jonathan Swift, Alexander Pope, Locke, Hume, and Gibbon; and to the United States through Thomas Jefferson and Benjamin Franklin. The human being was singularly important as the prime focus of time and creation.

All this force of reason *worked against and threatened the monarchy and its coterie of the privileged* (some 20,000 passports were issued in the two months following the Bastille Day for the upper class to emigrate [flee] from France). It even went against the Church which, late in the Revolution, was ordered to accede to the people, to give over (for considerations) its land holdings to create more farms to feed the people (the ninety percent agrarian population). The spirit of the times became people-centered to the extreme. Fears of famine, high unemployment, unjust laws, gouging by the monopolists, and being conquered by foreign powers made the populace (the so-called Third Estate) fertile for revolution. Without any doubt or hesitancy, the people were finally to have their say in how their life developed and progressed into the future.

The Revolutionary movement fulfilled itself in the political concept of the Republic: a government free from hereditary or monarchical rule, controlled by the people with a public welfare platform. All segments of society are represented in a Republic, and there are constitutional limitations on state powers.

A Republic is distinguished from a Democracy by its function through a representative assembly chosen by the people; while in a Democracy, the people participate directly in the government. The United States is a federal Republic (federated states under unified, representative rule but empowered locally); the USSR was a centralized Republic.

The First French Republic was established at the National Assembly on September 21, 1792.[404*]

---

404 First Republic: September 21, 1792, at 3:30 P.M. LMT in Paris. The third decree of the day by the National Assembly. See Campion, *World Horoscopes*, #106. This First Republic horoscope still defines modern France approaching the twenty-first century; it is the fundament of the French spirit, the break from long-established monarchy and the revolutionary press for individual freedom. It stands up to test after test in terms of old and modern events. *It supports importantly and essentially the horoscope of the Fifth Republic to portray present-day France.* (See "The Fifth Republic," page 187.)

Note: King Louis XVI was executed for international treachery (secret deals with Austria being discovered in his papers): he was marched on January 21, 1793, along roads lined with the National Guard and a silent populace to the Place de la Revolution, and guillotined [Cobban, volume 1, 211; "at 10:20 A.M. LMT," Campion]. This ended some 1500 years of continuous French monarchy.

The Napoleons

French political history from the First Republic forward has been turbulent. The First Republic gave way to another revolution and the rise of Napoleon, the great military leader who emerged from the French Revolution and the warring with Austria as a military leader of national prominence. He had developed tremendous public appeal through his victories and his intrigues to complete a new Constitution that reversed electorate powers from the people below to the heads of state above.[405]

Napoleon's exploits then grew into prodigious accomplishment: victories over England, Germany (Prussia), and Russia; elimination of the Holy Roman Empire (see page 154). Napoleon commanded and reshaped all of Europe. He crowned himself Emperor (transcending the Republic) on December 2, 1804.[406]*

Eventually, conquered enemies returned: successive defeats by Spain and Portugal, Alexander I of Russia, and the Prussians decimated Napoleon's army and reputation. His allied conquerors demanded complete abdication by Napoleon—on April 6, 1814—and placed him in exile upon the British-controlled island of Elba.

Napoleon engineered his return to try to rise again, but in a battle with the Austrians and British, he was defeated by the Duke of Wellington at Waterloo (now in Belgium). Napoleon then returned to Paris and abdicated for a second time on June 22, 1815. He was exiled to the island of St. Helena, and died there on May 5, 1821.[407]

Napoleon's first abdication was in favor of his son, Napoleon II (who had been proclaimed King of Rome upon birth). In this act, Napoleon gave up the concept of Empire, and a monarchy under this son was instituted.

---

405 In ratification of the new Constitution, created by Napoleon with the Abbe Sieyes, who had drafted the original constitution of the Republic and had been instrumental in the forming of the National Assembly, Napoleon removed any pretenders to leadership (including Sieyes). Napoleon was elected to the highest Electorate (the position with all the power to appoint the controlling Senate) by 3,011,007 votes to 1,562. [Cobban, Volume 2, 13]

406 Napoleon was born on August 15, 1769, on Corsica (Ajaccio), a French territory, in Italy. His birthtime is uncertain (speculation around 11:30 A.M.). The horoscope is defined dramatically by the Leo Sun square Jupiter in Scorpio (the sense of driving mission), with Jupiter opposed Uranus; with a Capricorn Moon conjunct Pluto. Napoleon's beginnings were meager: spurned as a foreigner and provincial, aloof, withdrawn, near the bottom of his academic class in military school.

407 His death is attributed to stomach cancer, yet theories exist about gradual arsenic poisoning through an assassination plot through over-medication.

Napoleon II was never to rule in actuality. He was kept a virtual prisoner in Austria. A second and exceedingly violent revolution erupted in France on February 22, 1848, and ended with King Louis Philippe (Napoleon II to the Bonapartists) abdicating on February 24. On that date, the Second Republic was proclaimed.

On December 20, 1848, Napoleon I's nephew, Prince Louis Napoleon, became President of France, the Second Republic, and began to plot to restore the empire. On December 2, 1852, he proclaimed the empire as reestablished, and installed himself as Emperor Napoleon III.[408*]

Prince Louis had been a long-time insurrectionist, punished with exile to the United States and to Britain; then, after another coup failure, escaping from prison in France, he hid in England once again. The second French Revolution in 1848 welcomed Louis back and gradually, through intrigue and a final coup, this driven man with the legendary name, became Emperor in the Second Empire, confirmed by popular vote.

This Napoleon III headed a dictatorship for some eight years, with military victories reinforcing his position. But times began to change—battles did not go his way, and the clerical opposition was strongly upset with his oppression of the papacy in Rome. Napoleon liberalized his government. He worked to expand the Empire, with explorations to China (with the British), building the Suez Canal, and losing out in Mexico (under United States pressure on the French to withdraw).

Napoleon was then goaded into war by Otto von Bismarck of Prussia (see "The Second Reich," page 155) in the Franco-Prussian war of 1870–71. Napoleon himself was captured on the battlefield, taken prisoner, and exiled to Britain. In France, the Empire declared him deposed in absentia, and a bloodless revolution was completed.

Alfred Cobban, eminent historian of France, saw the collapse of divine right as the rise of republican fervor but possessed of principles "too self-contradictory and too difficult to reconcile with hard political and social facts, to provide the ideological bases for a new

---

408 Napoleon III, son of Napoleon Bonaparte's brother, was born on April 20, 1808, at 1:00 A.M. LMT in Paris. [Taeger Archives, birth certification, 1*]: exact Sun-Mars conjunction in Aries, exact Mercury-Venus conjunction in Aries (idealism of tyranny); Capricorn Ascendant, Saturn in Scorpio square the Moon in Aquarius; combinations of authoritarianism and ego-aggrandizement with idealistic liberalism.

society. The new ruling classes that emerged from Revolution and Empire had used democratic and egalitarian ideas to justify their attack on the older privileged classes, but with no intention of allowing the same principles to be turned against themselves."[409]

Upon Napoleon III's collapse, the *Third* Republic was established on September 04, 1870, two days after the Emperor's defeat by Prussia. This Republic lasted for seventy years, until the German invasion of France in World War II.

The Vichy State

French politics were once again in disarray in the late 1930s and, considering the absence of any foreign policy and the rise of Hitler in Germany, France followed the leadership of the (Neville) Chamberlain government in Britain.

On September 29, 1938, Chamberlain, France's Daladier, Italy's Mussolini, and Hitler met at Munich. To allay concerns of war, the western powers yielded to Hitler's threats and agreed to the partitioning of Czechoslovakia, arbitrarily giving over part of that territory to Nazi Germany. England and France believed that the menace of war had been lifted. Additionally, two months later, German Foreign Minister Ribbentrop arrived in Paris to sign a Declaration of Friendship.[410]

But three months later, German troops, in disregard of the Munich Pact, invaded Czechoslovakia, as Great Britain and France watched helplessly. Chamberlain then promised Poland protection if Nazi aggression came their way.[411]

Reluctantly, Britain and France went to Russia to gain an ally and improve the balance of Europe in their favor. But Russia had just completed a non-aggression pact with Germany (August 21)!

On September 1, 1939, the Germans invaded Poland, and on September 3, Great Britain and France declared war on Germany.

On June 4, 1940, the victorious German Army entered Paris. France pressed for a separate peace with Germany, and this brought tension to the relationship between France and Britain. The French government was on the run, holding forth in various

---

409 Cobban, Volume 2, 134.

410 Ibid, Volume 3, 170–171.

411 Although France already had a treaty from 1921 to help Poland in the face of aggression, France was simply a witness to these early days of the World War. Chamberlain and British policy were out front. [Cobban, Volume 3, 173.]

cities, considering even a transfer of its center to North Africa. General Charles De Gaulle, serving as Under-Secretary of War, made a dramatic escape to England and appealed for continued resistance against the Germans.

But a French-German Armistice was signed on June 22: France was divided into two zones, the Occupied (60%) and the Unoccupied (40%), and the French military was disarmed. The attempt at a French government was transferred to Vichy in the central southwest of the country.

As is seen so often in French history, *there are factions that rejoice at national adversity*, including international war, because it brings about a collapse of the national government (Republic, Empire, Republic) of the moment.

For the most part, the French were resigned to defeat by the Germans. The Parliament that could be assembled voted (with only one dissent) and the Chamber of Deputies did as well (vote 395 to 3) to suspend the constitutional laws of the Third Republic and establish yet again a new régime.

The word "Republic" was avoided in this action; the "State of France" was used instead. The new government structure became a *personal* régime (reminiscent of Bonapartism) in the figure of an old, staid but charismatically popular military Marshall Henri Pétain. The government of Vichy consummated yet another National Revolution; July 10, 1940.

The Right Wing leaders tore down Third Republic infrastructure everywhere,[412] planning to rebuild France into an era of sound business practice, solid trade unions supporting professional corporations, with the interests of the workers and employers resolved. Anti-Semitic sentiments emerged in special laws that excluded Jews from all positions in government service, teaching, and state-subsidized industries, from managerial positions in the press, radio, and cinema. The urgency was for *nationalism* to save a defeated country.[413]

France suffered terribly: divided, with the richer portions of the land occupied by the Germans, with a British blockade closing Atlantic and Channel-port supply routes, suffering a bad harvest, and enduring stringent Vichy economic controls of rationing and wages and prices.

---

412 In fact, in Old Testament sensibility, many saw the war as the vindication of history for the sins of the Third Republic.

413 Cobban, Volume 3, 181–184.

Cobban sees the Vichy government as the central focus of the illusion that, by accepting the German Armistice, France was somehow removed from the war. A large faction of leaders believed that their prompt recognition of the new order in Europe, i.e., the German hegemony, would earn a reward from the Germans. Many believed an independent France was still possible. The Vichy propaganda became violently anti-British (the British were still fighting the Germans). Pétain and his Vichy government cooperated with Hitler.[414]

For a year, the situation in France remained essentially static. Then it changed with the German invasion of Russia in June 1941. In a national broadcast, Pétain described the Nazis as the defenders of civilization against France's political enemy, Communism (an echo of Hitler's war cry to arouse the German people). But the actions against Russia *released all French Communists*, the former enemies of France, *into the French Resistance Movement headed by De Gaulle in Britain*. In turn, the Communist infrastructure absorbed the French fighters and, exploiting the collaborative relationship with the occupying Germans, the Resistance grew almost overnight to a formidable force in France and later everywhere else in the international theatre of the European war.

The Vichy government had sentenced Charles De Gaulle to death in absentia. Great Britain had recognized him as head of the Free French movement. On June 3, 1943, De Gaulle founded the Committee of National Liberation with another anti-Vichy leader. Then, after the United States invasion of Normandy June 7–12, 1944 and the German's leaving Paris by August 25, De Gaulle himself entered Paris in triumph and set up a provisional new government.[415*]

De Gaulle presided over the provisional government until the new constitution was written and the *Fourth* Republic was founded, October 13/28, 1946.

---

414 Ibid, 186–187. Additionally: Fernandez-Armesto, 510, portrays the Vichy State as "a government of old soldiers and Nazi sympathizers [who] collaborated with the Germans against their fellow citizens; Jews and leftists were slaughtered and enslaved. [When the Germans fled in 1944,] Frenchmen [were left] at each other's throats."

415 Charles De Gaulle: November 22, 1890, at perhaps 4:00 P.M. LMT in Lille, France [Taeger Archives 1* but there is dispute about the time]: Sun in Scorpio opposed the Neptune-Pluto conjunction in Gemini (the signature of so many leaders during World War II), Jupiter square Uranus; Moon in Aries. De Gaulle died November 9, 1970.

The Fourth Republic

The constitution of the Fourth Republic was lackluster. It was close to that of the Third Republic installed after the French under Napoleon III were defeated by Bismarck. Three political parties were stirring the mix at this post-World War II time in France, and none was enthusiastic about the document. It was "the same old thing," only the *dramatis personae* were different. Although De Gaulle had denounced the constitution, withdrawn from active political life and registered upset through a political Union bearing his name, the new Constitution won the acceptance of the country by the narrow margin of nine million votes to eight million, with eight million abstaining.[416]

Parties politic—the Communist Party (receiving most votes in the November 10 election of the new Assembly; the way paved by Resistance cooperation during the war), the Popular Republicans, and the Socialists—ran things in the new Republic. The disarray of politics reflected itself in the make-up of the government: in seven years, there were fifteen cabinets (approximating the rate of change in the old Third Republic). In the election of December 1953, *thirteen* ballots were required for majority selection of a new Socialist President.

Early in 1957, negotiations began for a Common Market with Germany, Italy, and the Benelux countries. In March, the Rome treaty establishing the Common Market was ratified by the French Assembly. These developments gave the Fourth Republic some energy, the nation some evidence of belonging within Europe, and some prosperity.

Algeria

France's colonial concerns exploded in the Algerian bid for independence, begun May 13, 1958. Terrorism and counter-terrorism quickly escalated to a war that occupied French troops on the other side of the Mediterranean, kept France jolted out of full and orderly European cooperation, and severely upset fiscal security.

The threat to France was enormous. Charles De Gaulle was recalled to government on June 1, 1958, by the National Assembly to solve the government crisis. On December 21, De Gaulle was

---

416 Cobban, Volume 3, 206–207.

named President, and, following secret negotiations with the Algerian rebels, he decided for Algerian self-determination. This enraged French colonialists and confused and embittered the French Legionnaires; in more than seven years of battle, at least 100,000 Muslims and 10,000 French soldiers and many thousands of Muslim civilians were killed.

De Gaulle held firm, and Algeria gained its independence on July 3, 1962.[417] France and Algeria were to cooperate in economic and social affairs, and France was to retain for a limited period military bases in Algeria and the right to test nuclear devices in the Sahara (De Gaulle pushed France's atomic program into development).

The Astro-profile for Algeria shows a highly emotional nation, consumed with insecurities about its functioning *correctly*. This sense of rightness, of idealization, works best in isolation, incontrovertedly, independently. This spirit is focused within religion, learning, the arts. With a highly active military dimension, we can expect rebellion, enforcement, fundamentalist struggles "to get it right," upheaval within the very strength potential of Algeria, to become a nation of highest culture and study.[418*]

On June 10, 1965, there was a bloodless coup that overthrew the government. It was led by the defense minister (the military), Houari Boumedienne.[419*]

The new president got a secure hold on Algeria by the end of 1968. He nationalized the French oil and natural gas companies (with compensation), increased production to record levels by 1972, and improved export earnings enormously.

After Boumedienne's death December 27, 1978, the presidency was taken by the militant National Liberation Front (FLN), Colonel Chadli Bendjedid, who was then reelected in 1984.

---

417 Roberts, 849, 851, 881. Columbia, 66.

418 *Algeria Independence:* July 3, 1962, at 10:38 A.M. CET in Algiers. [Campion, *World Horoscopes,* #5] Sun-Moon in Cancer, Sun in Water Grand Trine with Neptune in Scorpio and Jupiter in Pisces upon the Descendant and square the Midheaven. Mars square Uranus, ruler of the 6th (military); Mercury in Gemini, ruling Midheaven and Ascendant in sextile. Mars-Neptune and Jupiter-Uranus quindeciles (upheaval). AP=Venus/Neptune, Sun=Neptune/Ascendant; Midheaven=Pluto/Ascendant.
   The tie with 1st Republic France is through exact opposition of *Mars* positions; with 5th Republic France, Algeria horoscope ruler Mercury tightly opposed (controlled) by France Saturn.

419 Boumedienne was born August 23, 1932. Algeria: SA Pluto exactly square Midheaven; SA Mars square Uranus. Tr Saturn opposed Ascendant, tr Uranus conjunct Ascendant, and more.

Opposition parties were legalized in 1989, and on June 12, 1990, the Islamic Salvation Front (the *fundamentalist* movement) won many votes in the first phase of national elections. To forestall an Iran-style fundamentalist takeover, the military staged a coup, took control, pressured Bendhedid to resign, and cancelled further elections.[420*]

Warring Islamic extremists began fighting to overthrow the military FLN. A major eruption broke out in downtown Algiers, with fourteen persons killed, on November 2, 1994.[421*]

The military-backed FLN administration has been unable to manage the government, and the economy has fallen into collapse. Terrorist attacks by militant fundamentalists have increased. Social chaos and civil war are threatened. In the elections of November 16, 1995, Independent Liamine Zeroual was elected compromise-President, for a term of five years.[422*]

■ Prediction ...

Islamic Fundamentalists Win in Algeria—President Zeroual's term will be severely interrupted December 1996-January 1997,[423*] during the first week of January 1999,[424*] during the first two weeks of May 1999, and/or around July 15, 1999.[425*]

The Islamic extremist movement will gain ground, will win the civil war, and Algeria will become a fundamentalist Islamic nation.

---

420 Algeria: SA Jupiter, ruler of the 4th (the party out of power) squared the Sun; tr Uranus-Neptune opposed the Sun.

421 Algeria: SA Neptune opposed Midheaven; SA Moon conjunct Uranus; tr Pluto square Uranus (ruler of the 6th, in the 12th), tr Uranus opposed Moon, tr Saturn square Midheaven.

422 Algeria: SA Saturn opposed Ascendant (exact in April 1996).

423 Algeria: SA Pluto square Sun, sesquiquadrate Mars, tr Jupiter-Neptune opposed Moon, tr Saturn applying square Sun; TP Mars square Neptune, TP MC-Pluto conjunct Ascendant.

424 Algeria: SA Pluto semisquare Uranus, SA Ascendant=Mars/Pluto, tr Pluto conjunct the fourth cusp, opposed the Midheaven; TP Moon conjunct Midheaven (1/9/99), TP Sun square Saturn.

425 Algeria: Tr Pluto still conjunct the fourth, SA Moon=Mars/Midheaven; TP Moon-Pluto conjunct Ascendant, TP Saturn opposed Venus, TP Mars opposed Midheaven, TP Jupiter squared Sun, TP Midheaven square Sun/Moon.

The Fifth Republic

The new government, under De Gaulle's presidential leadership, the *Fifth* Republic, was born on October 6, 1958, when the State Seal was affixed to the Constitution.[426*]

The Astro-profile of modern France combines the breakaway, explosive, revolutionary spirit of the founding of the First Republic and the prevailing political presentation of that spirit in present-day terms. The two profiles blend into one remarkably well: the spirit of France is adventurous, transcending basic conventions to establish the freest concept. Big ideas are adapted to social service. It is up-with-the-people in its drive, completely. Rebellion abounds, to the point of fanaticism and explosion. The fight for individuality is backed with nationalistic arrogance. Financial problems seem to persist interminably; legalisms and foreign concerns are problematic; social welfare, insurance (security) concerns, and problems with unemployment are endemic to the way of France for over 200 years.[427*]

Each shift for France to a Republic government and from Republic to Empire and back—except for the transition from the 4th to the 5th, which was like a twelve-year waiting period "to get it right" after the chaos of World War II—has been accompanied dramatically in its history *by enormous social upheaval, revolution and war.*

In September 1995, France exploded a nuclear bomb off Tahiti[428*] and sparked riots there and in capitals throughout most of the western world. Pacific nations broke off relations with Paris. Formal protests were lodged by more than twenty governments. French Embassies and cultural centers in Berlin (12,000 youths

---

426 The Fifth Republic: October 6, 1958, at 6:30 P.M. CET in Paris. This horoscope has tested well for present-day France. It is *an essential complement to the horoscope for the First Republic* (see page 178), the formative portrait, a startlingly valid portrait of spirit and time for La Grande France. The two work together undeniably. See similar earlier-chart co-reliance for Spain as well, page 193).

427 1st Republic: Sun in Virgo=AP and *Moon in Sagittarius in the 10 peregrine; Mercury unaspected in Virgo,* Saturn retrograde ruling the Ascendant =Sun/Moon. Saturn opposed Jupiter in Scorpio (sense of mission) conjunct Neptune in late Libra. Key: *Mars at the Midheaven squares the opposition of Pluto-Uranus,* 1st to 7th.

  5th Republic: Sun in Libra, *Moon in Cancer unaspected.* Key: Mars, ruling the Ascendant) squares Pluto (only square). Mars=Sun/Moon. Jupiter conjunct Neptune in Scorpio in the 7th, Jupiter ruling the 9th. Uranus=Sun/Saturn (ruler of the Midheaven); Venus=Neptune/Pluto (creativity, overindulgence).

428 The first Atomic Bomb explosion by France occurred in February 1960 (tr. Uranus square Pluto in the 1st Republic horoscope). This explosion in Tahiti occurred at 12:30 P.M. local time (21:30 GMT) on September 5, 1995, 1,000 meters below the Murora Atoll. (*The European,* September 7–13, 1995, 1).

protested), Chile (10,000), Sydney, Tokyo, and Manila saw riots and burnings of the French flag.[429]*

In December 1995, some two million French workers struck, and 160,000 of them took to the streets of Paris with students to protest, shutting down the postal service, closing schools, cutting phone service 40%, stopping public transportation, threatening electrical power shut-off to protest increases in taxes and cutbacks in welfare-state benefits, and unemployment. "National character shows at moments like these," comments the *New York Times*.[430] The chaotic traffic jams were "like nothing imaginable in either Germany or Britain." Paris was paralyzed for two weeks, in a decidedly French way for decidedly French reasons.[431]

Analysts observed that the strikes showed that there is no organized institutional dialogue and mutual respect between labor and capital in France. The French workers scream of their resentment of the "know-it-all" attitude conveyed by Prime Minister Alain Juppé and President Jacques Chirac.

The *Times* continues that President Chirac promised "profound change" when he took office in May 1995 for a seven-year term. He projects that change now to be two years into the future with belt-tightening and sacrifice for the people. And *The European* continues that, as the government goes, so goes the worker, beyond policy and welfare guidelines: 24.3% of the work force is employed by the government. It is an enormous problem: even in the midst of urban chaos, polls revealed that some 60–65% of the citizens understood and supported the strikers.

President Chirac is a tough man; forceful, experienced, knowledgeable. Former French President George Pompidou once dubbed him *le bulldozer*. His decision to resume nuclear testing to complete an experimental program that would support future simulated tests was "irrevocable." Analysts see that France—which is more dependent on nuclear power than any other nation—must also keep its nuclear force *credible* (modernized) as well beyond the

---

429 1st Republic: SA Saturn *conjoining the Midheaven*, tr Pluto *conjunct the Midheaven*; SA Neptune square the Uranus-Pluto axis; SA Jupiter opposed the Midheaven exactly; SA Moon square Sun; SP Mars exactly conjunct Saturn; tr Saturn at 22 Pisces conjunct Nodal axis (unpopularity). Key: *Tr Uranus conjunct the Ascendant.*

    5th Republic: SA Pluto just squared to *Midheaven*, SA Mars *just opposed the Midheaven*. Tr Saturn square Saturn

430 December 10, 1995, E5.

431 Also, *The European*, December 7–13, 1995, 2–3.

year 2015, when the present generation of warheads will have aged into obsolescence. More cynical analysts see the rough-and-ready Chirac proving to the French and the world that, because of his decision, "France is back"; that he is an authentic president.[432] The "national character" that is showing is that part of the French mystique that needs pressure, that needs upset and eruption to prove itself, to change itself. It is not a learned methodology; it is an expression intrinsic to the French. And it is Chirac.

And it is a spirit also recognizable as indigenous to western civilization; the *Marseillaise* "Allons Enfants de la Patrie; Aux Armes, Citoyens!" *("Let's go, children [offspring] of the Country; to arms, all citizens!")* is everyone's second most recognizable national anthem.[433 434*]

The major challenges that face Chirac and the Fifth Republic are unemployment, state finances, and an international policy that includes simultaneously the thrust toward European unity and the protection against Islamic terrorism that is threatening French security dramatically, in relation to immigrant flow from North Africa. These will always be the major stones around Chirac's neck.[435*]

And with all this unrest and fear and public outcry, we note that the present Fifth Republic has lasted thirty-six years (as of 1996), the second longest, after the Third Republic, constitutional span in France in two centuries. It will change.

---

432 *TIME* magazine, September 18, 1995, 85–86.

433 *The Marseillaise* was composed in 1792, three years after the storming of the Bastille, by Claude Rouget de Lisle, a Revolutionary engineer captain. It is named for its popularity with the soldiers from Marseilles. It was banned by Napoleon Bonaparte, his son (Napoleon II) Louis XVIII, and Napoleon III, understandably because of its rousing rhythms and text of revolt.

434 See the Astro-profile and history. But as well, note Chirac's horoscope (Birth Certificate reference, through astrologer Lynn Bell in Paris; Taeger Archives 1*): November 29, 1932, 12:00 P.M. GMT in Paris (Ascendant 20 Aquarius 47) an exact Sun-square-Mars aspect, Mars conjoined by Neptune in the 7th House (public charisma)! Additionally, *Chirac has Sun=Uranus/Pluto* (revolution, thrust of power), an echo of the 1st Republic Mars=Uranus/Pluto!

Chirac's Moon is in Sagittarius and it is peregrine in the 10th House (conjunct the Moon of the 1st Republic): rampant opinionation, unabashed speculation (ruling the 5th).

435 Chirac: Uranus in the second squared by Pluto in the 6th, ruler of the 9th, holding the Sun, squared by Mars-Neptune. The 2nd, 6th, and 9th Houses are extremely pressured: finances, (un)employment issues, and immigration and international markets.

■ Prediction ...

The Sixth French Republic Is Born July 1996-July 1998—
With the death of François Mitterrand, former two-term
socialist President of France (1981–1995), Chirac's predecessor
(for whom Chirac was Prime Minister from 1986), on January
8, 1996, an era in touch with the last World War, with the
Gaullist national resistance, ended. Mitterrand was a highly
decorated former member of the Resistance and a member of
the De Gaulle Assembly beginning in 1946. He was a leftist, a
liberal bridging relations with the Communists and formulating
France's modern Socialist Party.[436*]

Chirac is of the new generation of world leaders, dealing
with problems without anchor to mid-twentieth-century experience. He is positioned toward the conservative Right. The
new demands for internationalism within the European
Union—to relax national protectionism—the social unrest, and
a shrinking world now reminded of nuclear threat all call for
change in the government infrastructure of France.

If the world starts to shift away from utilization of nuclear
power, for example, France will have made a huge investment
and lost. If national safeguards keep foreign investment to low
levels, especially without participation by Japan with its electronics technology, France can only slow its progress. If methods for dealing with the nation's high unemployment rate do
not work, social unrest will escalate strongly.

The key unemployment issue is complicated by the very
high percentage of the unemployed being comprised of
unskilled workers and low-wage earners, with about one-third
of those being "long-term unemployed," i.e., without work for
more than one year. This is complicated by a net inflow into the
labor market of about 150,000 people, and all of these considerations are attached to the immigration concerns, punctuated
by rampant terrorism, and the European Union mood that is
decidedly anti-immigrant.[437]

---

436 Mitterrand was born October 26, 1916, at 4:00 A.M. in Jarnac, France (Taeger Archives
1*; well tested): Sun in Scorpio squared by Saturn-Neptune, Moon in the Libra Ascendant, Pluto conjunct the Midheaven, and Uranus without aspect in Aquarius.

437 Germany and Italy do not have this problem because of their lower birth rates. See *Foreign Affairs* magazine, November/December 1995, "Chirac of France," by Dominique
Moisi, Editor in Chief of *Politique Etrangere*, 8–13.

Chirac emphasizes military action as an essential instrument of diplomacy. This determination to be definite, to use force, is central to the French contribution to NATO policy with Bosnia—the stand for military intervention, which strongly influenced United States policy—and is key to Chirac's own "irrevocable" pursuance of nuclear testing, a decision that elicited disapproval from 60% of the French public, and his alarming move toward "Europeanization of the French nuclear deterrent" (as a deterrent factor for Europe to use as a whole); to the battle against Algerian terrorism in France focused upon the fundamentalist Islamic Armed Group (GIA) among the more than four million Muslims now living in France, demanding recognition, respect, and influence (see "Terrorism," page 132).

Dominique Moisi, Deputy Director of the Institut Français des Rélations Internationales, sees these challenges to France, to Chirac, as chiefly political, manifested in a series of scandals of corruption as well as in the terrorism, strikes, and street-rioting that are almost beyond the control of the government.

The French people are pressing for change. The new rise in value-added tax from 18.6% to 20.6% can backfire if there is a cutback in spending in protest. The growing social welfare funding gap will have risen from $281 billion in 1994 to $371 billion in 1995 and now looms dangerous, requiring even more taxation. Moisi concludes, "If Chirac fails to reconcile the French with themselves and their state, if a combination of social unrest and terrorist violence divides the society and fractures the culture, unsavory, undemocratic forces, such as Jean-Marie Le Pen's extreme right National Front, could become a much more serious and destabilizing political threat."[438]

Historian Alfred Cobban sees that the traditional enmity between the little people and the greats *(les petits, les gros) has survived intact in France through two centuries*, as "a class war of rich against poor, the unholy alliance of parties of the left and right [that have] a vested interest in its [the struggle's] perpetuation." It is still undecided in history if economic progress into the modern era—without the spirit of humanitarian reform—will indeed solve the rift, ease the tensions, and

438 Ibid, 8–13.

bridge the schism so that the pattern of social strife will cease to have relevance.[439]

Astrological analysis of France over 200 years, with a particular focus on the shift of each Republic to Empire and succeeding Republics, shows a French-characteristic pattern indeed, and it shows that this pattern is repeating itself now. France will announce a reformulation of constitution and government, the Sixth Republic, beginning dramatically, probably in October–December 1996, or shortly thereafter. It will be projected two years to completion, to Summer 1998. And this period will give Chirac time to complete the "profound" changes he promised upon his election.[440*]

If a plan for Reform is not announced by Fall 1996, France will erupt in tremendous revolt, and, characteristically, historically, revolution will again dictate change.[441*]

En route to this momentous time in French history, the financial crises will extend particularly strongly and painfully from Spring 1995 through October 1997. The international problems with political fallout from the nuclear testing, the pressures of European Union, and the immigration threats will be at their highest February–June 1996 and January– April 1997.[442*]

---

439 Cobban, Volume 3, 248–249.

440 *First Republic Chart—Shift to Napoleon Empire:* SA Midheaven exactly conjunct Moon, SA Uranus square Midheaven, tr Pluto square Moon, tr Uranus conjunct Sun; *Shift to the 2nd Republic:* SA Sun conjunct Mars-Midheaven, SA Moon conjunct Ascendant, tr Pluto at 25 Aries square the Ascendant exactly; *Shift to the 3rd Republic:* SA Pluto conjunct Moon, tr Saturn square Sun, tr Uranus conjunct 7th, tr Pluto square Pluto-Uranus axis; *Shift to the Vichy State:* SA Saturn conjunct Sun, SA Node conjunct Pluto, SA Moon conjunct Saturn, tr Uranus opposed Midheaven, tr Pluto square Sun/Moon; *Shift to the 4th Republic:* SA Pluto at 26 Cancer opposed Ascendant, SA Sun square Moon, SA Mars conjunct Saturn, tr Uranus conjunct Ascendant; Shift to 5th Republic: tr Pluto at 3 Virgo square the Moon; tr Neptune square Sun/Moon.

　Shift to "Sixth" Republic: SA Saturn conjunct Midheaven, December 1996, with tr Uranus=Sun/ Moon, tr Pluto conjunct Moon, SA Moon square Sun; tr Saturn square Ascendant and then conjunct Saturn 7/98 with SA Neptune building opposed Midheaven (exact June 1999); SA Pluto semisquare Jupiter, SA Ascendant conjunct Uranus (February 1998).

441 *Fifth Republic Chart—Shift to the 6th Republic:* tr Pluto square Pluto opposed Mars 1995-96, application of SA Pluto to conjunction with the Sun (exact June 1998); SA Uranus=Sun/Pluto, "new perspectives, sudden change, rebellion, reform" (August 1996), tr Saturn opposed Sun; tr Saturn conjunct Ascendant (June 1997).

442 Note Jupiter-Saturn Great Conjunction Chart for Paris, December 31, 1980 at 10:23 P.M., CET: tension routes are decidedly between the 2nd House and the 4th, involving Mercury tightly, ruler of Ascendant (people) and the Midheaven (government in power). In Spring 1997, tr Pluto opposes the Midheaven of this chart, tr Saturn opposes the Jupiter-Saturn conjunction and squares the Sun-Mercury conjunction, and tr Uranus squares the Moon, *simultaneously.*

■ Prediction ...

President Chirac Withdraws after One Term—President Chirac will see France through to its *Sixth* Republic. The framing of a new Constitution may precipitate new elections earlier than the ones presently scheduled in the Spring of 2002.

Between October 1999 and July 2000, probably in January 2000, Chirac will announce that he is withdrawing after his one term as president. The reason could well be ill health. He will leave much honored for his leadership.[443*]

Spain: The Reigns

The Celts, Phoenicians, Greeks, and Carthaginians in the 3rd Century B.C.E., searching for the limits to the Mediterranean sea; the conquering Romans seeking to expand the Empire; inland, mountain tribes fighting as family groups and feudal principalities; the Visigoths (Germanic sackers of Rome and Christian expansionists of the fifth–sixth centuries) taking over and organizing earliest religious and government structure; the Moselms (the Moors) from North Africa invading to defeat the Visigoth king(s) in the late eighth century—these are the dramatic and complex forces that defined early history on the enormous Iberian Peninsula.[444]

Throughout the Middle Ages, the Catholic states warred continuously with the Moors—and among themselves, in great political complexity, often using localized Moorish alliances(!) for added strength, one state against another. Gradually, they forced the Arabs out. The process was slow due to the protracted fighting among the Catholic Kings. The final victory rode the grand crest of the era's fervid Christian zeal and exploited the Moorish decline from the summit of its cultural and material achievements in the preceding centuries.

---

443 Chirac: tr Pluto conjunct the Midheaven 1 to 6/2000, with SA Uranus opposed Moon in the 10th ruling the 6th, tr Saturn square the Ascendant, SP Moon opposed Sun, and tr Uranus conjunct the Ascendant in 6–7/00.

444 The great Moslem hero *Jabal Tariq* led an army of 7,000 ashore by the massive pinnacle that dominates the entrance to the Mediterranean. The rock became a natural monument named for the hero, its name garbled through history into *"gibral'-ter"*). The Greeks specified Gibraltar as one of the Pillars of Hercules, the other Pillar being across the Mediterranean in northeast Morocco, marking the western limits Hercules defined for safe sailing.

Iberia entered the fifteenth century as an organization of three tense kingdoms: the dominant and geographically central Castile; Aragon in the northeast with predominant French influence; and Portugal, a western kingdom that gained its sovereignty from the others in 1143. The last Moorish outpost of Grenada (the kingdom to the south) surrendered in 1492.

Prince Ferdinand of Aragon and Isabella of Castile united Spain through their marriage on January 19, 1479, the day Juan II, King of Aragon, died. It was the beginning of Spain's formidable rise as a world power.[445*]

The Astro-profile of this unification of Spain responds reliably to major historical developments *for 496 years,* including and beyond the coronation of Juan Carlos in 1975 (see below). Spain is shown as innovative and experimental, with a broad international viewpoint; intensely Romantic, idealistic and didactic, with these energies promoted to convert (persuade) others. There is a self-destructive potential because of blind spots to national bad judgment, international policy not as right as the reigning monarch sees it to be. Religion and learning become very important and are used in strategic, coercive ways. There is disruption and upheaval and rebellion all closely tied to religion; national imposition upon the Spanish people and upon the world under its domain.[446*]

---

445 Ferdinand was born on March 10, 1452, in Sos (Aragon), Spain. A Grand Cross in Cardinal signs overwhelms a Pisces Sun-Neptune opposition and the Moon in Scorpio squared by Jupiter in Aquarius. The horoscope is very complicated, and so was he, fathering several illegitimate children (an heir apparent becoming insane as a child), wounded in battle, the early death of his beloved Isabella, a second marriage to the niece of the King of France, and death himself on January 23, 1512. Sun in Pisces, Moon in Scorpio.

Isabella was born on April 22, 1451, at Madrigal de las Atlas Torres (Castile), Spain, much stronger than her husband, with the Sun unaspected in Taurus and the Moon in Capricorn opposed Uranus (desire for influence, need to make things happen). Mercury square Jupiter-Pluto opposition. Axelrod & Phillips, 98 and 147.

446 Sun in Aquarius unaspected; Moon in Sagittarius in the 8th is squared by Pluto; *Sun/Moon=AP. Key: Mars opposed Saturn retrograde in Virgo.* Saturn rules the 9th. Note: Uranus-Neptune conjunction in Sagittarius opposed the Ascendant, in the 7th ruled by Pluto. Venus in the 9th, ruling the Ascendant, is in an Earth Grand Trine with Saturn and Jupiter in Taurus (rising in the Ascendant): a closed circuit of practical self-sufficiency, defensive, didactic, etc.; without Sun or Moon (separate profile; a split in character). Mars quindecile (upheaval) Pluto, ruler of 7th.

Eight tests (and more) prove this chart (SA, Transits): national bankruptcies (use mid-year, June 1 date) in 1569, 1607, 1627, 1647; War of Succession, January 1, 1702 (probable start date; see text later); Spanish-American War declared, April 25, 1898, Franco Revolution July 17, 1936, Juan Carlos inaugurated November 22, 1975. Researching these chart developments is *extraordinarily* rewarding and provides conclusive confirmation of the 1479 national chart as valid until 1975 and beyond. Use noon; probably the very time of the marriage of the rulers and unification of Spain. There are more tests developed in the presentation that follows.

In his written report of his first voyage, Christopher Columbus reminded Ferdinand and Isabella, the patrons of his mission: "You commanded that I should not go to the East by land, by which way it is customary to go, but by the route to the West, by which route we do not know for certain that anyone previously has passed."[447] The courage, the zeal, the innovation of imagination and exploration were brought into the purview of royalty. While clearly concerned with the acquisition of land to rule and wealth to spend, exploration was also buoyed by the philosophy that discovery, emigration, and colonization were the prerogatives of Christianity, to bring many and more into the Catholic realm. World triumph was conceived, fulfilled, and justified on behalf of God.

The Spanish Crown rode a mighty wave. The Pope at the time was Alexander VI, of Spanish birth (near Valencia), and he favored Ferdinand and Isabella for their help in securing his election. He gave the "Catholic Majesties" dominion over all the lands that they discovered three hundred miles west of the Azores, on the condition that the King and Queen converted to Christianity the peoples whom they found.[448]

And thus the Romance of the Crusades was revived, as was perception of Islamic threat and the spread of Judaism: the Catholic Kings expelled all Jews from Spain—some 400,000 of them, their confiscated property swelling the Spanish treasury; in 1499, the inquisitor general (the Office formed by Ferdinand and Isabella in 1478 and now stepped up in activity) mandated baptism of all Muslims in Spain under threat of expulsion from the country. Spain's monarchy was intent on becoming the "sword of Christendom."

At the same time, the demand for gold increased. Spanish and European monarchs wished to copy the Florentines and use gold for coins; gold was needed for vestments, churches, and tapestries. And thus, in tandem with the glories of New World discoveries and the growth of mighty nationhood, Spain birthed its "Golden Age."[449]

---

447 Hale, 45. Columbus: b. 1451-May 20, 1506; set sail from Palos, Spain ,August 3, 1492; first sighted land on October 12; returned to Spain March 15, 1493. Began second voyage to the New World from Cadiz, Spain, with seventeen ships and 1,500 colonists in November 1993.

448 Thomas, 59. The Papal Bull of May 4, 1493.

449 Ibid, 62. The phrase "the golden years" was coined in 1495 by the playwright Juan del Encina. Previous to discovery of gold in America, the gold of Europe came mostly from West Africa., and later from Australia as well. (See "Gold," page 87.)

Spain was taking in as well the spirit of humanism from Italy's Renaissance. There was a grand cultural awakening. Scholars were as prized as warriors, but beneath the cultural glitter and the shining gold, as beneath the rock called Gibraltar, there were rifts, fractures, politically and throughout the land. Old rivalries were resurrected as each faction gained more power; the Spanish Inquisition swept throughout the land in 1516 to capture, corner, and condition intellectual life.[450]*

For a long time, the sun always shone somewhere upon Spanish ships around the world, and conquests in Mexico (Hernando Cortez) garnered converts for Christ and brought back to Spain extraordinary amounts of gold, silver, slaves, power and prestige.

The War of Succession

Philip II (son of the Holy Roman Emperor Charles V), a great international monarch over Spain's world embrace from 1556 to 1598, was the great-grandson of Ferdinand and Isabella. In turn, Philip II's great grandson was Charles II, the last of the Spanish Hapsburgs (see footnote, page 154), another focus of the centuries of inter-breeding and suspect gene-pooling (with insanity, aberrance, and deformity occurring more and more frequently): Charles was physically crippled and mentally retarded. His mother, Mariana of Austria, was regent for him. Her bias in favor of Austria aroused opposition and she was forced into exile by Charles' illegitimate brother in 1677.

Spain was drastically on the decline in international politics, war, and finance. After a grand, lengthy summer, there had been a long fall, and a harsh winter loomed ahead. Charles died in 1700 *without leaving an heir.*

There were three pretenders to the Spanish throne: The Sun King, Louis XIV (see "Louis XIV," page 176), claiming the right through his eldest son (a grandson of Spain's Philip IV, whose daughter, Marie Therese, had been Louis' wife); the Prince of Bavaria; and the Holy Roman Emperor Leopold I. All three had family ties back to the royalty of Spain.

---

450 Development of the Spain horoscope through the dominating Saturn in Virgo, its opposition from Mars, becomes clear; Uranus-Neptune conjunction in Sagittarius in the 7th opposed the Taurus Ascendant.

England and Holland especially were against French and Spanish dominion: France and Spain were the biggest countries in Europe; such a tie would give the French awesome power and divert Spanish trade away from England and Holland.

Louis XIV tried to arrange a peaceful solution to this complex dilemma. France, England, and Holland arbitrarily divided up Spain's holdings, which ranged importantly into Italy (Milan, Naples, and Sicily). Louis then broke from that alliance and followed Spain's designation of an heir (through Charles' deathbed wish), who just happened to be a grandson of Louis XIV! Philip V became King of Spain in 1700. England, Leopold, and Holland then allied themselves against Louis, and war began early in 1702: the very significant *Spanish War of Succession.*[451*]

The French lost Bavaria and were forced out of northern Italy; the English seized Gibraltar (which it holds to this day 1995). Louis proposed peace to the Dutch in 1706, but the English pressed the war onward for another seven years with many campaigns in Spain. The Peace of Utrecht finally settled things. What was achieved was the Principle of Balance of Power, *that power took precedence over dynastic or national rights in the negotiation of European affairs.* May the strongest nation win! Military strength has been a political force ever since, especially in Spain.

Napoleon's Invasion

In 1808, Napoleon I, Emperor of France, invaded Spain. It occurred as the Peninsular War was being fought by France against Great Britain, Portugal, and Spanish guerillas. Under this tangled political skein, Spain secretly agreed to support the French (Napoleon) in its war against Portugal. Napoleon then, duplistically at the same time, began maneuvers to invade Spain and secure it for France.

Spain was humiliated; this time period was the nadir of its national history: Spanish King Charles IV and then his son, Ferdinand VII, abdicated successively, one day after the next. Napoleon installed his inept older brother, Joseph Bonaparte, as king of Spain. With Napoleon I overextended in his war with Russia and with

---

451 Using January 1, 1702, for the start of the War, the Spain horoscope (Ferdinand-Isabella, 1/19/1479) reveals the extraordinary measurements *SA Pluto exactly square Sun, SA Moon opposed Midheaven,* Progressed Ascendant exactly opposed Ascendant, tr Saturn opposed Saturn.

Britain's help, the Spanish resistance soon forced Joseph's abdication (1813) and the withdrawal of French troops from Spain. [452]*

By 1825, eleven of Spain's "discoveries" and holdings in Latin America had fought for and gained their independence. There were further wars fought about secession, there were more abdications; the country developed parties of extreme reactionaries, moderates and rabid separatists (including the Basques and Catalans; see below). An anti-monarchical Socialist scheme—human rights, representation, and welfare—was building as it had built and exploded in France at the end of the eighteenth century. The movement's battleground was international and it was harshest upon the soil of Spain's last remaining territories.

In the Caribbean, Cuba fought hard for its independence from Spain. A revolt was staged in 1868, to last ten years, over the issues of autonomy and slavery, but Spain reneged on its agreements to Reform, and yet another revolt was ignited in 1895 (the War of Independence).

In the United States, there was much sympathy for the human rights concerns in Cuba, and this sympathy was fanned strongly by American expansionists with many business concerns on the sugar-rich island just ninety miles south of the Florida Keys. Additionally, the United States was vigilant and defensive of Caribbean approaches to the future canal location across the Isthmus at Panama, to the Pacific.[453]

The new American president, William McKinley (inaugurated March 4, 1897), had promised to recognize Cuban independence and succeeded in obtaining limited self-government for the Cubans. But, there was an explosion on board the U.S. battleship *Maine* (260 killed) in Havana harbor. A naval court of inquiry determined that it had been blown up by an external bomb or mine, and McKinley blamed Spain. McKinley demanded from Spain an

---

452 Another spectacular proof of the 1479, noon horoscope for Spain; the abdications and war, May 5, 1808: SA Mars conjunct the Midheaven Sun, SA Saturn opposed the Sun, SA Uranus at 3 Scorpio square the Midheaven; SA Midheaven precisely conjunct the Moon; tr Neptune at 3 Sagittarius conjunct Uranus in the 7th, Uranus ruling the Midheaven; and the SP Moon exactly conjunct the Sun/Moon midpoint at 17 Capricorn. Tr Mars on that date was at 11 Taurus, just square the Sun.

453 Roberts, 659, 862. The Panama Canal was completed by the United States in 1914.
   Within the first twenty years of the twentieth century, the United States would intervene directly in the lives of the Caribbean Rrepublics. This policy finally gave way to Franklin Roosevelt's "Good Neighbor" policy (1931), ending its "gunboat diplomacy" protection of interests in Latin America.

immediate armistice with Cuba, the release of prisoners, and an American mediation position between Spain and Cuba.

McKinley asked Congress to authorize military force to bring about Spanish evacuation of Cuba. Congress recognized Cuba's Independence on April 19, 1898, and issued the ultimatum to Spain. The response from Spain was inadequate, and the United States declared war on Spain on April 25, 1898.[454*]

Navy and ground troops shattered the Spanish forces quickly, not only in Cuba *but simultaneously in Puerto Rico and the Philippines* (see "Philippines," page 73).

The Treaty of Paris, December 10, 1898, ended Spanish rule in Cuba, and, from the War, the United States gained the islands of Guam, Puerto Rico, and the Philippines; The United States became an overseas empire with accompanying military installation power and responsibilities, vital throughout the First and Second World Wars and into the Millennium.[455]

Cuba

Concurrent with the Treaty of Paris through which Spain gave up its sovereignty of Cuba, the United States occupied Cuba, and that occupation lasted almost four years. Full independence was granted to Cuba by the United States on May 20, 1902.[456*]

The Astro-profile for Cuba shows a headstrong, self-willed, stubborn country with a tremendous emphasis on materialism to show its value. There is bound to be over-analysis of everything, systems upon systems, complex, fiery, and extremist rhetoric to define the political position. Growth is very difficult because illusion supplants a practical plan. Therefore independence is

---

454 Spain horoscope: SA Mars tightly square Spain's 10th House Sun; SA Pluto conjunct the 7th cusp; SA Saturn had been square the Sun for the seven-year buildup of tensions; Saturn rules the international 9th. Tr Pluto was square the key Mars-Saturn axis in the horoscope (again, note Saturn rules the 9th).

455 And also the U.S. Naval base at Cuba's Guantanamo Bay, leased by Cuba to the United States in 1902; a point of tension with the Castro régime into the present.

456 The Cuban chart, May 20, 1902, at 12:00 Noon, LMT in Havana [Campion, *World Horoscopes*, #71] stands strong to every test; for example, the Castro revolutionary period 1955 [SA Saturn squared Cuba Pluto, ruler of the 4th (party out of power, revolutionaries) with tr Saturn opposed Mars, *tr Uranus opposed Saturn*, tr Pluto square Sun and Midheaven, opposed Ascendant!] through 1957 [SA Saturn squared Mercury, ruler of the Ascendant, with tr Pluto opposed the Ascendant and square the Sun and Midheaven, tr Neptune conjunct the Nodal axis].

toppled and there is reliance on other countries to define the national welfare.[457*]

World War I destroyed Europe's beet-sugar industry, and, with the concomitant rise of sugar prices throughout the world, Cuba entered a boom time, a glowing national Summer, in its early political existence, 1916–1923.[458*]

The boom collapsed, and price manipulations, corrupt management and administration, and fraudulent elections followed, working to recover the sweet dreams. A reform government lasted eight years, 1925–1933, and then Fulgencio Batista took charge, as military commander and then as president. Problems continued, and there was then a revolution led by political-activist lawyer Fidel Castro between 1955 and 1959. Batista fled Cuba on January 1, 1959.[459]

Castro's socialist regime purged all opposition, nationalized all American businesses in Cuba, and installed an infrastructure of far-reaching rigid reforms and controls that were modelled after the the Communist government in the Soviet Union. The United States broke diplomatic relations with Cuba in January 1961, and the infamous"Bay of Pigs" invasion staged by the United States with some 1,500 Cuban exiles trained by the United States Central Intelligence Agency (planned by Eisenhower, executed by Kennedy) was a failure in its attempt to unseat Castro and "free" Cuba, on April 17, 1961.[460*]

The Bay of Pigs fiasco led to the Cuban Missile Crisis on October 22, 1962, when the United States blockaded Cuba against delivery of missiles to Cuba by the Soviet Union. Soviet premier Nikita Kruschev backed down and agreed to remove all missiles and missile bases from Cuba. The United States lifted the blockade on November 20. The Cuban Missile Crisis was a turning point in the Cold War.

---

457 Sun in Taurus, Moon in Scorpio, Moon peregrine in the 3rd (communications, mind-set); Mercury ruler of Ascendant is conjunct Pluto in the 10th in Gemini and opposed *Uranus in the 4th*. Neptune is peregrine and equals the Aries Point(!). Mars in the 9th, ruling the 9th, is square Jupiter in Aquarius (international aid).

458 SA Sun conjoining Pluto and Mercury in the 10th, SA Moon opposed the Midheaven, SA Jupiter crossing the Descendant, SA Venus conjunct the Nodal Axis in the 9th (international trade relations) with tr Jupiter opposed Jupiter and square the Sun through most of 1920.

459 Axelrod & Phillips, 47.

460 Cuba chart: SA Uranus exactly conjunct Jupiter in Aquarius in the 6th (good fortune, optimism, with the military), with SP Moon trine Ascendant and sextile Node (positive confrontation); tr Mars opposed Saturn, tr Neptune conjunct Moon (deception of the maneuvers).

The Soviet Union and the communist bloc had taken up the trade deficit that had developed when the United States embargo began in 1961 and accounted for eighty percent of Cuba's international trade. The Soviet Union subsidized Cuba's economy, and when the Soviet Union itself collapsed 1991–92, Cuba reached its most constricted historical position. Cuban's foreign debt per capita became one of the largest in the world, and tens of thousands of immigrants swarmed to leave Cuba for the United States.[461]

Since the 1980s, huge Cuban populations within the United States have clamored for revolution to unseat Castro and to rebuild Cuba. Three major factions have been formed among the 600,000 Cuban Americans in the Miami, Florida, area: the Cambino Cubano, dedicated to peaceful transition to post-communist rule in Cuba, based on dialogue with Castro; the Cuban-American National Foundation, claiming some 200,000 members, formerly terroristically dedicated to forceful overthrow; and Alpha 66, an anti-Castro para-military group.[462]

■ Prediction ...

United States to Lift Trade Embargo of Cuba—The period from the Fall of 1994 to the Fall of 1995 saw renewed tensions out in the open in Cuba. With a country that was stronger and more fortified, a revolution would have "traditionally" taken place, complete with a new regime installed by early 1996. But Cuban people are too weak to rebel, and the Cuban rebels in the United States, while strong in numbers, are without resources to pull off a coup, since that action in Cuba would have to depend upon the Cuban people on the island, upon the Resistance that is so poorly formed.

As always, time creates change: charismatic leaders age and die, rebels finally negotiate, the children of exiles do not remember older times of loyalty and passion; radical doctrines mellow, and inflated needs for subsistence capital come to dominate national spirit. Cuba will begin to formulate a changed world-view late in 1996, occurring on a swell of protracted economic disappointment since the collapse of the Soviet Union and Cuba's hope for a return of international stature.

---

461 Williamson, Chapter 12.
462 *TIME* magazine, July 17, 1995, 22.

Castro can tighten Cuba's belt no further, nor can he delay further confronting the issue of isolation. Personally, Castro is projecting his future and his end: to fulfill his need to be honored and remembered as a humanitarian monarch, to make his place in history through benevolent power. In his desperate need for foreign investment, Castro will negotiate with other nations to invite their participation in a Cuban Renacimiento. Just as the Organization of American States lifted its sanctions of Cuba in 1975, after thirteen years of exclusion, so the United States, under pressure of business expansionism from sugar, tourism, and oil lobbies in America, will lift its embargo of trade and diplomatic relations between the Spring of 1997 and January 1, 1998.[463*]

A growth goal will be set by Castro timed for the Millennium. In all the excitement of Cuba's return to the international scene, the antiquated government and business infrastructures will be sorely taxed to adapt and function. Achievement of the national goals will be exceedingly difficult.[464] A whole generation will be required for the mindset of the people to broaden, to "get with the program." Key times for growth pains will be late in 1998, Summer 2000, and late Fall 2001.[465*]

The Spanish Civil War

The labyrinth of Spanish politics wove itself around monarchical movements (Alfonso and Charles parties), personality cults (Fascist dictators, the *Phalange* party), and numerous parties of socialist and communist bent, responding to the populist winds blowing Europe into the twentieth century.

---

463 Castro's birth year and place are ambiguous in the literature. The best testing I can do (see *Synthesis & Counseling*, 286–290, 652–654) suggests August 13, 1927, at 2:00 A.M. EST in Biran, Cuba (75W30, 20N45). The Sun is in Leo and the Moon probably in Aquarius, with a Fire Grand Trine, Gemini Ascendant, and an emphasized Neptune.

464 There is precedent for this in the best of times, i.e., during a sugar boom after Castro took power: the people broke all records for production but fell short of Castro's publicized and promoted quota expectations. This resulted in deep psychological disappointment, the sense of inferiority and futility among the people.

465 Cuba: Tr. Pluto opposed Sun, Midheaven, and square Ascendant 1995/96. *SA accumulated Square* June 1996, with tr Neptune conjunct Saturn retrograde in Capricorn. SA Jupiter conjunct Mars in the 9th, November 1996 with tr Pluto square Ascendant (last time). SA Sun square Midheaven in May 1997 with tr Uranus square Moon; *SA Sun conjunct Ascendant* in January 1998. SA Pluto square Uranus (ruling 6th, military, epidemic, labor force) with Ascendant=Mars/Pluto and Jupiter=Sun Moon in Fall 1998. Tr Saturn opposed Sun, Midheaven in Summer 2000.

Francesco Franco was a military man who earned a tremendous reputation and rapid promotion in the Spanish army in a 1912 war against Morocco, as commander of the Spanish Foreign Legion, and then as Director of Spain's prestigious military academy at Saragossa. The Republicans of the day then overthrew the dictatorship of General Jose Antonio Prima De Rivera in 1931, and accused Franco of having monarchist sympathies.

Through intrigue and the rise of the Conservative Right, Franco's lot changed, and a large conspiracy was mounted, erupting into the Spanish Civil War (an army revolt in Morocco against the Loyalist Republican government) on July 18, 1936, with Franco as its leader.

Immediately, Nazi Germany and Fascist Italy began to supply Franco with troops, planes, tanks, and other war materiel. In turn, the Soviet Union aided the Loyalists, and Great Britain and France tried to get 27 nations together to proclaim a non-intervention agreement. The agreement did not form, and Franco won successive battles throughout Spain; key cities toppled to his onslaught, and, with the fall of Madrid on March 28, 1939, and over one million people killed, Franco became de facto Fascist (the Falange Party) dictator of Spain.[466*]

Franco proved himself as cautious and methodical a politician as he had been a military strategist. He imprisoned and executed thousands of Loyalists and outlawed political parties. During the Second World War, he kept Spain officially neutral (as Spain had been during World War I under the reign of Alfonso XIII) while favoring the Axis forces.[467]

---

466 Franco was born December 4, 1892, in El Ferrol, Spain, probably close to 00:30 A.M. LMT (according to Penfield, church records, and Tyl testing): Sun in Sagittarius opposed Moon-Neptune-Pluto conjunction, 3rd–9th Axis, with this mighty axis squared by Mars; Mercury peregrine in Sagittarius, ruling the Ascendant and Midheaven; Jupiter opposed Saturn (prove-a-point signature).

In July, 1936, SA Uranus opposed his Midheaven, SA Node conjoined his Midheaven, tr Saturn opposed his Ascendant, tr Neptune squared his Sun; tr Jupiter conjoined his Sun.

Spain chart (1479): SA Mars-Saturn axis squared its natal position (as did everything else in the horoscope; 457 years, i.e., 10 accumulated semisquares; 5 accumulated squares). SP Moon conjoined Saturn and opposed Mars; tr Saturn opposed Saturn and conjoined Mars.

467 The Axis powers were those nations fighting against the Allied powers of the United States, Great Britain, and France during World War II: the Hitler-Mussolini, Berlin-Rome axis (military pact of 1939), with Japan, Hungary, Bulgaria, Romania, Slovakia, and Croatia joining in 1940.

At war's end, Spain found herself not entitled to any rewards of the Allied victory. Since Spain had no strategic alignment involving encroachment by the Soviet Union, the Allies had no incentive to share the spoils, as it were. Also, ignoring Spain was indirect "punishment" for the nation's falling to a dictator. It was "unthinkable" for Spain to be considered for benefit from the Marshall Plan aid for Europe. Additionally, in December 1946, the United Nations passed a resolution recommending a trade boycott of Spain, which lasted for three years. This was the beginning of Spain's dreadful *años de hambre*, "years of hunger."[468*]

Although the blockade was lifted in 1950, Franco continued with his harsh social regimen of frugality, control, repression, and isolationism, unable to buy foreign technology with which to catch up with post-War progress and modernization. Analyst John Hooper, in his humanistic study of *The Spaniards*, records the extraordinarily harsh conditions suffered by the people; that national income did not regain its pre-Civil War level until 1951, and personal income did not reach its 1936 level until 1954.[469]

Critically though, during these horrible times of insecurity, Franco *did* adjust his regime in 1947, on July 6, with the Law of Succession (recall the "War of Succession," page 196); Spain's sensitivity to head-of-state continuity and protocol).[470]

This Law declared that Spain was a *kingdom*, although it had no king, and Franco was its Chief of State for life; that Franco would be succeeded by "a person of royal blood" who would be approved by Parliament. Franco passed over the son of Alfonso XIII, the last Spanish king who had been deposed during post-World War I strife and the Republican uprisings, and chose *his* son (Alfonso XIII's grandson), Juan Carlos.

King Juan Carlos, The New Reign in Spain

With Franco's death on November 20, 1975, an era ended. The Generalissimo had made every important decision for Spain for 36 years. As Hooper observes, "His disappearance was of itself enough to justify a feeling of trepidation among supporters and opponents

---

468 The astrology: Spain (incredibly, yet again a proof)— *SA Saturn at 28 Sagittarius 40, 15 minutes of arc from exact conjunction with the Moon in the 8th;* SA Mars opposed the Moon; *tr Saturn at 9 Leo in December 1946, exactly opposite the national Sun.*

469 Hooper, 23–24.

470 Axelrod & Phillips, 101.

alike. But Franco had also left behind him a perilous gap in expectations between the people and their rulers."

On the day after Franco's death, Prince Juan Carlos was made to take an oath in front of members of Franco's Parliament, on his knees, with one hand resting on the New Testament, to swear loyalty to Franco and "fidelity to the principles of the *Movimento Nacional* and the fundamental laws of the realm."[471]

On November 22, 1975, Juan Carlos de Borbon y Borbon became King Juan Carlos I of Spain.[472*]

Juan Carlos's coronation created a companion horoscope for Spain, a modern outreach, if you will, of the basic foundation-of-Spain portrait created by the marriage between Ferdinand and Isabella in 1479. It is not unusual for national horoscopes to prevail over hundreds of years, and this one for Spain is undeniable in its validity still. The recent coronation is an embellishment to it.

Addition to the Astro-profile of Spain: the dimension of enormous self-confidence comes into Spain's portrait. There is an outreach to work with the rest of the world (an alteration of the international discovery thrust in the base horoscope). At the same time, within the centuries-old capacity to self-destruct through internal haggling, there is again an emphasis of the potential of rebellion, great political debates between the Conservatists (Monarchists) and the Liberals (the Socialists), between the nationalists and the separatists (among the Basques and Catalans, especially; see below). There are immigration concerns internationally and domestically, in the management of hordes of field workers who have swelled the cities of Spain seeking better jobs for over fifty years, and there are the concomitant concerns of employment, public health and welfare and social security.[473*]

King Juan Carlos is orientated to humanitarian or social service channels, all accomplished through innovative ideas, supported by

471 Hooper, 35, 37.

472 The "Borbon" references refer to dynastic family ties to the French Bourbon family that for generations ruled France, Naples and Sicily, and Spain, beginning in France in 1272. The rule in France was interrupted with Louis XVI's post-Revolution execution in 1793, and was restored with Louis XVIII in 1814. Meanwhile, Louis XIV's (the Sun King's) grandson came to the Spanish throne in 1700. The last Bourbon descendant to rule in Spain was Alfonso XIII, grandfather of Juan Carlos I, deposed after World War I.

473 Juan Carlos was crowned on November 22, 1975, at 12:45 P.M. CET in Madrid (Campion, *World Horoscopes*, #312): Sun in Scorpio, Moon in Cancer in the 6th square Venus-opposed-Jupiter. Saturn opposes the Aquarian Ascendant and squares Uranus, its ruler, positioned in the 9th. Mars is peregrine in 00 Cancer=the Aries Point.

technological development, especially in communications and education. He has strong stability of purpose and is determined to make
things happen. His serious demeanor, modest ways, and tight communication style belie a great store of energy and sports enthusiasm.

When a lieutenant-colonel in the Civil Guard marched into
Congress on February 23, 1981, with a detachment of men, to hold
every politician of note in Spain at gunpoint for almost twenty-four
hours, the country was on the brink of a military coup. Indeed, the
officer was a "military fanatic," but it was the King's quick wits,
steady nerve, and authority that saved the day: using a specially
designed communications center which he had had installed to
enable him to talk directly to the country's eleven captains-general
anywhere at any time [great respect for the military], Juan Carlos
assured all of them that the take-over attempt of the government
did not have his backing. The core military then responded against
the fanatic fringe. Thereafter Juan Carlos worked to persuade the
government to appease the military. This becomes a very important
consideration in government affairs in Spain.[474]

The military was/is comparatively ill-equipped in materiel and
technological support because of the hard times in Spain; implicitly they faced then and still do embarrassment in comparison with
the military forces of other countries. Spain is a huge country and
its military force is very small (even today, ranking 27th in active
troop strength among countries), but its sense of tradition, its history of involvement in government, is great. With the Napoleonic
invasion in 1808 (see "Napoleon's Invasion), the military was created to effect persistent intervention in government, which Hooper
sees as the hallmark of Spanish politics during the last century.
Since Napoleon in 1808, through some forty-four uprisings culminating with the Civil War in 1936, the military has established its
significance as interpreters of the will of the people.

It is no surprise that Spain's return to world fame in terms of
public outreach was not through the discovery of another new
world but through the bringing of the world to the New Spain,
through the Summer Olympic Games of 1992.[475*]

---

474 Hooper, 45.
475 Juan Carlos: born January 5, 1938, at 1:15 P.M. (Taeger Archives and others, Church
    Records) in Rome, Italy. Sun in Capricorn, Moon peregrine in Aquarius; Jupiter at the
    Midheaven in Aquarius opposed Pluto; Saturn square Mercury in zero Capricorn,
    square the Aries Point; *Jupiter=Sun/Moon.*

More than 14,000 athletes, representing a record 172 nations, gathered in Barcelona to compete for sixteen days in 257 events at Olympiad XXV. Television broadcast the games and the growth, maturation, and culture of modern Spain to hundreds of millions of people throughout the world.[476]

The Nations Within the Nation

In addition to the historical themes of development in terms of international discovery and loss, and re-ascendancy to world view; of the military as bridge between people and politics; of the insistence for monarchical leadership, there is the age-old strain of regionalism, the passionate emphasis of regional sub-entities within Spain that are constant considerations for the government and the King.

John Hooper observes that Spaniards tend to put their loyalty to their home region on a par with, or even ahead of, their loyalty to their country." Regional sentiment bedeviled attempts to build a strong unitary state in Spain during the sixteenth and nineteenth centuries. It is separatism in the shape of ETA (the Basque political party) and its supporters which now poses perhaps the greatest threat to the survival of democracy."[477]

Spain is nearly half again as large as reunited Germany and is almost twice the size of Italy and four times the size of England, thirty percent larger than Japan. The desperation of the hard times swelled the cities and left the agrarian plains sparsely populated. The effects of that time during and after the Civil War haunt Spanish government social programs still today. The countryside is dotted with widely spaced communities, dramatically separated from one another, kept that way by the dearth of navigable waterways, just as it was in early history. Regionalism is key for self, family, and ancestral identification.

Opening of Olympics: July 25, 1992, in Barcelona shows, in the New Spain coronation chart, SA Uranus precisely to the minute conjunct the Node in the 9th at the Midheaven (enormous public exposure), SA Ascendant at 20 Aquarius 37 square the Node, tr Pluto at 20 Scorpio also conjunct the Node, and tr Mars exactly opposed the Sun at the Midheaven, with tr Sun conjunct the Descendant!

In the Old Spain chart—astounding corroboration: *SA Moon conjunct Jupiter*, SA Pluto square Ascendant, SA Ascendant at 22 Libra square Venus, ruler of the Ascendant, in the 9th, tr Saturn conjunct the Sun at the Midheaven, tr Sun opposed the Midheaven. The SP Venus from 1479 was conjunct the Ascendant!

476 *The World Almanac*, 1996.

477 Hooper, 204, 208, Chapter 18. "ETA," *Euskadi Ta Askatasuna*, in the strange Basque language, "the Basque Nation and Freedom."

As in early times, the very earliest—perhaps 3,500 years ago, in parallel with the time set for the early settlements of Canaan, the time suggested for the Jewish Exodus out of Egypt (see "Exodus," page 106)—immigrants emerged in the northeast of Spain along the present-day border with France and human history there began. Were these earliest people the Basques?

The Basque language (*not* a Spanish dialect) is practically inscrutable to semanticists; it contains an echo of Caucasus and Georgian languages of the far Middle East and of the Berbers of North Africa. Basque body structure, the relative size of appendages, bone study, and especially startling revelations of blood analysis link the Basques together as *separate from the rest of European stock* yet strangely part of European evolution. Consensus at present establishes the Basques as possible direct descendants of Cro-Magnon man (French-area humans, 30,000 years ago, later than the German-area Neanderthal), Europe's aboriginal population.

The Basques are known to be fiercely independent. Only with Roman rule of Iberia were they effectively subjected to a central administration. The people were "innocent and quite unprepared for the new ideas that were to enter the country during the nineteenth century—and in particular the Napoleonic concept of a centralized state whose citizens should all be subject to the same laws." Since the Civil War, the Basques have energetically resisted centralization; they have persisted with their language, their laws, their customs, and, with explosive terrorism, have pressed those rights for political acknowledgment.[478]

Today, 25% of Spain's inhabitants speak a a second (regional) language in addition to or instead of Spanish. For self-protection and self-aggrandizement within a history of assaults and fractures, regionalism gives security and autonomy. Consequently, regionalism comes before nationalism: the town, the county, the cultural sub-group—all before the country. In their quest for autonomy within Spain, the Basques are the major focus of the sense of nation within the Nation; but there are the Catalans along the Mediterranean coast; there are the Galicians to the West; the Andalusians to the North, all making similar demands. It is an explosive situation for the present-day government of Spain. Unity is threatened; rebellion lives still.

---

478 Hooper, 223.

In 1978, Spain's constitution changed: the concept of "Autonomous Community" was introduced, with each such Community being made up of a single province or several neighboring provinces. Each Community was to have a President, a Governing Council, a Legislative Assembly, and a Supreme Court. All of this new infrastructure, catering to the regionalist demands, will require for administration an estimated 100,000 of the government's employees.[479]

A Socialist majority was elected to Parliament in 1982; Spain entered NATO on June 30, 1982; in 1989, Spain became head of the European Communities Council of Ministers (EC) and joined the European Monetary System, all paving its way into the European Market consciousness approaching the Millennium.

At the same time, though, these unifying, national accomplishments were jarred by a General Strike in 1988 that forced the government to increase unemployment benefits, yet the unemployment rate of 16.4% in 1990 was and still is one of the highest in Europe; there were terrorist bombings by the Basques in 1989, demanding full national independence; and the Socialist Workers' Party, after winning four consecutive elections 1982–1993, showed weakness nationally in the election of May 28, 1995.[480]

Will the army intervene?

■ Prediction ...

Upheaval in Spain for Drastic Government Change—Spain can not hold down or service the increasing demand of more people for a sense of security and self-reliance within the panoply of the government. Political infrastructure is overextended and exhausted. Sedition is forming and will erupt between November 1996 and June 1997. The King, the monarchy, can easily—and typically—become the scapegoat for government dysfunction, even with new leadership.[481*]

---

479 Ibid, 255, 261.
480 Under Spanish law, the unemployed cease to receive benefits after twenty-four months of no work. The assumption is that the family will support the worker. Hooper, 104.
481 *Old Spain:* SA Pluto square Neptune (May 1997), tr Uranus conjunct the Midheaven (2–6/96; 1–3/97); *New Spain:* SA Uranus conjunct the Midheaven (November 1996), SA Pluto square Saturn (August 1997); *Juan Carlos:* an extreme May 1997 with SA Pluto opposed Saturn, ruler of the Midheaven, tr Neptune conjunct the Midheaven, tr Saturn square the Sun, tr Pluto conjunct the Node; the King's Tertiary Progression for May 1, 1997 is dramatic as well with TP Saturn exactly square the Midheaven, TP Uranus conjunct the Ascendant, TP Moon exactly conjunct Mars, ruler of the 12th and more.

The monarchy, the King personally, is in danger, most especially between April 28 and May 10, 1997. This grand disorder will affect Spain's position within the European Union; Spain's problems will spill over into the rest of Europe, slowing the progress of the European Union, striking a chord with German and French domestic concerns.

The upheaval will last two years, until Summer 1999, with a mid-point climactic stage after Spring 1997 occurring in March 1998. The revolt will be seen as a "people's revolt" rather than a military coup. It will be sparked by the Basque demand for a separate nation. Other social welfare concerns will flood into the breach of government structure. Terrorism will predominate, and new political parties aligning themselves to voice the rebellious sentiments of the people will recall what Franco did when he amalgamated the three warring political parties (before outlawing them) into a new unity, the National Movement: *The Falange Española Tradicionalista y de las Juntas de Ofensiva Nacional-Sindicalista.* The concept of separation, of heterogeneity, acknowledged within traditional togetherness and protected by the military may be hard to pronounce and taxing to achieve, but it will be Spain's Millennial way toward nationalism organized through greater internal unity.

Royal England — For Succession to Succeed

The French Connection

The conquest of England by the Normans (from the area in Northwest France long contested between England and France) gave England a unified identity in 1066. The English king, Edward the Confessor (1042–1066), had grown up in the Norman court, the son of a Norman mother. He joined her and her new Danish husband in England and ascended to the throne in 1042. His efforts to unite all the rival earls throughout the land were unsuccessful.

Edward—who was at heart a French monk—reluctantly married the daughter of Godwin, the greatest English Earl, and stubbornly refused to give his wife a child (and England an heir).[482] There was a great falling out with Godwin because Edward favored

---

482 Delderfield, 20. Or "led a chaste life," depending on sources; see Longford, 41.

Normans when he filled key court appointments. A revolt was born, but Edward put it down and banished Godwin and his family. Edward then named William of Normandy (his second cousin) to be his successor.[483]

Edward was not inclined to secular affairs and gave all his time to the building of St. Peter's Abbey at Westminster (Westminster Abbey, which was consecrated on December 28, 1065) and a new palace nearby. Shortly before his death, Edward changed his mind about succession—perhaps on his deathbed—and named Harold, son of Godwin, as next in line.[484]

Harold I was militant and defensive in his brief reign, and he was defeated and killed in battle with William of Normandy, William "the Conqueror." William was crowned William I of England, ending the line of Anglo-Saxon kings, on Christmas Day, 1066, at Westminster.[485*]

The Coronation ceremony is cited as the "only recorded case of the Conqueror showing fear." The service was conducted by two prelates, the Archbishop Ealdred of York in English and Bishop Geoffrey of Coutences in French.

> But at the prompting of the devil, who hates everything good, a sudden disaster and portent of future catastrophes occurred. For when Archbishop Ealdred asked the English, and Geoffrey bishop of Coutences asked the Normans, if they would accept William as their king, all of them gladly shouted out with one voice if not in one language that they would.

> The armed [Norman] guard outside, hearing the tumult of the joyful crowd in the church and the harsh accents of a foreign tongue, imagined that some treachery was on foot, and rashly set fire to some of the buildings. The fire spread rapidly from house to house; the crowd who had been rejoicing in the church took fright and throngs of

---

483 Delderfield, 18–21.

484 Edward was canonized in 1161 by Pope Alexander III. His feast day is October 13.

485 This is the horoscope moment for England most studied by astrologers for the profile of England: December 25, 1066, set at 12:00 noon at Westminster. No exact time is known.
The speculative horoscope for England is defined in the main by the Moon in the last degree of Pisces (?) squared by Uranus, a peregrine Mars in Aquarius, ruler of the Aries Ascendant, and an Earth Grand Trine among Mercury, Neptune, and Saturn. Saturn rules the Midheaven and is retrograde. See Campion, *World Horoscopes*, pages 376–395.

men and women of every rank and condition rushed out of the church in frantic haste. Only the bishops and a few clergy and monks remained, terrified, in the sanctuary, and with difficulty completed the consecration of the king who was trembling from head to foot.

Almost all the rest made for the scene of conflagration: some to fight the flames, and many others hoping to find loot for themselves in the general confusion. The English, after hearing of the perpetration of such misdeeds, never again trusted the Normans who seemed to have betrayed them, but nursed their anger and bided their time for revenge.[486*]

Had the Normans not invaded England, England would probably have become part of the northern Scandinavian world.

The Norman Conquest created a social revolution in England. All the Saxon lands were divided up among the Normans, and the feudal system of land-holdings in return for military obligations was instituted throughout England.

The tensions between England and France never died: Richard the Lionhearted *(Coeur-de-Lion)*, for example, had little English blood and spent only ten months of his ten years' reign in England; there is doubt that he even spoke English. His successor was the cruel and avaricious King John, born in Oxford, who waged war with France and lost Normandy in 1204. In a fierce confrontation with the Pope about human rights (the Magna Carta), John was

---

486 Longford, 50, quoting the *Orderic Vitalis.* One must ask: if the guards were outside and the ceremony was taking place during daylight hours, i.e., noon for the timing of the horoscope, were torches indeed at hand outside for immediate deployment by the guards in panic as diversion from the tumult they supposed was occurring?

Might this scene inspire testing with a *different* time on that day (evening): perhaps 3:20 LMT, with the Moon in *Aries*, still square Uranus in Sagittarius, now *ruling* the 9th (empire) and 10th, with Pluto conjoining the Midheaven! The Moon rules a Cancer Ascendant in this option. Might research to the late afternoon time uncover a new, fundamental horoscope for England in place of the traditional "noon" chart on this coronation day?

Initial random time checks to check Angles are encouraging: *Magna Carta June 15, 1215:* SA Moon opp MC, SA ASC squ MC, SA Plu opp Ven, *SP Moon opp MC;* tr Ura opp Moon; *Ascendancy of the Tudor line, October 30, 1485:* SA Asc opp MC, SA Moon squ MC, SA Sun conj Plu in 10; Ura Return, ruler of MC; *Henry VIII break with Pope, July 23, 1529:* SA Nep opp MC. SA Asc squ Sun, SP Moon conj MC, tr Ura conj Asc, tr Sat squ Moon; *WWI,* SA Plu conj Asc, tr Plu conj Asc, SA Sun squ Mars, SP Moon conj Moon, tr Ura conj Mars in 9; *WWII:* SA Asc opp Nep, SA Moon squ Nep, SA Mars conj Asc opp Ura, ruler of 9 and 10; SP Moon conj MC, tr Plu conj Mars in 9, tr Ura conj Nep.

excommunicated and then finally surrendered to Innocent III, one of the greatest medieval popes.[487]

Edward I fought France (his wife's homeland) for five years, in the early 1270s. Then, intermittently between 1337 and 1453, during the reigns of five English kings, England carried on the "Hundred Years War" against France. The battles were over contested territory in France, commercial activity in Flanders, the French support for Scottish independence, and the claim of English King Edward III (through his mother, Isabella, daughter of French King Philip IV) to the French crown itself.[488]

In 1366, Edward III and Parliament repudiated the feudal supremacy of the papacy over England, claiming that King John had acted illegally (without the consent of the nation) in his surrender to Pope Innocent III.

The German House

Because King James II (of Scotland, 1685–88) appeared bound to impose Roman Catholicism upon the English people, a grand revolt rose up, and the King was deposed in the "Glorious Revolution." The revolt was led by his Dutch brother-in-law, William of Orange, who in turn became King William III. The Act of Settlement then barred royalty from marrying a Catholic or a Catholic becoming sovereign.[489*]

---

487 Innocent III reigned from 1198 to 1216: besides forcing King John of England to be his vassal, he pressed Holy Roman Emperor Otto to support Frederick II of Germany, initiated the disastrous fourth Crusade of 1202, and presided over the fourth Lateran Council (1215), which defined "transubstantiation" (the Communion symbolism) and established requirements for Church membership. He also defined the legal theory of the papal monarchy.

488 This claim was not surrendered until 1802, on March 27, at the Treaty of Amiens, ending the War of Second Coalition. Great Britain abandoned claims to the French throne, returned territorial gains to France, and withdrew from Malta. France agreed to abandon Naples.

489 King James II is not the King James who commissioned a new translation of the Bible. That king was King James I, grandfather of James II, who ascended the throne in 1603, called a conference in January 1604 "for the hearing and for the determining things pretended to be amiss in the Church." James I gave his approval for a new translation on February 10, 1604. Fifty-four learned men took on the task, and the first edition of the King James Bible was published seven years later. The Jupiter-Saturn Great conjunction chart for this period (December 18, 1603, at 6:50 A.M. in London) is strongly declarative about 9th House matters: the era of exploration and the translation of the Bible. Note that this Great Conjunction at 8 Sagittarius 19 was square Neptune at 6 Virgo in the 9th. In the conjectured 1066 chart (see footnote #485), 1066 Jupiter is at 7 Virgo. The Great Conjunction Chart's Sun was exactly conjunct 1066 Uranus, ruler of the 1066 9th House.

William III and his wife Mary II, who died at age thirty-two, had no children. William died in 1702, aged fifty-two, in a fall from a horse.

Anne, the second daughter of the deposed Catholic King James II (of Scotland), ascended to the throne, with her "dim" Danish husband. Anne was described as "an ordinary and at times vulgar" woman. She had seventeen children, all of whom died: twelve of miscarriages and five at an early age (hydrocephalus). Her child-bearing trials left her semi-invalided.

But Queen Anne reigned in a "brilliant age," 1702–14, articulated by brilliant thinkers, writers, architects, and scientists, including Swift, Pope, Christopher Wren, Locke, and Newton. Her affairs of State conducted by gifted diplomats were highlighted by the Union of England with Scotland, forming Great Britain in 1707.[490*]

The concern of formal succession became crucial at this time in England's (Great Britain's) history. A granddaughter of James I, the first Stuart King of England (1603–1625), offered the solution: she was named Sophia and she was the nearest *Protestant* relative of the early Stuarts. She had married Duke Ernest Augustus, a German Protestant leader of importance in the Thirty Years War 1618–48 (see page 154). Augustus had been given the rank of *Elector*—and his lands were called the Electorate—*of Hanover.* It was to their son, George Ludwig, that England reached to regain a new "House" of lineage for succession of the English throne.[491]

George I became the first Hanoverian king of England in 1714. There would be no separation from the Hanover line until 1837 when, to accommodate the succession of Queen Victoria—since Hanover did not recognize female succession—the "German Arms" were removed from the Royal Arms of England. Hanover was then taken into Bismarck's Germany, the second Reich (see "Second Reich," page 154).

In 1760, succession led to the great-grandson of George I: the infamous George III who reigned for fifty-nine years, overseeing extraordinary epochs of history: England's loss of the colonies in America during the American Revolution; the French Revolution and

---

490 Delderfield, 96. See Campion, *World Horoscopes*, #356.

491 Sophie was the fifth and only Protestant daughter of Elizabeth of Bohemia, James I's only daughter. The Succession Act deliberately passed over "superior" rights of the Stuarts represented by the *Catholic* James II. The outreach to Hanover was purely statutory. Delderfield, 102.

the Age of Reason (Enlightenment, see page 176); England's transition into the nineteenth century; its confrontation with and defeat of Napoleon (see page 179). George's mind was weak; by the end of his reign, blind for fifteen years, he was acknowledged as insane.[492]*

Yet, George III was simple, scandal-free (no womanizing), and pious, and it followed that he was respected and loved by many.

George resigned much ministerial power to William Pitt, son of the famous Minister William Pitt who had also served King George. He installed his eldest son to rule for him as Regent for the last nine years of his life. This son would become George IV.

England and Ireland were joined in 1801. The population doubled, foreign trade quadrupled, and the national debt sextupled because of the wars. Income tax was introduced upon the people to help pay for those wars. Great military leaders like Wellington and Nelson administered the strength of England; geniuses showed the light of England's literature and art: Johnson, Gibbon, Scott, Jane Austen, Byron, Coleridge, Wordsworth, Shelley, and Keats; artists like Gainsborough and Reynolds.

Queen of an Era

Queen Victoria came to the throne as the granddaughter of George III (after orderly but poor-performance succession by his two sons: the second one, William IV, having sired only two daughters, i.e., females barred from succession according to the Salic Law of the Hanover House). England separated from Hanover (Germany) to keep succession on English soil. Victoria was barely five feet tall, ascended to the throne at age eighteen, married a German Prince (Prince Albert, her first cousin), produced four sons and five daughters, survived seven attempts on her life, reigned for sixty-three years and gave her name to an era.[493]*

---

492 George III was born on June 4, 1738, at 8:00 A.M. LMT (source: Alan Leo), in London (Norfolk House at St. James's Square). Note the stellium in *Gemini* focused on *Mercury in Gemini*, ruling the mental 3rd. Mars in Aries squares the Moon-Uranus conjunction *in the 6th, ruled by Saturn conjunct Mercury*. The Sun in Gemini rules the Ascendant and is peregrine. Moon quindecile Mercury (upheaval); Saturn=Sun/Moon, Mercury/Neptune, Mercury/Venus. In personal description, observers noted his fast talk, his abundant gestures. His favorite food: sauerkraut with lemonade. Longford, 310.

493 Victoria was born May 24, 1819, at 4:15 A.M. LMT at Kensington Palace, London (Taeger Archives, biography). Note the New Moon Gemini birth and the Grand stellium (Aries and Taurus) *in her 12th House;* the Saturn-Pluto conjunction in the 11th was squared by the Uranus-Neptune conjunction on the cusp of the 8th, Uranus ruling the Midheaven. Jupiter was in Aquarius alone in the 10th.

When her beloved Prince Albert died—he had introduced the Christmas Tree to England from Germany, conceived and promoted the Crystal Palace Exhibition of 1851 which attracted some six million people and great profit, taught Victoria management skills, yet stayed quite in the background—Victoria withdrew into seclusion for five years, and did not open Parliament until 1866. Her period of mourning lasted for twenty-six years. Out of her pain, loneliness, and seclusion, she projected upon her country and an entire generation a prudery of sexual taboos. Also because of her seclusion, although attentive to details of government operation, her absence from government visibility and confrontation brought about a wave of unpopularity.[494]

During her reign, England went from coaches to modern transportation and communication; the Empire doubled in size: New Zealand, Canada, Australia, parts of Africa, and India all came under her dominion. Wars were fought in Afghanistan, Zululand, Egypt, the Sudan and South Africa. She [England] was related directly or through marriage to the royal houses of Germany, Russia, Greece, Romania, Sweden, Denmark, Norway, and Belgium.[495]

Victoria regained enormous popularity toward the end of her reign, celebrating in grand style her fiftieth and sixtieth Jubilee years as England's longest-reigning monarch. Her conscientiousness and strict morals helped restore the prestige of the crown and establish it as a symbol of national honor, unity, and public service.

Constitutional Upset

Edward VIII, Victoria's great grandson, was king without a crown. Dashing, popular Edward VIII ascended to the throne upon the death of his father, George V, on January 20, 1936. During the inter-regnum period before his planned coronation, problems that had been brewing for some time exploded into public view: his love affair with an American woman, Wallis Warfield Simpson.[496*]

---

494 Her Ministers were exceptional. Among them Lord Melbourne, Benjamin Disraeli, William Ewart Gladstone, Lord Salisbury. They were her eyes, ears, and administration.

495 Delderfield, 128–130.

496 Edward (later Duke of Windsor) was born June 23, 1894, at 10:00 P.M. at White Lodge, Richmond (London); Taeger Archives, church records. Sun in Cancer trine the Moon in Pisces in the 1st, with an Aquarian Ascendant. Mars in Aries squares the Sun, ruler of the 7th. Neptune-Pluto conjunction in the 4th, with Pluto ruling the 9th holding peregrine Uranus, ruler of the Ascendant. Jupiter, ruler of the Midheaven, is trine Saturn; AP=Sun/Moon (public projection); Venus in Taurus=Uranus/Midheaven (feelings exposed; promiscuity).

Edward and Wallis—a married woman, living with and about to divorce her second husband—were seen together everywhere in London: "Wallis [was] usually overdressed and bejeweled, would turn up on the arm of the heir apparent at parties, balls, and even the Royal Opera House. Her appearances were treated as sensational and, to many in the 1930s high society, as scandalous, because society knew she was a married woman, still living with her second husband."[497]

Edward's mother, Queen Mary (wife of George V), "feared for the monarchy itself" unless Edward put his personal life second to his position as king, representing the entire nation. "Britain could not support a twice-divorced woman as Queen."

The government indeed opposed the marriage. Edward resisted the opposition. Constitutional procedure was threatened. While there was precedent for a king's marriage to a divorced woman— Henry II to Eleanor of Aquitaine—the idea was intensely disliked. The public wanted the Georgian sense of duty preserved in the monarchy, not the introduction of "Edwardian charm."

The Church of England censured the entire concept of divorce. Edward was neglecting his "spiritual responsibilities." Edward's choice became a drastic one: sacrifice his scandalous relationship and become crowned King of England or abandon the throne for life with the woman he loved.

After his 325-day reign, on December 11, 1936, Edward VIII became the first English monarch to abdicate the throne. He presented his decision personally to the world over an historic radio broadcast. His younger brother became George VI—and it is he who would sire Elizabeth II, the present queen.

Edward was given the title of Duke of Windsor and exiled. He traveled a great deal, became Governor of the Bahamas, and then spent most of the rest of his life in Paris. He suffered cancer at age seventy-eight, was visited by Elizabeth, with great sympathies of an entire generation with him in retrospect. He died shortly after the Queen's visit, and his wife Wallis died fourteen years later. They are buried together at Windsor.

During the time period from Ascension to Abdication, SA Mars tightened opposition with Uranus; *SA Venus exactly conjoined the Sun, ruler of the 7th, in the 5th.* Tr Neptune squared Jupiter, ruler of the Midheaven, tr Uranus squared the Ascendant, and more.

497 Davies, 38.

The Problems Anew

Queen Elizabeth faces the same problems that have haunted the English monarchy routinely for almost a thousand years: concerns of succession, philandering males—in her case, going beyond her husband Prince Philip, to her son and heir apparent Charles and the "lesser royals" of the extended family—the harsh publicity given to family upset, collisions with the Church of England, financial pressures related to royal privilege, and the clash between tradition and modernization.

The Astro-profile of Queen Elizabeth focuses upon seriousness to the point of severity: she is an extremely stubborn woman with a tremendous need for recognition, respect, and appreciation. Her will, her sense of responsibility, is formidable, dominating everything about her. Everything is well organized to fulfill her leadership position, the monarchy for which she lives. Her sense of mission dominates her life and justifies personal sacrifice of her much warmer private self, her need for an authoritative man and the strong confirmation of personal love (apparently incompatible historically with a queen's reign, except in the case of Queen Victoria and her Prince Albert). Elizabeth is undoubtedly a lonely monarch.[498*]

In November 1992, at a celebration luncheon honoring her fortieth year as Queen, Elizabeth spoke not about the glories of her royal experience but, historically, she spoke candidly of the Winter of her reign, acknowledging her *Annus Horribilis*.[499*]

Elizabeth had lived an adult lifetime of silent endurance of adulterous peccadilloes by her husband, Prince Philip, the divorce problems of her sister Margaret and her daughter Anne, the marital debacle of son Andrew and the indebtedness of his wife, "Fergie,"

---

498 Queen Elizabeth II: born April 21, 1926, at 2:40 A.M. GMD at the home of the Duchess of York's parents, 17 Bruton Street, in London. (Carter; Taeger; birth certificate) Sun in Taurus, Moon in Leo, Mercury in Aries all peregrine, indomitably strong. Saturn, ruler of the 21 Capricorn 23 Ascendant, is *retrograde and/but conjunct the Scorpio Midheaven*. Mars-Jupiter rising in Aquarius opposes Neptune in the 7th, and this axis is squared by the Midheaven-Saturn focus (perseverance in spite of fears, breakdown of idealization, a heavy cross). Moon=Sun/Saturn (loneliness, personal needs under wraps, hurts); Pluto=Sun/Uranus (drive for power, new reality, driving reforms).

499 Please recall footnote #486 regarding research toward a more definitive grounding chart for England. In the conjectured chart for 3:20 P.M. LMT, December 25, 1066, in Westminister, progressed for Elizabeth's *Annus Horribilis*, we see SA Saturn tightly square Uranus, ruler of the Midheaven, on the 7th cusp; SA Mars=Sun/Moon and SP Moon (ruler of the Acendant) exactly conjunct Mars at the time of the Windsor Castle fire, November 1992. Tr Saturn was applying to the MC, tr Pluto to square the Midheaven.

the rumors about son Edward's homosexuality, and the international explosion of Prince Charles' marriage to Diana; the profoundly significant decision for the Royal Family to pay personal income taxes as everyone else does; the devastating fire at Windsor Castle that did $75 million in damage; the scandal-conditioned public opinion polls fearing for continuation of the Monarchy itself, casting an image of irrelevancy upon the Royals; a clash with the Church of England about the strictures of divorce and the succession to the throne, involving consideration of the Princes William and Henry of Wales, the sons of Charles and Diana; let alone the affairs of State that focused strongly on movements for Australia and New Zealand to leave the Dominion and become independent Republics (see "Australia," page 86).

For Elizabeth, these problems go beyond logistics; they spear to the heart of her belief in the divine right of Kings, the political doctrine that the monarchy is divinely ordained, that right of heredity can not be violated or dismissed, and that monarchs are accountable to God alone for their actions. Biographer Nicholas Davies focuses strongly on the life-changing impact her Coronation had on Elizabeth, June 2, 1953, for the first time given witness by the world through television: "At her Coronation she had been anointed sovereign by the Archbishop of Canterbury in Westminster Abbey before the sight of God; in effect, she had married the monarchy ... Elizabeth viewed the burden of monarchy with desperate seriousness."[500]*

It is from this perspective that Elizabeth—never having been exposed to normal life, privately schooled in her castle, attended to day and night by servants, meeting no one who was not aware first of royal protocol, isolated from the life-pressures and changes of her times—must judge the future of her Monarchy, the succession to the throne in a passage that is Divinely inspired. That Monarchy is now stained by scandal; all her actions must be justified with the Church of England. Elizabeth must lead

---

500 Davies, 115. At the Coronation, Elizabeth experienced SA SP Sun exactly opposed the Midheaven, SA Pluto exactly conjunct the Moon, and *tr Neptune exactly square the Ascendant-Descendant axis*. Tr Neptune had just moved off exact opposition to her Sun, ruler of her 7th. Davies states emphatically that, with Charles and Anne already born of her marriage with Philip, i.e., the heirs in place, she "banned Philip from her bed. Her royal duties did not include or necessitate any further sexual activity with her husband." Davies mentions the birth of Andrew and Edward in 1960 and 1964: "It is not known when Elizabeth allowed Philip back into her bed, but, in 1960 ..." (206).

England's history through the Millennium into new, more modern times.

■ Prediction …

Prince Charles Will Not Be King of England—There is an interesting set of astrological measurement variables that emerges from study of the horoscopes (the Astro-profiles) of the ten English monarchs from George II born in 1683 to Queen Elizabeth II. Charting five key measurements, 60% of all the monarchs had measurement one, 60% measurement two, 70% had the third one, and 40% and 30% had the next two, respectively. The startling observation in this overview is that Prince Charles, heir apparent to the throne, does not have any one of the measurement variables of the monarchs in his horoscope.[501*]

This fact, when combined with the possible reality of Charles not being named successor to Elizabeth, could explain a dysfunctional variable Elizabeth shows in her horoscope.[502*]

Prince Charles is born to express life in the "grand manner." Yet, if the emotional component gets the upper hand in his life, the structure of it all will collapse.[503*] Charles desperately needs a sympathetic audience for his position in life to flourish, and

---

501 The variables: *a strong contact between Saturn and Neptune* (conjunction, semisquare, square, trine, or opposition; a contact that stands out among these horoscopes) 70%, perhaps capturing the sense of divine right (the trine was weakest in occurrence); *the Midheaven Ruler engaged somehow with Jupiter, 60%* (the classic success indicator, the monarchical suggestion); *the Ascendant or Midheaven ruler retrograde, 40%* (a search for a negative; but here, not clearly one, it seems); *a non-retrograde planet conjunct the Midheaven* (5-degree orb; for Midheaven emphasis) *40%*, significant but not dominant among the sample; *a retrograde planet conjunct the Midheaven, thirty percent* (perhaps suggesting the negative: George V (grandson of Victoria and Elizabeth's grandfather) had retrograde Jupiter in *Sagittarius* in the 9th, corroborated by the trials of WWI, world depression, the Empire's foreign members demanding self-government); his son George VI (after older brother Edward VIII's abdication, Elizabeth's father) had retrograde Jupiter in Leo in the 10th, reigning at the time of lowest prestige for the throne in 100 years, due to the preceding abdication), who redeemed respect by taking a vital morale-building role during WWII, visiting installations, etc. (Jupiter ruled the 3rd.) And *Elizabeth*, with Saturn retrograde ruling her Ascendant, suggesting personal sacrifice, which will include her son.

502 I.e., the Saturn retrograde at the Midheaven. Additionally, Elizabeth's Jupiter is conjoined by Mars and is exactly opposed by Neptune retrograde in the 7th. Jupiter rules her 11th, her public popularity and her son's marriage (the seventh of her 5th), and Jupiter rules her 12th. This powerful Mars-Jupiter-Neptune axis is squared by Saturn at the Midheaven.

503 This insight for Sun in Taurus, Moon in Scorpio is from Lewi and Tyl studies of luminary polarities some fifty years and thirty years ago, respectively. See Tyl, *Synthesis & Counseling*, Section I, D, pp. 65–102.

this audience is not his estranged wife Diana and it is not his mother. The Queen dominates Charles, and he is forced to follow her way; privately, he retreats into a world of smouldering ambition in which he achieves a lone self-sufficiency.[504*]

▪ Prediction ...

Charles and Diana Divorced by September 1996 [Written December 1995]—Charles and Diana will have worked out a divorce settlement by September 1996. Through divorce, Diana would be able to remain a "Princess," but that would probably be conditional on her not remarrying. Her children will maintain their succession to the throne, second and third in order after their father. Her settlement will certainly include property and, according to royals-watcher Andrew Morton, "two incomes: one for life, as the mother of two heirs to the throne, and one which she would forfeit if she married again."[505*]

The divorce laws (the Divorce Reform Act of 1969 and the Matrimonial Causes Act of 1973) give Charles the leeway to divorce Diana upon "the irretrievable breakdown of [his] marriage." With the sole exception of George I (reign 1714–27), a divorced person has *never* succeeded to the throne of England. [Some sovereigns have been divorced *after* being crowned.] To marry again, after divorce, Charles would need permission of the Queen and the Privy Council and would probably remove himself from succession. The singular reason for divorce from everyone's perspective appears to be to settle tensions formally, to define Charles's position legally, and—on a personal level—

---

504 Prince Charles was born on November 14, 1948, at 9:14 P.M. at Buckingham Palace, London (news record). The Sun in Scorpio rules the Ascendant and is squared by Pluto (blanket over a grenade); the Moon in Taurus is conjunct the Nodal Axis in the 10th and is part of an Earth Grand Trine (practical self-sufficiency, defense position); Uranus rules his 7th and squares the Aries Point(!); note that *Neptune tightly opposes the Midheaven*. No monarch beginning with George II had Neptune in touch with the Midheaven in any way. [Three had supportive contact with the ruler of the Midheaven.] Charles's Neptune=Sun/Saturn, "sadness, loss of hope, delusions within relationship, aloneness."

505 Morton, 157–160 for notes about the Laws; for the prediction, note that Charles has SP SA Sun square Midheaven, SA Pluto semisquare Sun exact in December 1998, after SA Moon=Mars the preceding August. SP Moon exactly opposite Saturn. Additionally, see next footnote.

to give Charles the freedom from his mother that can then unlock his own personality. Within this freedom, he will have forfeited the throne by gaining permission—through great struggle with the legal councils—to remarry late in 1998.[506*]

■ Prediction ...

English Order of Succession is Changed—Compelled by circumstances related to Charles's private life— which transcend her sense of hereditary ordainment—a personal tragedy involving Charles (Spring 1997 is critical), his plea to remarry granted at the end of 1998 (when he is fifty), and/or a studied choice to designate youth to lead England upon her death in the next century, Elizabeth will announce a change in succession to herald the Millennium, probably in Spring 2000, naming Prince William of Wales as her heir, the next King of England.[507*]

The Astro-profile that emerges from Prince William's horoscope shows an inordinate need for security, emotional and home security, driving his life. There is enormous sensitivity and self-protection about him. His home is his castle in every sense of the idiom. He is diplomatic, patient, and if his sensitivities are not met with high values of emotional response, he withdraws into loneliness, much like his father. Like Edward VIII (the Duke of Windsor; see page 217) and again like his own father, Prince William will be confused, disappointed, and constricted by affairs of the heart. His mother, Diana, will be extremely important to him as a source of strength in trying to project himself as a king. His tendency is/will be to accept diffi-

---

506 Princess Diana was born July 1, 1961, at 7:45 P.M. GMD in Sandringham, England (Taeger, according to stepmother, and Church records): double-bodied sign (Gemini) on the 7th holding Mercury, in Cancer retrograde, conjunct Sun. Note: Mercury is Quindecile the Ascendant (upheaval in marriage) and Venus, ruler of the Midheaven, is quindecile Neptune. *In Spring 1996, SA Pluto squares Sun in the 7th, ruling the 9th; tr Pluto squares Mars, ruler of the 4th; tr Neptune conjoins Saturn, ruler of the 2nd.* Divorce.

507 *Elizabeth:* SA Venus opposed MC *(Venus rules her 9th, grandchildren),* with tr Pluto square Venus; she will be 74 then; she will have made this decision with or because of Charles in March 1999. Charles: SA Uranus square Sun, tr Uranus square Sun, tr Saturn opposed Sun in Spring 2000, Sun ruling his Ascendant, aged fifty-one; *Prince William (June 21, 1982, 9:03 P.M. GMD, London):* SA Saturn conjunct Midheaven, tr Neptune square Midheaven, Spring 2000, aged 18; *Prince Henry (September 15, 1984, at 4:20 P.M. GMD in London):* tr Saturn conjunct the fourth, SA Pluto applying to conjunction with the Midheaven, Spring 2000, aged fifteen.

culty and immerse himself in hard work and discipline, just the
advice his mother will give him.[508*]

There are astrological indications that can not be overlooked, though, that suggest that Prince William's reign could
well begin precipitously between September 2001 and March
2002, when he is eighteen and one-half. Romance/marriage
upheaval will mark his reign, or prevent/curtail it.[509*]

Prince Henry of Wales, heir apparent to his older brother,
is the stronger of the two brothers, more fit to the throne since
his emotional needs are less pronounced than are those of his
brother or his father. He inherits a severity from his grand-
mother; he is extremely organized and administratively stolid.
He likes to figure things out and work details to exhaustion. He
is extremely opinionated and will put a clear strength-of-will
stamp upon the monarchy when he is king. He will be old-
school effective rather than new-school popular.[510*]

It must be noted that this Prince Henry, the younger of the
two Princes of Wales, sons of Charles, will go through a terribly trying time in the Spring of 1997, when he is twelve and
one-half. This may be his reaction to all the family changes, his
parents' divorce, the awareness of succession changes brewing,
some separation from his brother or worse, a death in the family that jars everyone. It is a very lonely and sad time, which will
stir the young adolescent deeply.

Summer 2001 will see perhaps the most important development to that date of his life.[511*]

---

508 Prince William: Sun-Moon in Cancer in the 7th, Mercury, ruler of the 7th, is quindecile
Neptune retrograde (upheaval) rising on the Ascendant (an echo of his father's Neptune-Venus conjunction opposed the Midheaven). The Sun-Moon conjunction is
squared by the Mars-Saturn conjunction in the 9th. *Jupiter is retrograde on the Midheav-
en, ruling the Ascendant;* Saturn only quintile Neptune; Pluto, ruling the Midheaven, is
retrograde. AP=Sun, Moon/Neptune; Midheaven=Venus/Mars, Uranus=Sun/ Midheaven (sudden upset, changes of position), Ascendant=Sun/Neptune.

509 *Elizabeth:* SA Sun conjunct Pluto and SA Pluto=Sun/Mars with tr Saturn conjunct her
fourth, September 2001–February 2002. *William:* SA Mercury (ruler of the 7th)=Ascen-
dant, SA Node square Midheaven, tr Jupiter conjunct Sun; Henry: SA Pluto conjunct
Midheaven, tr Pluto conjunct Mars; Charles: tr Uranus square Sun.

510 Prince Henry: Sun in Virgo, Moon in Taurus, trine; Saturn rules the Capricorn Ascendant and is conjunct the Midheaven, in Scorpio, and *peregrine.* Mars in Sagittarius is
square the Sun; Mercury in Virgo dominates along with Saturn and is squared by
Uranus. Pluto=Sun/Uranus; Saturn=Sun/Jupiter; Sun=Mars/Neptune, and the Nodal
Axis is quindecile to the Midheaven and to Mars.

511 Spring 1997: SA Pluto conjunct Saturn with tr Neptune square Pluto, tr Saturn square
Ascendant, followed by SA Neptune=Ascendant in October 1997. In 2001, July: SA
Pluto is exact conjunct the Midheaven with tr Pluto conjunct Mars.

7

THE LONE SUPER POWER

Wars and Rights: The Themes that Thrall America

On January 1, 1892, on a small piece of land just out into the harbor bay water off the southern tip of Manhattan Island in New York, Ellis Island was opened to the world as a processing station for immigrants from Europe to the United States. Beneath the torch of the Statue of Liberty, already astride the island for six years, Ellis Island was laid out and planned to admit one million immigrants annually. The United States became the golden goal for much of the rest of the world, attracting about 60% of the world's immigrants between 1820 and 1930.[512*]

Immigration Groundswell

This gateway opened wide some fifteen years of enormous immigration to the United States. Forty-one percent of urban newcomers to New York and, through New York, to cities westward, arrived from abroad. In the early 1890s, four out of

---

512 Tr Pluto, having come from the United States' 9th House (7 Gemini 14 rising chart: U.S.A. July 4, 1776 at 2:13 A.M. LMT in Philadelphia, PA), *was at 7 Gemini* 17. SA Jupiter was exactly square Pluto *in the 9th*. SA Midheaven was applying to conjunction with the Ascendant; SA Moon was just separating from conjunction with Uranus at the Ascendant, and more: a new world-perspective for the country.
　　The "Statue of Liberty Enlightening the World," a gift from the people of France (sculptor Auguste Bartholdi of France), was dedicated by Grover Cleveland, with the last rivet put into place, on October 28, 1886.

five New Yorkers were foreign-born, a higher proportion of aliens than was present in any other city of the world. There were twice as many Irish in New York as in Dublin, as many Germans as in Hamburg, and half as many Italians as in Naples. Chicago claimed the largest Bohemian (Czech) community in the world, and by 1910, the size of the Polish population there ranked behind only Warsaw and Lodz.[513]

While the immigrants fled ethnic, religious, and political persecution in their homelands, they were lured as well by promises of good fortune made by American industry spearheading an expansionist era in the United States. The immigrants represented cheap labor, and encouragement by the Federal government was provided through the Contract Labor Law of 1864—twenty-eight years before the modern era of immigration organization beginning in 1892—which established a lien program on immigrants' future wages to pay for the immigrants' passage. That early program had already brought in over twenty million immigrants, some ten million of them after the United States Civil War, and so many more were to follow.

Before 1880, immigrants were mainly of German or Celtic origin from northern and western Europe. From 1890 on, Latin, Slavic, and Jewish immigrants became the dominant groups.

In 1921, Congress moved to curb immigration sharply with a quota system.[514*]

The Immigration & Nationality Act of 1952 set a new quota system with limits to 700,000 immigrants annually, acknowledging family member status, preferences for spouses and children, "adversely affected" countries of origin, etc.

In 1988, a deadline of May 4 was established for illegal aliens to come forward, to apply for amnesty under a United States Immigration and Naturalization Service policy. One million four-hundred thousand did so, 50% of them living in California. Across the nation, 71% of the aliens had entered the United States from Mexico.

In 1995, as of April 1, the United States has a higher proportion of immigrants than at any time since before World War II. About

---

513 Tindall, 790–793; and *Almanac*.
514 May 19, 1921: SA Neptune conjunct MC, SA Uranus=Sun/Moon, SA Ascendant square Pluto.

8%—or some twenty million—of Americans were *not* born in the United States; about one out of every twelve persons.

Immigration brings extraordinary problems to every developed nation in modern times, complicating population control, housing construction, unemployment and health benefits, education services, and crime prevention. Germany showed extraordinary largesse to the world through its open border policy and "Asylum Act," which, with the extraordinary inflow of Near East people and the whole of East Germany itself, now has had to be amended (see "Immigration Problem," page 162). The French see swollen unemployment numbers with refugees from war-torn Algeria, its former colony; the Spanish are still trying to cope with the internal immigration flood from rural areas to urban areas, a rebound from the Revolution sixty years ago (see page 205).

The governmental concepts of a Republic, of a Democracy, put the people forward. Their welfare becomes the *sine qua non* of national unity, peace, and productivity. As the world grows closer together, *it grows toward profitably established Republic centers,* the European Union, the United States, Australia and New Zealand in the southern Pacific area.

As it always has, migration flows in the main from East to West and, in the northern hemisphere, from South to North (North to South in the southern Hemisphere). The United States fights an extended and expensive border war with Mexicans in particular *to stem the enormous flow of illegal immigration.*

The immigration problems focus at the very core of United States identity. The famous inscription upon the base of the Statue of Liberty reads in part: "Give me your tired, your poor, Your huddled masses yearning to breathe free, The wretched refuse of your teeming shore. Send these, the homeless, tempest-tost to me, I lift my lamp beside the golden door!"[515]

This poetic address to the world is a vivid depiction of the Astro-profile of the United States: there is a tremendous emotional projection to the world; innovative social service creates the posture of the humane aristocrat, the benevolent facilitator, fulfilled through money (Foreign Aid) and international trade of inventive

---

515 The inscription poem, *The New Colossus,* was written by Emma Lazarus (1849–1887), an American poet and essayist of a Sephardic Jewish family; she was an early champion of Jewish nationalism.

technology (communications and travel innovation, weaponry, pop-ular culture, information services) and military power. As well, there are ominous threats to other countries when American attentiveness intrudes on other countries' governmental policies. There is a charismatic allure internationally founded on natural resources and the riches gained from them; on national wealth, which is overspent, incurring problems with debt. There are problems with youth, with national morals, with religious guilt. The international "caretaker" role at the core takes on the caste of arrogant self-righteousness. Power is all.[516*]

The Development toward Foreign Imperialism

The United States is completely focused upon foreign involve-ment—from its original receptivity to (constructionist reliance on) immigration to build the nation to its armed occupation of other countries to keep the peace and reach out to other countries. This core of the nation's Astro-profile developed naturally [according to the horoscope] against the initial contrapuntal plan that had been emphatically laid out for the nation by George Washington, at the end of his second term late in 1796. Washington's Farewell Address pointed up the objectives and methods of what he thought would be a successful republican foreign policy: "The great rule of conduct for us in regard to foreign nations is, in extending our commercial relations, to have with them as little political connection as possible ... It is our true policy to steer clear of permanent alliances with any portion of the foreign world."[517*]

---

516 Sun in Cancer, Moon in Aquarius in the 10th (take charge). Saturn, ruling the 9th, square the Sun. Sun rules the 4th (natural resources). Venus-Jupiter and Sun in the 2nd; Sun square Saturn, ruler of the 8th (debts). Mercury, ruler of the Ascendant opposes Pluto in the 9th (Aircraft is the United States single largest export (at 5%). Mars square Neptune; Moon-Mars-Saturn Air Grand Trine (intellectual and social self-sufficiency): Pluto=Moon/Jupiter, Sun/Moon, power.

517 Roberts, 615. This can anchor well the *retrogradation* axis Mercury (Ascendant ruler) and Pluto, 3rd to 9th International policy, agreements, etc; as well as international trade, information exchange, travel, tourism, etc.); i.e., the contrapuntal national policy.

While this is the essence of Washington's philosophy, the first half of this extended quote used by Roberts does not appear in the full text of Washington's "farewell address" (which was never orated, but instead was published at Washington's request in Claypool's *American Daily Advertiser*, September 19, 1796). The text began with a para-graph about the need for the public to be enlightened and then proceeded with "It is our true policy ..." In a letter to James Monroe three months earlier (August 25), Washing-ton had expounded on this theme "as my decided opinion that no nation has a right to intermeddle in the internal concerns of another ... maintain(s) a strict neutrality and thereby preserve peace ..." See Seldes, 441.

Indeed, this *anti*-imperialist philosophy prevailed into American history, reiterated by presidents John Quincy Adams, Woodrow Wilson, Richard Nixon, and others. All wars were portrayed as defensive or aiding the cause of truth, freedom, and independence in other countries.[518]

There was the defensive war with Great Britain in 1812, which was provoked by shipping-lane interference during various blockades imposed by Napoleon between Europe and the West Indies. Britain began seizing American ships that were infiltrating the trade routes, and detaining sailors with British backgrounds. Border disputes followed, including those in North America between the United States and British Canada.

The war began June 18, 1812, and ended December 24, 1814, with almost 7,000 deaths and casualties. The battles raged along the Canadian border in the Great Lakes regions, Baltimore Harbor, in Washington, D.C., with the burning of the city and the White House, and at New Orleans, this big battle fought after the end of the war before the truce was ratified.

It was a fumbling and inept war, redeemed for the Americans only by Andrew Jackson's strategically heroic victory at New Orleans, and by morale-boosting catch-phrases of bravery like "Don't give up the ship" and "We have met the enemy and they are ours." It was a war that amounted to a "Second War of Independence," a defensive reiteration against the most powerful nation on earth at the time. The new young nation had held its own; it had new symbols of its nationhood and a new roster of heroes. The United States was definitely to be taken seriously internationally.

All conquered territories were then restored, and boundary commissions were established for all future negotiations. National confidence was restored for the nation, and expansionism began to push westward into territory beyond the Mississippi (now owned by the United States through the Louisiana Purchase from France in 1803). These western lands were protected by the Native Americans for themselves, and they had been armed previously by the British (as allies in the War of 1812). American

---

518 Kissinger, 35, 48, 706.

expansionism now extended into those Indian lands, almost erad-icating the native population.[519*]

The Monroe Doctrine followed in 1823 (December 2) as a very strong declaration of this American policy especially toward the new states of Latin America, newly independent from European dominion. It stated that any attempt by European powers to inter-fere with the powers' old colonies in the *western hemisphere* would not be tolerated by the United States and that the Americans them-selves were not to be considered as subjects for any colonization by those powers. As well, it was stated that *the United States would remain neutral in any European power struggles.*[520*]

In 1845-49, President James Polk was intent on continuing land expansion, specifically to acquire (purchase) California as a state. Negotiations had been started with the Texans about their entrance into the Union. When the population in Texas had shifted to favor Americans, Texas had begun a long fight to be free of Mexico; the battle of the Alamo in 1836 had become a historic symbol of the Texas effort to independence. The time was ripe in 1845 for annex-ation of the huge territory by the United States.

The Mexicans resisted American annexation of Texas, and a contingent of Mexicans attacked American soldiers north of the Rio Grande. This was the aggressive act needed to justify counter-attack and war—just what President Polk wanted. He and the Con-gress quickly declared war on Mexico, on May 13, 1846. The United States deployed about 78,000 troops in a series of battles that finally led to Mexico City, which the Americans took on Sep-tember 14, 1847.

---

519 June 18, 1812, the beginning of the war: SA Ascendant and Uranus tightly conjunct the national Sun; SA Mars conjunct Mercury, ruler of the Ascendant; SA Saturn, ruler of the 9th, square the Moon at the Midheaven; tr Saturn, ruler of the 9th, opposed Jupiter, tr Uranus square the Moon.

   The Louisiana Purchase involved Louisiana, Arkansas, Iowa, Nebraska, both the Dakotas. Minnesota west of the Mississippi, most of Kansas, Oklahoma, Montana, Wyoming, and a big portion of Colorado for the price of $11.25 Million. *Tr Pluto from the 9th House was at 7 Pisces square the U.S. Ascendant;* SA Venus exactly opposed *Pluto in the 9th;* SA Uranus conjoined Jupiter, SA Ascendant conjoined Venus (both conjunctions in the 2nd), with tr Uranus square Venus in the 2nd.

520 SA Uranus exactly conjunct Mercury (opposed Pluto in the 9th), i.e., forceful interna-tional doctrine. Uranus rules the Midheaven. This represents yet another excitation of the 3rd–9th axis, the involvement of Pluto from the 9th; Uranus, ruling the Midheaven, from the Ascendant.

By the treaty of 1848 (February 2), Mexico ceded claims not only to Texas but also to California, Arizona, New Mexico, Nevada, Utah, and part of Colorado. The United States paid Mexico $15 million to complete the deal.[521]*

Within the expansionist thrust now complete all the way to the West coast, new problems arose practically everywhere: quarrels and disputes about boundaries, states' rights, the outreach of federal law, and, most important, the issue of slavery—the cheapest labor. An anti-slavery movement arose, anchored to the premise that free land—like Texas, annexed from Mexico where slavery had been abolished—should not then become a slave state. There were many new territories between the Rio Grande and the far northwest; slavery had to be checked.

A proviso was passed to protect the new territories, in theory, but the issue did not go away, and slavery did flourish, in Texas and throughout the South and in the new Territories of Nebraska, Kansas, New Mexico, and Utah.

America became mighty in its size. A spirit of youth—"Young America"—filled the nation with bombast and buoyant optimism. There was rampant enthusiasm for economic growth and territorial expansion. Historian George Brown Tindall describes the super-confidence and "anointed" self-image of American imperialism: "The dynamic force of American institutions would somehow transform the world." Disheveled by revolution and social upset, Europe could no longer stand as tall, did not loom as large as the United States.[522]

Detour from Greatness

The years devoted to building the nation up had misdirected and overshadowed thought about sectionalism within the nation, the separatist movement that threatened to tear the young nation apart. Specifically, the tensions were between the agrarian South—bound to the plantation structure and slavery mechanics of production—and the industrializing North. With the deaths of Henry Clay and Daniel Webster, the country found itself without leaders of national

---

521 Tindall, 525–526. February 2, 1848: SA Ascendant opposite Midheaven, SA Pluto square Jupiter, with tr Uranus exactly square the Sun and tr Jupiter exactly square the Moon.

522 Tindall, 588.

stature; the sectional politicians took over: W. H. Seward and Charles Sumner for the North and Jefferson Davis and Robert Toombs for the South.

The Republican Party was born in the North, and its first candidate, Abraham Lincoln, won the election in 1860. South Carolina protested the election results by seceding from the Union on December 20, 1860. Immediately, South Carolina was followed out by six other states: Mississippi, Florida, Alabama, Georgia, Louisiana, and Texas.[523*]

Lincoln's government was concerned about Federal property remaining within the seceded states; forts, courts, supply houses, train depots, etc. Lincoln decided to keep Fort Sumter in South Carolina, and it was there upon the fort that the first shots were made by the South to begin the Civil War, the War between the States. Some three million would serve and over 400,000 would die—three times as many American fatalities as would be incurred in World War I, seven times as many as in Vietnam.[524*]

American Imperialism Becomes International

Through the Mexican War, the United States united many more territories, and the growing nation reached the Pacific. Through the Spanish-American War (See "Spanish-American War," page 198)—beginning April 25, 1898, deploying some 300,000 troops, and lasting seven and one-half months—the country became installed internationally: gaining the territories of the Philippines, Guam, Puerto Rico, and the occupation of Cuba. The country gained an overseas empire with accompanying military installation power and responsibilities that became vital throughout the First and Second World Wars and remains strategically key into the Millennium.[525*]

---

523 South Carolina; secession took place at 1:15 P.M. LMT in Charleston, SC. See Tyl, Ed, *Astrology Looks at History* (Llewellyn Publications, 1995), "Lincoln, the South, and Slavery," by Marc Penfield.

524 Ibid, page 249. The start of the Civil War is timed through Bruce Catton, historian of the Civil War, and astrologer/historian Marc Penfield: 4:30 A.M. LMT at Fort Sumter in Charleston, SC. Tr Uranus was at 9 Gemini and tr Mars at 6 Gemini, conjunct the U.S. Ascendant and Uranus.

525 United States, April 25, 1898: SA Saturn exactly conjunct the 13 Aquarian 38 Midheaven; SA Ascendant exactly square Jupiter (expansionism); tr Neptune conjunct Mars (complicated motives); and tr Saturn and Uranus tightly bracketing the Descendant at 7 Sagittarius.

Within the first twenty years of the twentieth century, the United States would also intervene directly in the lives of the Caribbean Republics. This expansionism finally gave way to Franklin Roosevelt's "Good Neighbor" policy (1931), which ended America's "gunboat diplomacy" protection of its interests in Latin America.

The Link with God

Out of the War of 1812 (page 229), along with international stature, came as well America's link with God. The British were attacking Fort McHenry in Baltimore Harbor. All through the night of September 13, the British bombarded the Fort to no avail and finally abandoned the battle at 8 in the morning on the 14th. Francis Scott Key, a Washington lawyer, poet, and volunteer artillery man, was in the battle, captured by the British and detained on deck of one of the warships. As the North built up its victory throughout the night, Key was deeply moved by the battle and noted his poetic inspiration on the back of an envelope as the confrontation was coming to a close, at the "dawn's early light" early on the 14th, as he was being released and going ashore. This was the vivid poem "The Star-Spangled Banner," which gained immediate popularity.[526]

In the fourth verse of Key's poem (completed on September 15) appears the phrase: (to fit the first-verse anthem-line "Gave proof through the night that our flag was still there") "And this be our motto: 'In God is our trust.'" The poem was later adapted to the music of "To Anacreon in Heaven," an English drinking song, was played at presidential ceremonies in 1916, and adopted by Congress as the National Anthem on March 3, 1931.[527]

---

526 Tindall, 351. Almanac: the Battle began at 7:00 A.M., September 13, 1814, and lasted, without cessation, for twenty-five hours. The British fired more than 1,500 shells, each weighing as much as 220 pounds. The United States sank twenty-two British vessels, which blocked any further British advance through the harbor. The flag that Key saw now hangs in the Smithsonian Institution; it is thirty by forty-two feet, with fifteen stripes and fifteen stars (the original thirteen colonies plus Kentucky and Vermont).

The astrology of the battle victory and Key's inspiration: September 14, 1814, in the dawn's early light, say, at 5:20 A.M., twenty minutes before sunrise. Mars-Mercury were exactly rising at Baltimore (bombs bursting); *the Sun and Jupiter were in exact conjunction exactly square the U.S. Mars;* Saturn was at 24 Capricorn exactly opposed the US Mercury and conjunct the "international" Pluto in the U.S. 9th. Note the position of Neptune: square the dawning Ascendant, Mercury and Mars, opposing the Midheaven. Munkasey gives "flag" a 4th House reference, here ruled by *Jupiter.*

527 Anacreon was a Greek poet (c582–c485 B.C.E.) who celebrated wine and love in simple verses, very popular in eighteenth-century Europe.

During the Civil War, "In God We Trust" was inscribed on United States coins. The sentiment found its way into morale-building speeches delivered to Union soldiers. It disappeared and reappeared on various coins until 1955 when Congress ordered it placed on all paper money and all coins.

God condones. God shows favoritism.

God inspires and invigorates the sense of belonging, which is the essence of nationalism. God ordains the imposition of belief and policy. Early on in history, God motivated Crusade after Crusade (see page 138). God [Allah] motivated *Jihad* and the spread of Islam. God inspires political movement and justifies political action. God [originally Yahweh] confirms the existence of the Jewish people in the "promised" land. Self-belief becomes the toxin within nationalism that eats its way into the histories of war. It appears essential to the human condition.

With regard specifically to the United States, Irish Statesman Conor Cruise O'Brien sees the Declaration of Independence as "the supremely sacred scripture of the American civil religion. Jefferson's role as the man who wrote down the scripture is analogous to the role of the Prophet Muhammad (Mohammed or Mahomet) taking down the Blessed Koran at the dictation of an angel of God."[528]

O'Brien makes a grand point that the ideas of the "Enlightenment" (See "Enlightenment," page 176) are far more solidly established in America than anywhere else, because there, as nowhere else, "they are firmly embedded in the massive edifice of sacral nationalism [through Jefferson and Franklin]."[529]

During the 1980s, as the Cold War came to its crest and end, President Reagan projected the "Evil Empire" identification upon the Soviet Union. It was a large and comforting point for America: God *had to be* on the side of the United States against godless Communism.[530]

---

528 O'Brien, 58.

529 A second motto of the United States, *E Pluribus Unum*, Latin for "Out of many, One," sounds deist, elitist as well, but that was not its original intent. It refers to the unification of the original thirteen colonies. It was chosen by John Adams, Benjamin Franklin, and Thomas Jefferson for the Continental Congress (the body of Delegates representing the colonies, before and during the Revolutionary War; beginning September 5, 1774) and is now inscribed on the great seal of the United States and on many U.S. coins.

530 Reagan: "The Soviet Union is the focus of evil in the modern world" (March 1983; see Ambrose, Chapter 15). The subsequent "Evil Empire" political references made many *Biblical* references come to life. Reagan had a deep regard for Old Testament prophesy and tapped into the enormous belief reservoir in the United States linked to Millennialism:

American foreign policy was gnarled by World War I, by the world view and by the competition with allies and enemies; and it was burnished by victory. It shone for the future. President Wilson decided that it was in the best interests of the world that the great America's values and structure be extended far and wide.

A "Social Gospel" had developed in America. It was born out of the bloom of social observers and philosophers who were inspired by the intellect of the Enlightenment from late eighteenth century France and Europe. American literature flourished with a cluster of literary geniuses living in New England. All of them depicted man overcoming evil as his own human nature improved. An era of Romanticism ushered in an era of Temperance in 1832–35 and onward.[531]*

Man's improvement was also tied to his political institutions, the governmental structure of his life. President Wilson believed that the United States could bring peace, freedom, and justice to the world by an act of will alone, a decision, a pronouncement from America on high. This was then developed further through the United States' second world victory, World War II.

This sentiment driving national policy had roots laid down long before, during the revolutionary formation of the nation itself, from the seed-idea that the British rebel, American Revolutionary states-man Thomas Paine saw in the victory of the War of Independence: that the American cause is "the cause of all mankind."[532]

Political analyst William Pfaff observes: "As a neutral power during the first two years of the First World War, the United States considered itself uniquely above the struggle, morally different, 'the Great Neutral,' conserver of sane and just peacetime values and the exponent of 'peace without victory.' *The Wabash Plain Dealer* said in 1914, 'We never appreciated so keenly as now the foresight exercised by our forefathers in migrating from Europe.' However, this

---

that Jesus will come to earth again to oversee an apocalyptic upheaval [*apocalyptic*, Greek derivation: unveiling that which is hidden] to purify the world for one thousand years. A Gallup Poll in 1983 confirmed that 62% of Americans had "no doubts" that this would occur. Apocalyptic belief thrives on through best-selling books and magazines and tele-vision presentations of the world's most celebrated evangelists. *The belief is born of crisis:* the more crisis the nearer the Apocalypse and then the grand peace of the world. See Boyer, especially Chapter 5, "Ezekiel as the first Cold Warrior."

531 See Tindall, 494–496. Astrologically, tr Uranus was at the Midheaven of the United States chart, and tr Neptune was conjunct the United States Pluto (1835): *inward change, spiritual perspectives, revolutionary turns.*

532 Pfaff, 180–182; reference to Paine's *Common Sense*, 1776, still available in bookstores.

conviction of American moral superiority and distance was by 1917 transformed into a campaign to crush 'the military masters of Germany' by means of the War that would end War. The United States now was held not only to possess superior motives to those of its allies, but to have a moral commission to reform Europe."[533]

It followed then that the president of the great American nation was indeed President of the free World, representative of *the good for all*.[534*]

The United States in Charge of the World

It is clear that the United Nations organization, which has no enforcement power of its own (see United Nations, page 24), relies on the United States for its muscle. In turn, the United States uses the United Nations for exposure and foil in international diplomacy. With the changes now transpiring at the United Nations, with its role retreating from world policing to world information service, the U.S. position is changing as well: the United States will become *more directly* the arbiter of world conflict.[535*]

Witness the first two crises *after* the fall of the Soviet Union, i.e., after the end of the Cold War: the eruption in the Persian Gulf and the Civil War in Yugoslavia. With Iraq's infraction of United Nations warnings, the United States had leave for its free operation as the only superpower in the world, advancing to the Gulf and attacking Iraq. President Bush insisted that this was an emphatic statement of U.S. policy: that the United States would punish aggression to ensure the new world order. "In other words, the United States would act as world policeman defending the status quo."[536]

With the rise of the turmoil in the Balkans, the United States acted with relative restraint, perhaps because the Persian conflict had been so expensive, perhaps because oil supplies were at stake

---

533 Pfaff, 181–183.

534 Astrologically, in this study, we see the natural development within 9th House concerns from internationalism to philosophy, to religion, to foreign policy, to trade, etc. The United States has Pluto in Capricorn in the 9th opposed Mercury, ruler of the Ascendant. Saturn rules the 9th and squares the national Sun in Cancer.

535 There are ten very close contacts between the horoscope of the United Nations and the horoscope of the United States: U.N. Sun=U.S. Sun/Moon, Jupiter square US Sun, Neptune-Venus square Jupiter, Pluto opposed Midheaven, Mars-Saturn conjunct Mercury, *Moon conjunct Mars*, Uranus trine Moon-Midheaven, and U.N. Midheaven opposed U.S. Sun.

536 Ambrose, 378–380.

in the Gulf and not in the Balkans, perhaps because international disapproval of the Balkan upset throughout the United States was not so pronounced. The United States finally *did* take action, on behalf of the United Nations and NATO, accomplished a tenuous peace, and now is beginning a projected year-long military occupation in Bosnia.[537*]

As predicted in our discussion of the Balkans (see "Balkans," page 149), Serbia will probably break the peace in May–June 1996 or March–October 1997 at the familiar city centers in Croatia. The United States will be forced into military action.[538*]

The imperial internationalism of U.S. foreign policy is debated by a political theme of isolationism, hearkening back to George Washington's espousal of separatism in his Farewell address of 1796 (see page 228) and to the Monroe Doctrine (see page 230). The relations with Russia, Germany, and Japan were at the center of that policy consideration: all three had been defeated in World War II; the United States had rescued them; the United States *had to police them;* could it possibly have left them alone after all that had happened? The imperial view would win. It is part of the U.S. birthright.

The Shift to Economic Power

The end of the Cold War changed the parameters of world power. Since military might belonged solely to the United States, i.e., no one anywhere in the world could challenge U.S. military strength, so military strength was no longer an issue in the international mix. Instead, there was a shift made to *economic power.*[539*]

---

537 The U.S. military intervention in Bosnia occurred in the Fall of 1995 with tr Uranus (always associated with American militarism throughout its history) exactly conjunct Pluto in the national 9th House. At the same time, SA Ascendant was exactly square Saturn (the national position of control and enforcement). Additionally, SA Jupiter was conjunct the Midheaven.

538 SA Neptune=Sun/Moon *(deception within the treaty as well as extreme political division about intervention)* April 1996, with tr Neptune conjunct Pluto; Spring 1997, SA MC conjunct *Neptune* with *tr Neptune still square the midpoint of Sun/Moon. SA Pluto square with the Ascendant building (exact November 1997)) with tr Pluto opposed Ascendant.* Also: see footnotes in "Balkans" section, beginning page 149.

539 My extensive research on the Quindecile aspect (1/24 of the circle, 15 degree intervals, specifically the 165-degree aspect) reveal undeniably the dynamic of upheaval and captivation. In the U.S. horoscope, there is a quindecile of importance between Pluto and the Sun (and contraparallel), within 9 minutes of arc of precision: the stormy tie between money and power, military power and economic clout, the two working hand in hand in (as) foreign policy, in upheaval and unsettled obsession.

In economic power, the United States is no longer as powerful as it was just ten years ago. Ambrose and others point out that from the end of World War II into the beginning of the 1980s, the United States was the world's largest creditor nation, i.e., more money was owed to the United States than to any other nation. Then, at the beginning of the 1990s, this position completely reversed itself, with the United States now *the largest debtor nation in history*.

Germany and Japan had become the leading creditors, but the German position was then deeply upset by the drains of unification (see page 166), and the Japan position was continuously jarred by its world banking problems and graft-ridden, unstable government (see page 48). The United States had become the nation with the least amount of savings; a fall of over one trillion dollars from surplus to deficit within ten years. (With Japan rising $600 billion in the same time span, as comparison.)[540]

In the early 1980s, the United States had become the world's largest exporter, but by 1991, Germany, with a work force one-fourth the size of America's, had taken the lead. Ambrose reveals that Citicorp and Chase Manhattan banks were the two largest banks in the world in 1980, but by 1991, the world's ten largest banks were all *Japanese*, with Citicorp ranking twenty-seventh.

The key here is that the American attitude of supremacy is one thing but—now, for the first time in history—its capabilities of backing up the grand expectations are less than they have been in this century. The close-down of the federal government at the end of 1995 and early in 1996, the urgency for a balanced budget are signals of the beginning of an all-out effort by the erstwhile shining nation to ward off its Winter.

■ Prediction ...

United States Takes its Might to the Millennium—The threat of atomic war is almost nonexistent: there is little competition; the threat of retaliation is daunting; some ten treaties since 1963 have diminished arsenals severely, curtailed testing, and improved cautions; fallout experience and studies show that even how the wind blows during an atomic explosion (or leakage) can endanger nations beyond the target area, to the planet itself.

540 Ambrose, 379–380. McRae 147.

Yet, the United States birthright is to "take care of the world," to do it with aid and might, and this concept of "caretaker" is gradually being displaced by the concept of being "policeman" of the world.

The United States will move into Israel concomitant with and instrumental to the peace treaty between Israel and Syria (see page 124). The move could be approved by Congress in May 1996, with the peace signed in June or July, but Israeli elections and new leadership there could delay this.

The United States military presence will remain in effect in Bosnia, and the situation there will erupt strongly *at the same time* as the occupation of the Golan Heights is installed.

This will arouse enormous debate in the United States, quite possibly just preceding the presidential election. The initial condemnation of the idea of peace-keeping in Bosnia has quickly changed to a stance of American military honor; the United States is simply incapable of turning its back on Israel for a host of reasons (the ties between the two countries are considerable; see page 113). Elections in Israel and in the United States may suspend the time table of these highly probable developments

The United States is dedicated to military containment of others, to intervention, to making *the American cause* the cause of all mankind. As President Bill Clinton insisted in his State of the Union Message, January 23, 1996: "Our [sixth] challenge is to maintain America's leadership in the fight for freedom and peace. Because of American leadership, more people than ever before live free and at peace, and Americans have known 50 years of prosperity and security ... All over the world, people still look to us. And trust us to help them seek the blessings of peace and freedom. But as the cold war fades, voices of isolation say America should retreat from its responsibilities. I say they are wrong."

■ Prediction ...

United States Military in Iraq—Further militaristic outreach will take place *during, perhaps throughout, the period from October 1997 to January 2000.*[541*]

The United States will establish a presence in Iraq shortly after the overthrow of Saddam Hussein, beginning late in 1996; the upheaval in Iraq lasting approximately ten months. Then, in late Summer 1997, the United States will enter Iraq to help with Aid and policing an orderly installation of a Republican/Democratic government.

In essence, the "job" of Desert Shield/Desert Storm has not been finished: the United States learned, through its victories over Germany and Japan, that reconstruction, enormous foreign aid, magnanimous treatment to the conquered country not only assuages conscience but *protects the future,* defends the American position in times ahead.[542] The United States feels the responsibilities of victory strongly. In Iraq, the reconstruction has yet to be done. Surely the promise of this is circulated among rebel factions to encourage revolution. The key times are coming soon, and the United States will establish a mighty presence within the oil-rich Persian Gulf area.

The United States' enormously enhanced position in the Middle East will confront the Japanese strongly with its hegemony of the Pacific. As the ends of the world come closer together, China will be forced to respond, to come all the way into new government strength, republican freedom, and enormous trade activity (see "China Abandons Communism," page 66). The Koreas will unite similarly (see "Korea Unified," page 73). Integration will become the international, economically expedient mode of power. America remains the mighty catalyst. (See the Pacific Market Section, beginning on page 39.)

---

541 *SA Pluto square Ascendant* in November 1997 with *tr Pluto opposed the Ascendant and Uranus* from September 1997 to January 1999. *Tr Uranus conjunct the Midheaven* March–June 1998 and February 1999. SA Pluto square Uranus with SA Venus conjunct the Midheaven and SA Uranus=Sun/Pluto in July 1999, with tr Uranus conjunct the Midheaven a final time October–December 1999. Then the build-up to SA Jupiter conjunct Moon in August 2000.

542 As opposed to the vindictive Treaty of Versailles ending World War I, which kept shame and discontent alive in Germany.

The Social Problems

In his State of the Union Address, January 23, 1996, President Bill Clinton devoted much time to "Strengthening Families." It was his "first challenge" to the country to strengthen the nation. The challenge involves improving education, reforming taxes, and fighting crime and extends to cleaning the environment, humanizing and downsizing government, and managing the on-going population (immigration) problems.

These concepts are not the intrinsic concepts of American politics or, indeed, one political party; rather, they are the enduring threads in the fabric of American life, the structure of its identity. They are presented regularly in every political campaign and election effort; they follow every war time or international outreach with aid, as if the extra-national activity had misdirected the nation from the core business of its own survival, betterment, and profit.[543*]

In American history, these concepts emerged with insistent emphasis in literature, religion, and politics in the aftermath of the carnage (brother against brother) of the Civil War and the Emancipation Proclamation that freed the slaves. The Astro-profile for the twentieth century (see also "Century Signatures," page 12), besides presaging the enormous tensions of international war, also shows extreme social awareness, the values of humankind in society. Certainly these considerations gain in drama and contrast against the horrors of war, and such are the lessons of history. Societal pain and social betterment were/are as much keynotes of the twentieth century as was war.[544*]

---

543 It is important to see the point of the discussion in this section in parallel with the key elements of the U.S. Astro-profile, its horoscope: keep in mind please, Sun in Cancer (Family security) *squared by Saturn* in the 5th (children, teaching), ruler of the 9th (education, religion, internationalism); the Gemini Ascendant with Uranus in Gemini in conjunction (the people known for creativity, diversity, entrepreneurial spirit, rebellion, spontaneity, technological inventiveness, social awareness, entertainment); Uranus rules the Midheaven, holding the Moon in Aquarius (the humanitarian, take-charge need), in an Air Grand Trine with Mars and Saturn. Note also *the power Pluto in the 9th*, opposed Mercury retrograde (Ascendant ruler) in the 3rd (the tension among internationalism, education, philosophy, power, mind-set, trade, and *the tug of all this against the domestic needs symbolized by the Ascendant and by the Sun complex*).

Note the extreme emphasis of the 2nd House: wealth and prestige, holding the Sun and Venus-Jupiter. The Sun's square from Saturn is then the struggle with debt (by citizens and nation), with Saturn's rulership of the 8th (others' monies).

544 In the Century chart for Washington, D.C., or any capital city for midnight, Jan 01, 1900, Jupiter is in Sagittarius and widely sextile Venus in Aquarius, and Venus rules the Ascendant! Venus is sextile Uranus. Note as well that the spine-structure aspect of the United States horoscope (the Mercury-Pluto opposition) *is repeated dramatically here in the Century horoscope*, with the Node involved as well (great publicity, international exposure and spread).

Late in the nineteenth century, Darwinism[545] was pervasive in social thought. The grand wave of the western Enlightenment (see page 176), the praise of Reason, now was modified/fueled *with an emphasis on experience*, with learning and developing out of the past. This went beyond the Enlightenment's creation and assessment of knowledge through reason alone.

German scholarship flourished. History—from past events (archaeology was born to give scientific grounding to historical Romance) to current events—became detailed. Documents and manuscripts and the evidence of chains of events were all re-studied and analyzed in a reality check on development. The truth about things was to be found in their origins.

This affected religion, especially the Judeo-Christian legacy of the Jews being the Promised People (see page 104). Nations rushed to justify their own existences with as much age, god-endorsement, and value as they could. Long-held historical conflicts gained a vividness, and, as well, points of new political leverage. National ethnic and land borders were electrified with detailed definition and rationalization. A century of wars like none other in history followed.

With the rise of this people-sensitivity, especially in Austria, Germany, and the United States, there was the rise of "psychology," detailed understanding of what makes people behave as they do, linked to their past development. William James of Harvard (1841–1910) is credited with the beginning of psychology in America and, of course, Sigmund Freud, Alfred Adler, and Carl Jung in Europe.

James theorized a social philosophy of "pragmatism" (solving problems in the world of action, as opposed to the realm of idealism), understanding why behavior took place, the relationship between cause and effect. Historian Tindall observes, "Pragmatism reflected a quality often looked upon as genuinely American: the inventive, experimental spirit."[546]

After James and deeply influenced by him, educational reformer John Dewey (1859–1952) worked with ideas as "instruments." He saw education as the process through which society

---

545 Charles Darwin (born February 12, 1809; 6:00 A.M.?, "early in the morning" according to biography; in Shrewsbury, Great Britain) was a naturalist who, after a scientific world expedition (1831–1836), first formulated the theory of *Evolution by Natural Selection*. He published *Origin of the Species* in 1859. His findings challenged all social and religious thought of the time.

546 Tindall, 806.

would gradually progress to optimum security. The young needed not just knowledge of the world but *a critical intelligence* in order to cope with a complex, modern world ever in development. Dewey engineered the shift in education away from authoritarian methods and abstract knowledge and toward experimentation, practice, and deductive reasoning.

The genius writers of the era—Mark Twain, William Dean Howells, Emerson, Longfellow, Lowell, Holmes, Henry James, Bret Harte, Frank Norris, Jack London, Theodore Dreiser—captured the spirit as well, depicting a nation reunited after War and assimilating the diversity of its peoples and cultures. There were still the flow of immigrants, the race issues, and a great exodus of people out of the countryside into the more prosperous, industrialized urban culture—with its new telephones, its new street lights, the new streetcars, newspapers, magazines, and amusements. Stereotypes were born for the South, the Yankee North, the Black, the landed gentry, the immigrant worker, the politician, etc. The academic discipline of Sociology was formulated to deal meaningfully with observed human causes of *social effects*. Social views were articulated, enriched, and proved by detail.[547*]

Most of the churches of America responded as well. Many denominations adopted "earthly functions" in addition to saving souls, devoting their revenues to community service and care for the unfortunate. Educational programs were instituted to teach working people in the evenings.[548] The Catholic Church initially lagged behind the social movement, because of a dictum issued by Pope Pius IX (1846–1878), a *Syllabus of Errors:* the pope was deeply suspicious of modernism, and his position made "erroneous" the ideas of progress, liberalism, rationalism, and socialism that were current then.

Under Pius IX, the Church faltered in its attention to social programs and awareness, although the Catholics themselves (especially the immigrant population in America) were among the victims of slums. Pius IX's successor was the energetic Leo XIII (1878–1903),

---

547 This close of the nineteenth-century period was lived under the mundane signature of the Neptune-Pluto conjunction in Gemini (inward change, spiritual perspectives, awareness of power, analysis), occurring three times in 1891 and 1892 (first time: August 2, 1891, at 7:17 P.M. Greenwich Time) at *8 Gemini, exactly upon the United States Uranus (and Ascendant)!* Most WW II leaders were born with this signature.

548 Tindall, 814–815; The Baptist Temple in Philadelphia grew tremendously in its membership and its night school grew into Temple University, for example.

and it was his encyclical *Rerum novarum* ("Of modern things") that brought Catholics into the mainstream reform movement.[549]

All of these concerns for people and their betterment are exacerbated by War. Barbarism, threat to nationhood, and the possibility of loss threaten security and call attention to the need for as much security as possible. The Civil War had accomplished this awakening of social values in the United States, and so then did World War I.

The First World War was a great shock to sensibilities. It was a blow to the reigning idea that civilization was progressing. The young of the nation had been marched off to die on foreign soil, far away, for a cause of distant significance. Insecurity ran rampant through the crowded urban centers teeming with immigrants from abroad. *Old World* ties were resurrected—the "old" security—and a nativism (harkening back to former nationality) was piped into the fractured sense of American nationalism.

Radical groups formed to defend their social values. Racism and militant religiousness were resurrected, those very forces that had driven so many out of Europe to America. Strikes by workers expressed socio-economic fears. Ethnic (nativistic) cliques fought corporate and government authorities. Crime got organized.

The celebrated Sacco and Vanzetti robbery and murder trial in Massachusetts (Spring 1920) cast a shadow of criminality and sedition upon all immigrant Italians. Popular books promoted negative stereotypes, created further prejudice, and birthed out-and-out discrimination. A push to curb immigration was born, and the Emergency Immigration Act of 1921 was enacted, reducing immigration quotas from Europe severely. A loophole in immigration law kept the gate wide open for new arrivals from within the Western Hemisphere greatly increasing the inflow of Hispanic Catholics.

The Ku Klux Klan was originally started late in 1865, seven months after the close of the Civil War, to intimidate blacks and, later, the carpetbaggers (Northern opportunists) seeking to exploit southern reconstruction for profit. After World War I, the Klan adopted a new form that was promoted as "100% American." America is no melting pot, Klan founder William J. Simmons warned ... "It is a garbage can!" The Klan, by going nativist, had now gone national, and the promotion of hate and separatism

---

549 Ibid, 815; also Cheetham, 272–275.

spawned big business. Tindall observes that the Klan, with all its secrecy, ritual, anonymity, and fiery intensity, brought drama into the dreary routine of a thousand communities.[550*]

Christian fundamentalism entered the social struggles of fear as well. The new ideas of Darwinism were a "modern scholarship" that threatened the old secure teachings. The Fundamentalist Movement was born (c. 1910). Its leader was the superb orator and famous politician William Jennings Bryan (who had lost the Presidential election twice to William McKinley in 1896 and 1900).[551]

Bryan denounced Darwin and this led to a bill to outlaw the teaching of evolution in public schools and colleges.

Prohibition as well was a manifestation of moral righteousness movements that were engineered to heal the disorientation caused by World War I. The women's Temperance Union and the Anti-Saloon League stopped "working on" individuals and addressed the nation. By 1910, the pressure was everywhere to outlaw alcohol; Protestant churches rallied behind "dry" political candidates. Thousands marched on Washington. The 1916 elections finally produced a two-thirds majority for *prohibition*, in both houses of Congress. Tindall describes, "Soon the wartime spirit of sacrifice, the need to use grain for food, and wartime hostility to German-American brewers transformed the cause virtually into a test of patriotism." On January 16, 1919, the Eighteenth Amendment to the Constitution—"Prohibition"—was adopted, outlawing the manufacture, sale, transport, importation, or exportation of intoxicating liquors in the United States and its territories.[552*]

And Al Capone—Italian leader of organized crime—by 1927 was earning $60 Million per year.[553]

---

550 Ibid, 987. On Thanksgiving night, November 25, 1915, near Atlanta, "bathed in the sacred glow of the fiery cross, the invisible empire was called from its slumber of half a century to take up a new task." *The event chart:* Water Grand Trine (defensive, closed circuit of emotional self-sufficiency) among Moon-Saturn in Cancer, Jupiter, and Mercury in Scorpio (squared by Mars). For the *U.S.: tr Saturn was conjunct the national Sun, and tr Uranus at 12 Aquarius 14, conjunct the tr Nodal axis, was conjunct the US Midheaven at 13 Aquarius 38;* SA Mars was square the U.S. Nodal Axis exactly!

551 "Fundamentalism" established five points as fundamental to the faith: a Bible above error, the Virgin Birth, God's Forgiveness of Sins, the Resurrection, and the Millennial Second Coming of Christ.

552 *The event:* curiously again, Mercury was opposed Jupiter-Pluto, Capricorn-Cancer. *For the U.S.:* this Pluto-Jupiter conjunction was conjunct the national Jupiter-Sun, and tr Neptune was at 17 Leo opposed the national Moon at the Midheaven. Startlingly, SA Neptune was at 11 Aquarius 52 conjoining the U.S. Midheaven, and SA Uranus and Ascendant were tightly square U.S. Pluto in the 9th (Laws)!

553 Tindall, 994.

In the midst of all this difficult adjustment at practically every level of American life and image, there had been another Constitutional Amendment passed, the XVIth, providing a legal basis for imposing *federal income taxes* on individuals and corporations. It became law on February 25, 1913. This law was then doubled (from a base of 1% of income to 3%) to support an improved Navy during World War I.[554*]

These same issues—social security, education, pride, ethnic nativism, prejudice, religious fundamentalism, organized crime, taxes, social services—are the hallmarks of every political campaign still, at the threshold of the Millennium. After every diverting war effort or Foreign Aid maneuver, the issues arise anew with great urgency.

■ Prediction ...

Social Services Dominate Millennium Election—The United States' budget problem will have risen above politics and settled into balanced accord early in March, probably on March 6, 1996, and announced shortly thereafter to suit political expediency.[555*]

At the same time, the economy—not its finances, i.e., the organization of money sources and concerns, not the circulation of the monies—of the United States has reached a peak plateau, as reported by President Clinton in his State of the Union address, January 23, 1996: "Our economy is the healthiest it has been in three decades. We have the lowest combined rate of unemployment and inflation in twenty-seven years. We have created nearly eight million new American jobs ... Our leadership in the world is strong, bringing new hope for peace."[556*] This excellence should continue through to the election time at the end of 2000.

---

554 The enactment of the Income Tax amendment, February 25, 1913, shows for the U.S. SP Moon at 14 Aquarius 57 tightly conjoined with the national Midheaven (the Moon rules the 2nd House) and SA Jupiter was tightly square the Moon in the 10th. Tr Jupiter was at 11 Capricorn in the 8th (taxes) opposed the U.S. Sun at 12 Cancer in the 2nd. SA Moon at 1 Cancer 40 was conjunct Venus at 2 Cancer in the 2nd.

555 Prediction made January 2, 1996: tr Jupiter will have been exactly opposed the national Sun in 12 Cancer on March 6, with Tertiary Progression showing TP Moon exactly conjunct the 4th, TP Mars opposed the Moon, ruler of the 2nd, TP Sun opposed Pluto, TP Jupiter exactly square the Ascendant.

556 *SA Jupiter conjunct the Midheaven* (exact February 1996) and SA Midheaven=Jupiter/Ascendant.

In parallel, there are continual drains of attention, prestige, and monies abroad—in the Balkans, Israel, Iraq, and other places of unrest. The United States will continue to neglect its home front. The tremendous point of debate in the *Millennium* Election in 2000 will finally be social services (the "Me-2" generation?). Americans will be looking back on a century of military projection, wars, international outreach, and seeing in dramatic relief the social problems at home. Only then will the press be on as never before for health-education-and-welfare programs of enormous scope and import, for resuscitation of family values, for increased containment of crime—all the issues of social importance that were discussed but will not have been acted on politically for twelve years previously will dominate national consciousness.[557*]

The argument in the United States polarizes to expenditures abroad vs. solving problems at home. Within vision at this time will be the specter of greatest moral decay in the United States, escalating (or more appropriately, falling to its nadir) as politics churns to get solutions working. The rebuilding of American life will however begin in earnest in the Spring of 2003.

United States Presidents and Death

Four American presidents have been assassinated. Astrologically, we learn a great deal from their death times and horoscopic circumstances.

Abraham Lincoln, Republican, was the "anti-slavery" candidate in the election of 1860, which he won with a minority of the popular vote. By the time of his inauguration in March of 1961, ten states had seceded from the Union (see page 232). The Civil War then erupted one month into Lincoln's first term. As Commander in Chief of the military, Lincoln fought hard to keep the Union together militarily and as well politically in its democratic structure; preserving the Union was his foremost objective. In the midst of the War, he issued his Emancipation Proclamation to free the slaves, in effect January 1, 1863, which fulfilled the objectives of the abolitionists who promoted the war so strongly.[558]

---

557 *SA Mercury square Ascendant*, SA Saturn semisquare Sun, SA Ascendant=Sun/Pluto, and tr Uranus square the Aquarian Moon in the Midheaven and ruling the 2nd.
558 Roberts, 620.

Lincoln was reelected in 1864 and inaugurated on March 4, 1865. The War ended on April 9 with Lee's surrender to Grant at the Appomattox Court House in Virginia. And then in Ford's Theater in Washington, D.C. during an evening play performance on April 14, Lincoln was shot by John Wilkes Booth, an actor and die-hard pro-slavery rebel. Lincoln died early in the morning the next day.[559*]

James Garfield was the twentieth United States President. During the Civil War, Garfield had served as a colonel from Ohio and been promoted for gallantry to major general. He entered Congress as a radical Republican and then became a Senator. He was selected for the presidency as a compromise candidate. He promoted conservative fiscal policies and improved Latin American relations considerably. The nation was outraged when Garfield was shot and mortally wounded in the Washington train station on July 2, 1881, just four months after his inauguration. He died on September 19. His assassin was Charles Guiteau, a lawyer and disgruntled federal office seeker, declared insane at a celebrated trial.[560*]

William McKinley, the twenty-fifth President and also a Republican, had also served in the Civil War and achieved the rank of major. He became governor of Ohio and, from there, was elected to the Presidency in 1896. He responded to the Havana harbor explosion of the battleship *Maine* and declared war on Spain on April 21, 1898 (see "Spanish American War," page 199). Through this War, the United States assumed its position as a world power.

McKinley was reelected in 1900, again defeating William Jennings Bryan who espoused an anti-imperialism platform. On September 6, 1901, six months after his second inauguration, while welcoming people at the Pan-American Exposition in Buffalo, New York, he was shot by an anarchist (against government authority), Leon Czolgosz, and died eight days later. McKinley's Vice President, Theodore Roosevelt, succeeded him.[561*]

---

559 Lincoln (born February 12, 1809, at 7:20 A.M. LMT, in Hodgenville, KY; time from Marc Penfield rectification; see Tyl, Ed., *Astrology Looks at History*. St. Paul: Llewellyn, 1995. "Lincoln, the South, and Slavery" by Penfield). SA Pluto exactly opposite Uranus in the 8th, SA Mercury on Nodal axis (public), SA Mars square Jupiter, ruler of the 10th; tr Saturn exactly square the Moon and more. For the *U.S.*: SA Pluto square Mercury, ruler of the Ascendant; SA Node on the Moon in the 10th (public); tr *Pluto at 12 Taurus* tightly square the Midheaven; tr Saturn exactly square Pluto.

560 Garfield (born November 19, 1831, at 3:25 A.M. LMT in Orange County, Ohio; time from Doane, *Horoscopes of the U.S. Presidents*). SA Neptune exactly opposed Saturn, SA Pluto exactly opposed Mercury, ruler of his 12th. For the U.S.: SA Saturn conjunct Pluto, SA Uranus precisely square Mars, SA Node square Moon; tr *Neptune at 16 Taurus* square Moon/Midheaven.

561 McKinley (born January 29, 1843, at 7:00 A.M. LMT (Doane) in Niles, OH): SA Neptune square Saturn in Capricorn in the 12th, SA Uranus exactly opposed the Midheaven, tr

John F. Kennedy, a Democrat from Massachusetts, the thirty-fifth president, had served with distinction in the Navy in World War II. He was the youngest president ever elected at age forty-three, in the election of 1960, and was the first Catholic to serve in the Office. Kennedy oversaw the debacle of the Cuban Bay of Pigs invasion of Cuba but then triumphed in the Cuban Missile Crisis showdown with the Soviet Union (see "Cuba," page 199). He resisted Soviet efforts to expel the Allies from Berlin, championed European plans for the Common Market, and, at home, backed early civil rights legislation and strongly promoted space exploration. Kennedy was shot and killed by Lee Harvey Oswald during a motorcade parade in Dallas, Texas on November 22, 1963.[562]*

Four presidents—William Henry Harrison, Zachary Taylor, Warren Harding, and Franklin Delano Roosevelt—died of natural causes while in Office.

Harrison, our ninth President, was inaugurated on April 4, 1841 at the age of sixty-eight. He delivered his Inaugural Address in the pouring rain and died of pneumonia thirty days later on April 4.

Taylor, our twelfth President, inaugurated March 4, 1849, was known as "Old Rough and Ready" because of his boldness as a general in the Mexican War; he had defeated General Santa Ana's forces and become a national hero. He died suddenly on July 9, 1850, having contracted a severe fever during long exposure to the sun at the laying of the cornerstone of the Washington Monument five days earlier.

Warren Harding died after only thirty months in Office, on August 2, 1923, of ptomaine poisoning and pneumonia. His winning platform had been promoted by the slogan "return to normalcy," a reaction to the restraints with which the nation had complied during World War I. He rewarded political cronies with government positions, and his administration was rife with dishonesty and graft.

Saturn on the Node. For the *U.S.*: SA *Saturn at 16 Aquarius*=Moon/Midheaven; SA Node on Uranus, SA Moon on Mars exactly, tr Saturn opposed Sun.

562 Kennedy (born May 29, 1917, at 3:00 P.M. EST in Brookline, MA; accepted record): at death, his entire horoscope was 38' of arc before the accumulated semi-square Solar Arc; SA Mars conjunct Pluto, *SA Neptune exactly conjunct Moon*, SA Sun conjunct Midheaven (fame from death); tr Neptune opposed Mars in the 8th, tr Saturn square Mars. For the *USA:* SA Midheaven exactly opposed Moon in the Midheaven, SA Node conjunct the Midheaven, *tr Saturn at 17 Aquarius* conjunct Midheaven/Moon, *tr Neptune at 16 Scorpio* square Moon/Midheaven.

Franklin Roosevelt was the only United States President to be elected to four consecutive terms (now limited to two by the Twenty-second Amendment to the Constitution, ratified February 27, 1951). Roosevelt began as a U.S. Senator from New York, then Assistant Secretary of the Navy, and ran unsuccessfully for Vice President in 1920. He suffered a severe attack of polio in August 1921 and became partially paralyzed. He returned to politics in 1924 and was elected governor of New York for two terms and then became Democratic President in 1932.

Roosevelt initiated "New Deal" legislation in the aftermath of the Great Depression of 1929, launched the "Good Neighbor Policy" in Latin America, recognized the Soviet government, and administered American and Allied involvement in World War II. He was reelected for his *fourth* term in 1944, was inaugurated January 20, 1945, and died suddenly of a cerebral hemorrhage on April 12, 1945.[563]*

The astrological signature for assassination of the president in office is very clear-cut. It is similar for the president dying in office because of health concerns. And it is also present in the astrology of the one President who resigned the office during his term, Richard Nixon. Nixon had begun his political career as a Republican congressman and a prominent member of the House's anti-Communist Un-American Activities Committee. He became a Senator and then Vice-President to Dwight Eisenhower in 1952.

In 1960, Nixon ran for President against John F. Kennedy and lost narrowly. He recovered his popularity, based chiefly on foreign policy experience and the famous "Kitchen Debate" with Soviet Premier Khrushchev in Moscow (July 25, 1959). In the election of 1968, with President Johnson's refusal to run again, Nixon won and became the thirty-seventh U.S. President.

Nixon faced up to the Vietnam War crisis abroad and enormously adverse public opinion at home. Eventually, with Secretary of State Henry Kissinger's diplomatic power and insight, Nixon arranged a cease-fire agreement with North Vietnam (January 27, 1973). Nixon

---

563 W. H. Harrison born February 9, 1773, at 10:38 A.M. LMT in Berkeley, VA (all data, Doane); Taylor born November 24, 1784, at 10:56 A.M. LMT in Orange County, VA; Harding born November 2, 1865, at 2:00 P.M. LMT in Blooming Grove, OH; F. D. Roosevelt born January 30, 1882, at 8:00 P.M. LMT in Hyde Park, NY. All very instructive for study; note *tr* Neptune at 16 Aquarius conjunct the U.S. Moon/Midheaven spot for Harrison; *tr* Neptune at 17 Leo opposed U.S. Midheaven for Harding. Including deaths during one's term, these eight horoscopes show emphasis of the 13–16 degree area of Fixed signs (the U.S. Moon-Midheaven) in six cases, 75% of them.

made a historic visit to the People's Republic of China (February 22–March 1, 1972), which reopened contact with the mainland Chinese for the first time in more than twenty years, and Nixon became the first American President to visit Moscow three months later.

Nixon's second term in office, 1972–1976, was aborted by the scandal of the Watergate Affair, which exposed wide-spread corruption, public misinformation, misuse of the Central Intelligence Agency, and a grand shift of power to the White House away from Congress and the judiciary. Nixon resigned the Presidency in great shame on August 9, 1974. He was pardoned a month later by his successor, Gerald Ford.[564]*

■ Prediction ...

Extreme Danger for the United States President—The signature for a president not finishing his term in office is about to occur once again, definitively in 2004, in the heightened and intense configuration corroborating assassination or death in office in the past. An earlier, imminent period, less definitive but also promising threat, attack, upheaval, presents itself in 1997–98.

With the United States ostensibly occupying Israel and Iraq, with fanatical terrorism raging in both those countries and the Islamic world against the United States in 1996–97 (see page 124 and 240), a wave of terrorism will have mounted throughout western countries and come to focus in the Middle East, in Israel. The terrorism will be Islamic in rationale and revengeful in motivation, with nuclear blackmail involved as tactic. As the tensions grow through the Millennium, we can expect a serious threat to the person of the President of the United States to grow as well. The time period is October 1997–June 1998.

There will be strong military action taken by the United States abroad in its imperial control position in Israel, Iraq, and Bosnia. Additionally, there will be trade tensions with the Pacific Market, with Japan and with China. Japan will continue to have its crises of leadership along with fanatical student upris-

---

564 Nixon was born January 9, 1913, at 9:30 P.M., PST in Yorba Linda, CA (published record): at resignation, SA Neptune was square his Pluto in the 10th, tr Uranus was square Neptune; for the U.S.: SA Pluto at 13 Leo 35 was precisely opposite the U.S. Midheaven and the SA Ascendant was square Neptune; *tr Saturn was exactly conjunct the Sun, tr Uranus exactly square Mercury, ruler of the Ascendant.*

ings (see "Japan," page 52); China will be taking its steps of leadership change, assimilating Hong Kong, and managing major new uprising of students (See "China," page 66).

The first period of clear danger is between October 1997 and June 1998. The nation's international position is highly charged and in upheaval. The U.S. purview and resources are spread thin. Domestic issues are being neglected. There is a revolt by students in the United States. The Millennium intensity mounts for social change, change in international policy, and creation of a new national image, promised for so long, so long in forthcoming.

The definitively dangerous period then follows for the time overlap of the next two presidential terms. It is extensive: between March 2003 and December 2005, bridging from one president (presidential term) to another (election year 2004). The particular emphasis on the time of highest peril is between March 28 and June 15, 2004; with a second concerted period of danger later in the year, especially in December. A final period of potential attack, less pronounced than the other two periods, is between February and April, 2005, several months into the presidential term begun with inauguration in January 2005.[565*]

---

565 More specificity for these times will be dependent on the horoscopes of the individual presidents. We have observed the transits that aggravate the 13–16 degree-area of fixed signs concomitant with presidents taken out of office. The planets Neptune, Mars and Pluto are involved. Astrologer Michael O'Reilly has researched this signature, using the United States chart with Scorpio on the Ascendant and a 15 Leo 58 Midheaven. The difficulty among several of the charts suggested for the United States is that the angles are usually close harmonic echoes of each other. For example: O'Reilly's Midheaven is 15 Leo 58 and the Gemini rising chart used in this book's references has a Midheaven of 13 Aquarius 38.

My research agrees with O'Brien, as shown in the earlier footnotes, and I project the following: May–June 2004 shows tr Neptune conjunct the Midheaven (13 Aquarius), tr Uranus square the 7 Gemini Ascendant and natal Uranus, tr Saturn closing to conjunction with the U.S. Sun, tr Jupiter square Uranus, and, very importantly, as we have learned from the assassination cases, tr Pluto opposed the U.S. Mars. SA Mars conjoins the Nodal axis, on the South Node arm in the 9th (in public, a foreigner, or abroad); SA Uranus opposes Mercury, ruler of the Ascendant, from the 9th.

Curiously, SA Moon exactly squares Jupiter and SA Venus exactly conjoins the Moon; this occurs often among these chart examples, i.e., a "soft, successful" aspect to connote the fame from death symbolism. Note: Kennedy had SA SP Sun conjunct his Midheaven; Garfield had the SA SP Sun opposed his Midheaven; Lincoln's death for the U.S. showed its SP Ascendant at 17 Leo opposed the U.S. Moon.

Note as well the Jupiter-Saturn Great Conjunction horoscope (May 28, 2000, at 3:59 P.M. GMT, 11:59 A.M. EDT in Washington, D.C.): Jupiter-Saturn exactly upon the Midheaven over Washington, squared by Uranus; the Great Conjunction at 22 Taurus 43 is on the Israel Sun in 23 Taurus, the chart's Sun is exactly on the United States Ascendant, and the Sun is opposed by Pluto from the fourth!

8

OLD PATTERNS AND OTHER WORLDS

Out of the histories of nations—even from these cursory overviews focused on particular themes—it is easy to extract constants. First, histories deal with time, and time is change. It is within change—the happenings that articulate time and seem to justify it—that we capture the metaphor of the seasons, the ebb and flow, the rise and fall, the expansion and coalescence in the life of nations.

The holistic idea of a living earth is an old idea. It can be traced to an Egyptian sage/pharaoh/philosophy named Hermes Trismegistus. The wisdom linked all of Nature into an animate whole: what is above in the heavens corresponded to—and, indeed, actually shared a causal relationship with—what was below on earth. This togetherness of macrocosm and microcosm is symbolized by the ordered swirl of our Universe echoed among the spinning atoms of earth matter.

Hermetic philosophy foretold Christianity's teachings about heaven and earth and the interrelationship of these realms within the spirit of humankind, the Above and the Below synthesized within the human experience. Hermetic philosophy inspired Plato and the Platonists. It was the seed that led to the bloom of astrology, the essence of Renaissance thinking, and the birth of a magical religion that animated with operational unity and wisdom everything in our awareness.

In this view, nothing is alone, independent, immobile. Everything is universally animated somehow around the Sun in stellar terms, around the human being in mundane terms, around the state in political terms. There are cycles and rhythms, the kinds of measurements that guide us in our development and inspire the thought that history repeats itself. There is no death; there is only change.[566]

In a particularly astrological sense and, as well, in the sense of world togetherness, we can say that there is nothing new under the sun, but that the Sun is ever new.

The constants of these histories confirm that individuals naturally seek security to survive, bond with others to improve that security, enlarge the group for strength, define the group for recognition, stake out territory to live, expand its space, compete with other spaces, win until there is the loss to dominant force, assimilate the conqueror's traits, and then press growth further at new levels with new concerns for survival within a new cycle.

Through this concept also flow the thoughts of Charles Darwin, the link between animal and human behavior made geopolitical (see page 242). Similarly, the German geographer Friedrich Ratzel (1844–1904) also developed an extremely influential concept—*anthropogeography:* the importance of land location determines human activity. Ratzel saw the state (nation) in constant struggle for survival, with the stronger state expanding at the expense of the weaker neighboring state in order to prolong its life cycle. Ratzel postulated that once a state loses its expansionist impulse, it goes into a rapid decline, which, in many cases, ends in its eventual demise.[567]

This is an extremely important insight: Japan, for example, throughout its history—and especially with the industrial revolution, with a birth rate stimulated early on to augment the work force—developed continuously beyond the threshold of its land's capacity to support life and industry securely. Expansionist invasions were essential for survival; the outreach by distance increased; the stakes rose; and finally defeat occurred, the historical season changed. The cycle began/begins again, with Japan westernized in the values of the conqueror. The new Spring and

---

566 Key exponents of this philosophy were Marsilio Ficino and Giordano Bruno in late sixteenth-century Italy and—most influential to the twentieth century—George Friedrich Hegel (1770–1831), the key German exponent of the Englightenment. Hegel captured the historical development of the world in terms of the World Spirit (the Weltgeist), within his constructs of thesis, antithesis, and synthesis, assimilating polarities into new wholes of meaning. Karl Marx was a major follower of Hegel.

567 Freedman; Efraim Karsh essay, "The Causes of War," 65–68.

Summer have bloomed in the light of economic power, economic competition, outreach, a buy/sell-and-conqueror strategy. (See pages 39, 43, and 53.)

The focal points of geography have dominated Israel's entire national history for over 3,000 years (see page 120). In negotiations now with the Palestine Authority and with Syria, the issue of giving land "back" to all sides is as insoluble as it is intolerable.

A celebrated German geopolitician named Karl Haushofer (1869–1946) took Ratzel's fundamental ideas and developed them into a categorical imperative: the ideal of expansionism is to gain possession of an adequate living space ("Lebensraum," *lay'benz-rowm*). This concept is so important to a state that "the preservation and protection of that space must determine all its policies." And further: specific continental areas (the Balkans east into Eurasia) were linked with maximum political power.

Ratzel's and Haushofer's work greatly influenced Hitler.[568]

The theories begged the introduction of value judgment: are there good states and bad states; is expansionism all right if the motives are professedly altruistic, as in the formal U.S. policy of protecting the peace everywhere and anywhere?

The value judgment is impossible: in war, it is never clear who initiates a war; it is always the other side; there is always an earlier point of antagonism, a former issue, that can be pointed up as cause—and those points can refer back in time considerably as we have seen in the crises in the Middle East, the conflict between Islam and Judaism especially. (See "Israel," page 103, especially beginning page 104.) The adversary is always vilified and condemned in religious terms, as evil, satanic, against human existence. It is as in days millennia ago when battles were between communities representing different gods portrayed in idols, personified in leaders.

As a group of individuals highly identified for maximum meaningfulness and strength, the nation lives within its own political idealism. Individual interests are subordinated to the common good, to the world stance of the nation. Nations do not recognize a higher authority than their own.

---

568 Haushofer was a professor of geography at the University of Munich. One of his students was Rudolph Hess, who introduced Haushofer to Hitler. Haushofer became one of Hitler's closest foreign policy advisors. In 1946, Haushofer and his wife poisoned themselves in suicide.

While there are more and more separatist nations on earth as we reach the Millennium, the pressures of interdependence among them are considerable: resources of the earth must be shared to keep nations alive, and there is not enough aid from the dominant nations to take care of everyone else. In the process of resource exchange (commerce), profit easily breaks away from charity, business and politics quickly leave the human being behind within the collective following the national routine. Social movements in the wings around the national core take form, much as cells subdivide to propagate. Liberalism and conservatism polarities cluster themselves into powerful political forces.

This internal process of change begins when more state attention is demanded for the human being. Health and social welfare and employment benefits—the personal rewards of national membership—lead national temperament. Education guides the way of protest—how to articulate the protest, students demanding a voice, the thrust of youth for its future. Revolution occurs to turn things around to new points of view.[569]

Change begins externally as more Lebensraum is needed, as more food and fuels are required. Expansionism is vitalized by the life-or-death needs of the people and the national machinery of production.

Change is confirmed by victory as new growth or is re-channeled by defeat into reconstruction. Charismatic leaders age and die. New leaders emerge with adjusted vision. Radical doctrines are fulfilled through success or fragmented by failure.

It is difficult, for example, to read the *Communist Manifesto* today, with respect, reason, or reward; the times now are no longer right for the doctrine. "Working men of all countries, Unite!", the Manifesto's closing command, is unwieldy; in many senses of the reference, there are too many national borders, generational mind sets, and variegated needs for the message to cross effectively. The Manifesto's initial charisma was related to the time of its conception by Karl Marx (and Friedrich Engels) in 1847–48, a period of enormous social unrest centered particularly in France—the revolution that birthed the Second Republic (see page 180). Uneducated, demoralized, and hungry ears listened to the class-struggle concepts and flaming language as they would to a trumpet alarm from the heavens. The appeal lay in

---

569 It is important to realize that wars are actually fought in the main by the young.

the structure of it all, so detailed and grand in its plan, so idealistic in its conception, and so determined in its presentation. Military power was the instrument for class domination.[570*]

Inexorably, the growth among all nations facing the same problems is idealistically toward one world state. Can world government equate with perpetual peace? Is not world government actually tyranny fulfilled by the dominant nation?

■ Prediction ...

The World Moves to World Government—For the next twelve years, until the end of 2008, theorization about world government (community) will be a major topic of international political discussion. We can expect enormous changes in the role of the United Nations among the countries of the world (see page 20), through the Vatican among the Christian faiths (see page 26), and among the enormous marketing centers established in the Pacific (see pages 39 and 55) and in Europe (see page 149). Communism will have vanished with China's change of philosophy and Korea's unification. Middle East tensions will be contained by American "occupations" in Israel and Iraq.

The answer will be found through the structures of information and trade and tourism, the international cooperation required to fulfill these dimensions for the security of nations and people. The more informed the world is, the less violent it is: motives are clarified, intent is broadcast, and the opinion of the people is registered more than ever before in history, more than ever could have been imagined.[571*]

---

570 Karl Marx was born May 5, 1818, at 2:00 A.M. in Trier, Grmany [Taeger Archives 1*, Church Records through Ebertine]. This remarkable horoscope shows a New Moon birth in Taurus, with Venus in Taurus conjunct Mercury in Gemini (idealism); Saturn-Pluto rising (destroy for renewal; enormous power) squares Uranus, ruler of the Ascendant, in the 10th conjunct Neptune (revolution). Mars=Sun/Pluto. The *Manifesto* was written in German and published for the first time in London on the eve of the French Revolution of 1848. Marx: SA Sun opposed Midheaven, SA Ascendant square Uranus, tr Saturn conjunct Saturn (he was only thirty years old!).

571 Pluto in Sagittarius. The last transit through Sagittarius 1748–62 coroborated the period of the Enlightenment in France (see page 176). At the dawn of the Millennium, it corroborates the "information highway," the extraordinary internationalism of information exchange, trade, tourism, immigration, and the philosophy unifying all of these concerns within the values of law and order and religion. Pluto is in Sagittarius 1995–2008; in Capricorn 2009–23.

In the Summer of 2013, the United States will put its entire authoritative history behind a bid for world centralism. There will have been a tremendous three-year build-up, punctuated brutally by the death of a president in 2012 (perhaps March or September, by assassination), the second in the new Millennium (see page 254). It is a time of potentially the greatest international crisis. It is the time of potential establishment of United States dominance and leadership of the world.[572]*

The Confirmation of the World Leader

The world "leader" will actually be a communications and trade center construct to which all countries agree for leadership, arbitration, and world security (health, education, employment). The United States becomes the central monitor, having proved its altruism as conclusively as it had proved its power.

But this can not occur without some special new dimension—not necessarily a new weapon but a new state of affairs that turns world belief and resources toward the United States. What could be the conclusive confirmation of righteousness—of being chosen—to make such world hegemony by the United States possible?

Confirmation comes from a higher source, as the popes confirmed the righteousness of two centuries of Crusades (see page 140). Confirmation could well come to the concept of world government organization through contact with intelligence from outer space, through their model and instruction.

---

572 U.S.: SA Neptune square MC (2009), SA Neptune at 16 Taurus in 2012 with appropriate Saturn transit of Pluto; SA Saturn conjunct Ascendant, SA Mars conjunct MC, SA Pluto conjunct Neptune, SA Moon conjunct Saturn all in the Summer of 2010. Tr Pluto opposed Sun, tr Uranus square Sun, tr Saturn square Midheaven.

■ Prediction ...

United States Achieves Contact with Outer Space Intelligence—As early as 2004, possibly in the late Summer, the United States could well be in first contact with intelligence from outer space.[573]*

A new frontier will present itself. The image of earth, the development of its nations, the wisdom of its laws, the illumination of its religions will be challenged in ways never before anticipated. A superior intelligence will have chosen to touch the earth.

As medium to the new frontier, the United States will appear to have been "chosen" as the outer space channel. Will that occur by virtue of the nation's technology or will the outer space intelligence (OSI) have made a selection, an endorsement among the earth's nations? The United States implicitly and explicitly becomes superior as well. Over a period of eight years, this intermediary position will face great challenge on earth. Will the United States share access to OSI; will the OSI approve of sharing; will the OSI criticize our world to help it, to control it?

It is testament indeed to the constants in human nature and national awareness that, even today, as fanciful projections are made into our future with outer space, we humans approaching yet another Millennium still make our projections in terms of the fight for security, the defense of borders, and the confirmation of human rights: we will conceive all of this expansion potential yet once again in terms of wars ... wars among the stars.

---

573 In the study of the astrology connected with first flights, first launches, catastrophes, and space accomplishment, two degree-areas come clearly to the foreground: 17–20 Sagittarius and 0–5 Virgo. This area is punctuated strongly in the United States horoscope once again in 2004, keyed by tr Pluto in 20 Sagittarius, tr Uranus at 2–7 Pisces, and more.

■ Bibliography

* Marks books of exceptional readability and special value to the issues of this volume and its preparation.

Ancient History

Drews, Robert. *The End of the Bronze Age*. Princeton, NJ: Princeton University Press, 1992.

Gellner, Ernest. *Plough, Sword and Book — The Structure of Human History*. Chicago: University of Chicago Press, 1988.

* Grant, Michael. *The Ancient Mediterranean*. New York: Penguin, 1969.

* Grant, Michael. *The History of Ancient Israel*. New York: Scribners, 1984.

Oates, Joan. *Babylon*. New York: Thames and Hudson, 1986.

Redford, Donald B. *Egypt, Canaan, and Israel in Ancient Times*. Princeton, NJ: Princeton University Press, 1992.

Ruby, Robert. *Jericho — Dreams, Ruins, Phantoms*. New York: Henry Holt, 1995.

Thompson, Thomas L. *Early History of the Israelite People — From the Written & Archaeological Sources*. Leiden, The Netherlands: E. J. Brill, 1994.

Faith, Ethics

Armstrong, Karen. *A History of God.* New York: Ballantine, 1993.

* Boyer, Paul. *When Time Shall Be No More.* Cambridge, MA: Harvard University Press, 1990.

Cohn, Norman. *The Pursuit of the Millennium.* New York: Oxford University Press (1957) 1990.

Eliade, Mircea. *A History of Religious Ideas.* Chicago: University of Chicago, 1978.

Fox, Thomas C. *Sexuality and Catholicism.* New York: Geroge Brailler, 1995.

Maccoby, Hyam. *Judas Iscariot and the Myth of Jewish Evil.* New York: Macmillan, 1992.

Millard, Hoffmeier, Baker, Eds. *Faith, Tradition & History — Old Testament Historiography in Its Near Eastern Context.* Winona Lake, IN: Eisenbrauns, 1994.

* Peters, F. E. *Muhammad and the Origins of Islam.* New York: State University of New York, 1994.

Petersen, David, L. *Prophecy in Israel.* Philadelphia: Fortress Press, 1987.

Plantinga, Cornelius, Jr. *Not the Way It's Supposed to Be — A Breviary of Sin.* Leicester, UK: Apollos, 1995.

History, Commentary, and Reference

Ambrose, Stephen E. *Rise to Globalism: American Foreign Policy since 1938.* New York: Penguin Books, Seventh edition, 1993.

Appleby, Joyce; Hunt, Lynn; & Jacob, Margaret. *Telling the Truth about History.* New York: Norton, 1994.

* Axelrod, Alan & Phillips, Charles. *Dictators & Tyrants.* New York: Facts on File, Inc., 1995.

* Barber, Benjamin R. *Jihad vs. McWorld.* New York: Random House, 1995.

* Carruth, Gordon. *The Encyclopedia of World Facts and Dates.* New York: HarperCollins, 1993.

Cobban, Alfred. *A History of Modern France.* Three Volumes. London: Penguin Books: 1990.

Cheetham, Nicolas. *A History of the Popes.* New York: Barnes & Noble, 1982.

* Chernow, Barbara A. and Vallasi, George A., Eds. *Columbia Encyclopedia*, Fifth Edition. New York: Columbia University, 1993.

* Craig, Gordon A. *The Germans.* London: Penguin Books, 1991.

Davues, Nicholas. *Queen Elizabeth II.* New York: Birch Lane Press, 1994.

Delaney, John J. *Dictionary of Saints.* New York: Doubleday, 1980.

Delderfield, Eric R. *Kings & Queens of England & Great Britain.* England: David & Charles, 1994.

Di Scala, Spencer M. *Italy from Revolution to Republic.* Boulder, CO: Westview Press, 1995.

Fairbank, John King. *China — A New History.* Cambridge, MA: Harvard University Press, 1992.

* Fernandez-Armesto, Felipe. *Millennium — A History of the Last Thousand Years.* New York: Scribner's, 1995.

Freedman, Lawrence, Ed. *War.* Oxford, England: Oxford University Press, 1994.

Friedman, George & Lebard, Meredith. *The Coming War with Japan.* New York: St. Martin's, 1991.

Friedman, Thomas L. *From Beirut to Jerusalem.* New York: Doubleday, 1989.

Frum, David. *Dead Right.* New York: HarperCollins, 1995.

Garrett, Laurie. *The Coming Plague: Newly Emerging Diseases in a World Out of Balance.* New York: Penguin Books, 1994.

* Hale, John. *The Civilization of Europe in the Renaissance.* New York: Atheneum, 1994.

* Hooper, John. *The Spaniards.* London: Penguin Books, 1987.

* Hobsbawm, Eric. *The Age of Extremes — A History of the World, 1914–1991*. New York: Pantheon Books, 1994.

Jarausch, Konrad H. *The Rush to German Unity*. Oxford, England: Oxford University Press, 1994.

Kegley, Charles W. Jr. *World Politics: Trend and Transformation*. New York: St. Martin's Press, Fourth Edition, 1993.

Kissinger, Henry. *Diplomacy*. New York: Simon & Schuster, 1994.

Lall, Arthur. *The Emergence of Modern India*. New York: Columbia University Press, 1981.

Lewis, Bernard. *Islam in History*. Chicago: Open Court, 1993.

Longford, Elizabeth, Ed. *The Oxford Book of Royal Anecdotes*. Oxford: Oxford University Press, 1984.

Malcolm, Noel. *Bosnia*. New York: New York University Press, 1994.

Mansour, Camille. *Beyond Alliance: Israel and U.S. Foreign Policy*. New York: Columbia University Press, 1994.

Martin, Malachi. *The Keys of This Blood*. New York: Simon & Schuster, 1990.

* McRae, Hamish. *The World in 2020: Power, Culture and Prosperity*. Cambridge, Mass: Harvard University Press, 1994.

Mitchell, B. R. *European Historical Statistics 1750–1970*. New York: Columbia University Press, 1978.

Morton, Andrew. *Diana — Her True Story*. New York: Simon & Schuster, 1992.

O'Brien, Conor Cruise. *On the Eve of the Millennium*. New York: Simon & Schuster, 1995.

Parker, Geoffrey. *Philip II*. Chicago: Open Court, 1995.

* Pfaff, William. *The Wrath of Nations: Civilizations and the Furies of Nationalism*. New York: Touchstone, 1993.

Richler, Mordecai. *Oh Canada! Oh Quebec!* New York: Knopf, 1992.

Riley-Smith, Jonathan, Ed. *The Oxford Illustrated History of the Crusades*. New York/Oxford:1995.

* Roberts, J. M. *History of the World*. New York: Oxford University Press, 1993.

Seldes, George, Ed. *The Great Thoughts*. New York: Ballantine, 1985.

Sharp, Harold S. *Footnotes to World History*. Metuchen, NJ:Scarecrow Press, 1979

* Shanks, Hershel, Ed. *Ancient Israel*. Washington, D.C.: Biblical Archaeological Society, 1991.

Sinclair-Stevenson, Christopher. *Blood Royal — the Illustrious House of Hanover*. New York: Doubelday, 1981.

Smith, Hiedrick. *Rethinking America*. New York: Random House, 1955.

* Tindall, George Brown. *America: A Narrative History*. Two Volumes. New York: Norton, 1984.

Tholfsen, Trygve R. *Ideology and Revolution in Modern Europe*. New York, Columbia University Press, 1984.

Thomas, Hugh. *Conquest*. New York: Simon & Schuster, 1993.

Toffler, Alvin and Heidi. *War and Anti-War*. New York: Warner Books, 1995.

Tucker, Robert C., Ed. *The Marx-Engels Reader*. New York: W.W. Norton, 1972.

van Wolferen, Karel. *The Enigma of Japanese Power*. New York: Vintage Books, 1990.

Whitrow, G. J. *Time in History*. London: Oxford University Press, 1988.

Williamson, Edwin. *The Penguin History of Latin America*. London: Penguin Books, 1992.

Withers, E. L. *Royal Blood*. New York: Doubleday, 1964.

World Almanac, 1996. New York: Funk & Wagnalls, 1995.

World Bank. *World Development Report 1995*. Washington, D.C./ New York: Oxford University Press, 1995.

Astrology

* Baigent, Michael; Campion, Nicholas; Harvey, Charles. *Mundane Astrology*. Wellingborough, England: Aquarian Press, 1984.

* Campion, Nicholas. *The Book of World Horoscopes*. Second Edition, Bristol, England: Cinnabar Books, 1995.

_____. *The Great Year — Astrology, Millenarianism and History in the Western Tradition*. London: Arkana, 1994.

Carter, Charles E. O. *An Introduction to Political Astrology*. London: Fowler, 1969.

Doane, Doris Chase. *Horoscopes of the U.S. Presidents*. Hollywood, CA: Professional Astrologers, Inc., 1971 edition.

* Hand, Robert. *Planets in Transit*. Gloucester, Mass.: Para Research, 1976.

Mann, A. T. *Millennium Prophecies*. Longmead, UK: Element Books, 1992.

McCaffery, Ellen. *Astrology and Its Influence on the Western World*. New York: Samuel Weiser, 1970.

Munkasey, Michael. *The Astrological Thesaurus: House Keywords*. St. Paul, MN: Llewellyn, 1992.

Taeger, Hans-Hinrich. *Internationales Horoskope Lexikon*. Three Volumes. Freiburg: Hermann Bauer, 1992.

* Tyl, Noel. *Synthesis & Counseling in Astrology — The Professional Manual*. St. Paul, MN: Llewellyn, 1994.

* _____. *Prediction in Astrology*. St. Paul, MN: Llewellyn, 1991.

van Norstrand, Frederic. *Precepts in Mundane Astrology*. New York: Macoy, 1962.

■ Index

Stay in Touch. . .
Llewellyn publishes hundreds of books
on your favorite subjects

On the following pages you will find listed some books now available on related subjects. Your local bookstore stocks most of these and will stock new Llewellyn titles as they become available. We urge your patronage.

Order by Phone

Call toll-free within the U.S. and Canada, 1-800-THE MOON. In Minnesota call (612) 291–1970. We accept Visa, MasterCard, and American Express.

Order by Mail

Send the full price of your order (MN residents add 7% sales tax) in U.S. funds to :

Llewellyn Worldwide,
P.O. Box 64383, Dept. K-737-4
St. Paul, MN 55164–0383, U.S.A.

Postage and Handling

- $4.00 for orders $15.00 and under
- $5.00 for orders over $15.00
- No charge for orders over $100.00

We ship UPS in the continental United States. We cannot ship to P.O. boxes. Orders shipped to Alaska, Hawaii, Canada, Mexico, and Puerto Rico will be sent first-class mail.

International orders: Airmail—add freight equal to price of each book to the total price of order, plus $5.00 for each non-book item (audiotapes, etc.).

Surface mail: Add $1.00 per item

Allow 4–6 weeks delivery on all orders. Postage and handling rates subject to change.

Discounts

We offer a 20% quantity discount to group leaders or agents. You must order a minimum of 5 copies of the same book to get our special quantity price.

Free Catalog

Get a Free copy of our color catalog, *New Worlds of Mind and Spirit*. Subscribe for just $10.00 in the United States and Canada ($20.00 overseas, first class mail). Many bookstores carry *New Worlds*—ask for it!

SYNTHESIS & COUNSELING IN ASTROLOGY
The Professional Manual
Noel Tyl

One of the keys to a vital, comprehensive astrology is the art of synthesis, the capacity to take the parts of our knowledge and combine them into a coherent whole. Many times, the parts may be contradictory (the relationship between Mars and Saturn, for example), but the art of synthesis manages the unification of opposites. Now Noel Tyl presents ways astrological measurements—through creative synthesis—can be used to effectively counsel individuals. Discussion of these complex topics is grounded in concrete examples and in-depth analyses of the 122 horoscopes of celebrities, politicians, and private clients.

Tyl's objective in providing this vitally important material was to present everything he has learned and practiced over his distinguished career to provide a useful source to astrologers. He has succeeded in creating a landmark text destined to become a classic reference for professional astrologers.

1-56718-734-X, 924 pgs., 7 x 10, 115 charts, softcover $29.95

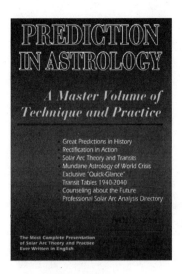

PREDICTION IN ASTROLOGY
A Master Volume of Technique and Practice
Noel Tyl

No matter how much you know about astrology already, no matter how much experience you've had to date, you'll be fascinated by Prediction in Astrology, and you'll grow as an astrologer. Using the Solar Arc theory and methods he describes in this book, the author was able to accurately predict the Gulf War, including the actual date it would begin and the timetable of tactics, two months before it began. He also predicted the overturning of Communist rule in the Eastern bloc nations nine months in advance of its actual occurrence.

Tyl teaches through example. You learn by doing astrology, not just thinking about it. Tyl introduces Solar Arc theory in terms of "rapport" measurements, which you begin to do immediately, without paper, pencil, or computer, dials, or wheels. Just with your eyes! You will never look at a horoscope the same way again!

Tyl, in his well-known, very special way, also gets personal. He presents 30 Aphorisms, the keenest of maxims, the most practical of techniques, to create predictions from any horoscope. And as if this were not enough, Tyl then presents 20 Aphorisms for Counseling. Look for Tyl's "Quick-Glance" Transit Table, 1940-2040, to which you can refer more quickly than a computer. The busy astrologer will use this Appendix every day for many years to come.

0-87542-814-2, 360 pgs., 6 x 9, softcover   **$17.95**

HOROSCOPE FOR A NEW MILLENNIUM
E. Alan Meece

For anyone interested in the meaning of the great events of our time, and for those who want to know how these events might affect their lives, *Horoscope for a New Millennium* offers the first revealing mirror of humanity in this age. Understand the great moments of history—and of the upcoming critical and progressive opportunities—through astrology presented as a fascinating, gripping story of our evolution from social enslavement to individual freedom ... and acceptance of personal responsibility within the planetary environment.

Scan the vast landscape of human destiny for the larger astrological rhythms and prophetic insights. Then focus in on our own times with the engaging narrative that traces the path of our transition from one Age to another. When the book becomes a crystal ball to divine where we're headed, discover what it means for you, with intriguing prophecies of specific events. Find out how we will soon find ourselves entering a "new Golden Age"—if we make the right choices.

1-56718-461-8, 432 pp., 7 x 10, softcover **$19.95**

NOSTRADAMUS 1999
Who Will Survive?
Stefan Paulus

What significant event did the 16th century prophet Nostradamus predict for the seventh month of 1999? Nostradamus predicts that a large comet will have a close encounter with the earth at that time. Could Nostradamus' "King of Terror" be lurking in that comet's tail?

Author Stefan Paulus presents Nostradamus as no one has done before. In a book that is both believable and highly readable, he pieces together the jigsaw puzzle of Nostradamus' final prophecies, correlating them to what is going on in current environmental trends. Only Paulus explores the link between the prophecies and a battle-by-battle vision of a near-future World War III. Only Paulus correlates Nostradamus' predictions with unfulfilled Biblical prophecies, particularly those from the Book of Revelation, and he explains how they could come true in ways compatible with modern scientific knowledge. In addition, Paulus compares Nostradamus' predictions with Islamic prophecies that are already being fulfilled at this time.

1-56718-515-0, 336 pp., 6 x 9, softcover   **$14.95**

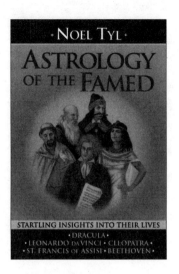

ASTROLOGY OF THE FAMED
Startling Insights Into Their Lives
Noel Tyl
The lives of Cleopatra, Dracula, St. Francis of Assisi, Beethoven and Leonardo da Vinci take on exciting new dimensions in this work by master astrologer Noel Tyl. History buffs and astrologers alike will be amazed at how he merges the technique of rectification with the adventure, genius and drama of five of the most unique and provocative lives in all of history.

Astrologers use rectification when they don't know someone's birth date; they work backward and allow life events to determine the time of birth. To determine the birth month of Cleopatra, for example, Tyl transplanted himself back to 69 B.C. and walked through her footsteps to translate her actions into a horoscope that symbolizes her life's events and her character.

And there is so much more to this book than rectifications. There is good solid history and analysis of the personalties. Tyl then uses astrology to color in their motivations and mind-sets over the black-on-white historical facts.
1-56718-735-8, 384 pp., 6 x 9, softcover $19.95

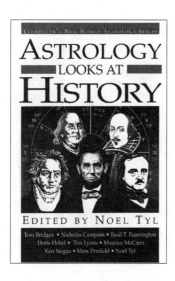

ASTROLOGY LOOKS AT HISTORY
edited by Noel Tyl

This book shows astrology performing at its very best through rectification (working backwards to determine someone's correct birthtime), capturing in astrological terms the fascinating lives of geniuses
who have touched the development of the arts, sciences and government in Western history. *Astrology Looks at History* reveals the details
of personal development in the lives of 10 notables, and illuminates
their interactions with the world as they changed it.

- Scholars are one day off on Shakespeare's birth;
  astrology establishes that he was murdered! – Maurice McCann

- Why such a powerful man named Machiavelli was so withdrawn,
  reclusive, and realistic – Basil T. Fearrington

- Astrology studies with keen historical grounding the many times
  lightning struck in the life of Benjamin Franklin – Tim Lyons

- The meanings between the lines of Edgar Allen Poe's tortured
  life, sensitive spirit and wondrous imagination – Doris Hebel

- Historical detail about Slavery, Jamestown, and Lincoln reveals a
  country in the making – Marc Penfield

- What do the Creation of the World, the horoscope of astrology
  and Jack the Ripper have in common? – Nicholas Campion

- Astrology times Nelson Mandela's past and projects into the
  future – Noel Tyl

1-56718-868-0, 464 pgs., 6x9, 92 charts, softcover $16.95

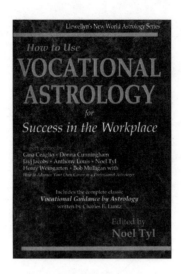

HOW TO USE VOCATIONAL ASTROLOGY
FOR SUCCESS IN THE WORKPLACE
edited by Noel Tyl

Announcing the most practical examination of Vocational Astrology in five decades! Improve your astrological skills with these revolutionary new tools for vocational and business analysis! Now, in *How to Use Vocational Astrology for Success in the Workplace*, edited by Noel Tyl, seven respected astrologers provide their well-seasoned modern views on that great issue of personal life—Work. Their expert advice will prepare you well for those tricky questions clients often ask: "Am I in the right job?" "Will I get promoted?" or "When is the best time to make a career move?" With an introduction by Noel Tyl in which he discusses the startling research of the Gauquelins, this ninth volume in Llewellyn's New World Astrology Series features enlightening counsel from the following experts: Jayj Jacobs, Gina Ceaglio, Donna Cunningham, Anthony Louis, Noel Tyl, Henry Weingarten, and Bob Mulligan. Read How to Use Vocational Astrology today, and add "Vocational Counselor" to your resume tomorrow! Includes the complete 1942 classic by Charles E. Luntz Vocational Guidance by Astrology.

0-87542-387-6, 384 pgs., 6 x 9, illus., softcover   **$14.95**